BRITISH HIGHER EDUCATION

BRITISH
HIGHER
EDUCATION

Edited by

TONY BECHER

University of Sussex

London
ALLEN & UNWIN
Boston   Sydney   Wellington

Allen & Unwin, the academic imprint of
Unwin Hyman Ltd
PO Box 18, Park Lane, Hemel Hempstead, Herts HP2 4TE, UK
40 Museum Street, London WC1A 1LU, UK
37/39 Queen Elizabeth Street, London SE1 2QB

Allen & Unwin Inc.,
8 Winchester Place, Winchester, Mass. 01890, USA

Allen & Unwin (Australia) Ltd,
8 Napier Street, North Sydney, NSW 2060, Australia

Allen & Unwin (New Zealand) Ltd in association with the Port Nicholson
Press Ltd
60 Cambridge Terrace, Wellington, New Zealand

First published in 1987

British Library Cataloguing in Publication Data
British higher education.
1. Education, Higher – Great Britain
I. Becher, Tony
378.41   LA636.8
ISBN 0–04–370170–1
ISBN 0–04–370171–X

Library of Congress Cataloging-in-Publication Data
British higher education.
Includes bibliographies and index.
Contents: Introduction / Tony Becher – The political context of higher
education / Stuart Maclure – Central control of the university sector /
John H. Farrant – [etc.]
1. Education, Higher - Great Britain. 2. Universities and colleges – Great
Britain – Administration. I. Becher, Tony.
LA637.B727 1987   378.41   87–990
ISBN 0–04–370170–1 (alk. paper)
ISBN 0–04–370171–X (pbk.: alk. paper)

Set in 10 on 11 point Bembo by
Computape (Pickering) Ltd, North Yorkshire
and printed in Great Britain by Billing and Sons Ltd,
London and Worcester

Contents

1

Introduction

TONY BECHER

THE UNDERLYING RATIONALE

During the past two decades, the higher education system in Britain has changed in a diversity of ways at a variety of different levels. It would be fair to say that anyone who graduated before the mid-1960s, unless he or she had kept in reasonably close touch with subsequent developments, would find the contemporary landscape almost completely unrecognisable.

In 1962–63 there were 31 universities and 188 colleges fully or mainly engaged in higher education, and a total full-time and part-time student population of some 333,000. In 1984, more than 500 institutions were engaged in some form of higher education, and the full-time and part-time student population stood at 886,000. The budgetary allocation from public funds in 1962–63 was estimated as £219 million, while the counterpart figure in 1984 was £3,300 million.

Besides such quantitative differences, one of the more significant qualitative changes lies in the political framework: in particular, Parliament has begun to take an unprecedented interest in policies for higher education. The mechanisms for central funding and control have been modified: the University Grants Committee's role has shifted significantly over the past few years, and the public sector institutions have become subject to the rationalizing influence of a National Advisory Body. Increases in the size of universities, with growing demands for accountability and financial management, have led to a stronger and more professional administration at the institutional level than was ever envisaged during and before the 1950s. The more recent types of academic body – the polytechnics and colleges of higher education – have generated their own set of management practices and problems. The academic structure of many institutions has been broadened to produce a more elaborate network of committees. New specialized fields have proliferated in

1

almost every disciplinary area, giving rise to increasingly complex arrangements for teaching and research. Curricular patterns have diversified from the traditional single-subject honours programme to a wide range of modular and interdisciplinary courses. There have also been a number of innovations in teaching and learning, as well as in methods of assessing student performance.

This bewildering array of developments may – at least in part – help to explain why even those directly involved in academic concerns seem often to have an imperfect understanding of contemporary higher education: a difficulty shared by staff on both sides of the so-called binary line, student union leaders, lay governors and interested politicians, not to mention the much larger numbers of people with more selective interests in the system as a whole (prospective students, teachers of A-level courses, parents of undergraduates, employers, and the tax-paying public).

This book is written predominantly for the former category of reader, though it is hoped that a number of the latter will also find it of interest. Its intention is to present a balanced portrayal of contemporary higher education, bringing out the positive features while acknowledging the inherent limitations. At a time when the defects of the system have been widely proclaimed, there is a case for displaying it as it actually works, and thus demonstrating its underlying rationales and values, its functional connections and its basic processes. In this way it is hoped to offer an account of the academic world in two senses of the term: not only a statement of what it does, but also a clear justification for its continued existence.

A MAP OF THE SYSTEM

It seems appropriate, in the course of introducing a book about higher education in Britain, to provide a brief conspectus of the enterprise as a whole. This is easier said than done because, although reference is made in the pages that follow – and in many other contexts – to the higher education system, the actuality is far from systematic. As with so many other aspects of British life, it is a product of tradition and pragmatism rather than of logic and the rigorous application of principles. Almost every generalization that can be made about it is subject to one or more qualifications.

In such circumstances, a choice has to be made between attempting to produce a detailed, accurate but complex and confusing Ordnance Survey or an artificially simplified but more easily intelligible sketch-map of the territory. The latter course will be adopted here. There seems little point in alienating the reader with an over-elaborate account by way of introduction; in any case, some of the more significant complexities and anomalies are discussed in subsequent chapters.

It is probably easiest to visualize higher education in terms of different levels of generality (and to some extent of power and influence). We might conveniently distinguish five such levels: government; the central authorities; the individual institutions; their several components; the individuals – academics and others – who people them.

The level of government in the system as a whole is represented in England by the Secretary of State for Education and Science, and in Scotland, Northern Ireland and Wales by the Secretaries of State for those countries (though the Secretary of State for Education and Science is alone reponsible for the universities in England, Wales and Scotland). The relevant government departments who act under their authority are the Department of Education and Science, the Welsh Office, the Scottish Education Department and the Department of Education for Northern Ireland. The ministers concerned are responsible for framing national policy and obtaining the necessary resources for the system as a whole. In this, they are subject to cabinet and parliamentary constraints, much as their departments are constrained – with other government ministries – by the Treasury.

By long-standing convention, the Secretary of State for Education does not directly determine the allocation of funds for individual universities, but delegates this task to the main central authority within the university sector, the University Grants Committee. Since 1968, when the first of the new polytechnics was designated, a separate public sector of higher education has grown up, with quite different funding arrangements and a different structure of central authorities. Foremost among these is the National Advisory Body, set up in 1982, whose remit in respect of English polytechnics and colleges is very roughly comparable with that of the UGC in relation to the distribution of resources, but which is (as its name implies) advisory to ministers rather than in possession of delegated powers. Its Welsh counterpart, the Wales Advisory Body, has a similar remit. The situation is further complicated in that the majority of public sector institutions in England and Wales (but not in Scotland) are maintained by local rather than central government – so in their cases the Local Education Authorities comprise an important intermediate level of control below the Department of Education and Science and NAB/WAB.

3

The UGC and NAB/WAB have a common concern for ensuring value for money and, hence, for the maintenance of quality within their respective sectors. However, neither operates any direct form of quality control. In the case of the universities, the standard of educational provision – or, at least, the assessment of student performance on degree courses – is monitored by external examiners (usually senior academics from other institutions) appointed by the universities themselves. The polytechnics and colleges of higher education are subject to the scrutiny of the Council for National Academic Awards. Unlike the universities, they are not chartered bodies, and so cannot award their own degrees. Their courses are subject to periodic validation by CNAA (though some well-established institutions enjoy greater autonomy than this implies) and the Council acts as their degree-giving body. They are also open to investigation by HM Inspectorate in a way that universities (with the exception of aspects of the work of departments of education and adult education) are not.

A significant number of degree courses (e.g. in medicine, law, engineering, accountancy, social work) lead to professional qualifications or to exemptions from professional examination requirements. In such cases, the professional bodies concerned usually impose their own demands on the curriculum and examinations. In this respect they may be counted among the central agencies for quality control in both the autonomous (university) and public (polytechnic and college) sectors.

In research, the main form of quality control is through the government-funded research councils and through a limited number of charitable trusts, most of whom award grants on the basis of advice from independent leading academics in the relevant field. The total funds awarded – in most subject areas other than the humanities – are held to give an approximate indication of merit.

The first tier of the system, then, comprises the ministers and central government departments ultimately responsible for British higher education. Its articulation with the rest of education and the public services is explored in Chapter 2. The second tier, which is the theme of Chapters 3 and 4, is less easy to delineate, especially in relation to the public sector. As we have noted, the key bodies are the UGC and NAB, but alongside them are ranged the professional bodies, research councils and private trusts, covering both sectors. In addition, on the side of the polytechnics and colleges have to be included the CNAA, HM Inspectorate and the Local Education Authorities. The catalogue could in each case be extended, but these are at least the main elements. In Scotland, control over the public sector is centralized in the Scottish Education Department, so the second tier is considerably weaker.

The third tier is relatively simple, in that it consists of three main categories of institution on the autonomous side and three on the public. The university sector comprises two federal groups of institutions – the Universities of London and Wales, each with their constituent colleges – and a central core of forty-three individual universities, a few of which (Cambridge, Oxford and Durham) are made up of constituent colleges, but the rest of which have a unitary structure. In addition, the Open University, the University of Buckingham, the Cranfield Institute of Technology and the Royal College of Art are all regarded as university-level institutions, although not on the UGC list. The public sector in England and Wales comprises thirty polytechnics – many of them formed as a result of mergers between a number of previously free-standing institutions (colleges of technology, colleges of education, further education colleges, colleges of art and design) – and some eighty or so smaller maintained, direct-grant and voluntary colleges of higher education (because these institutions are the most vulnerable in the system, and are liable to be closed down when resources are scarce or the teacher employment market is in decline, it is always hazardous to give a precise figure). The origins of the latter colleges have lain for the most part in the initial training of teachers, but they have now diversified to provide a somewhat broader range of degree courses (mostly in the humanities and social sciences). There is also a large penumbra of colleges of one kind and another that offer a limited number of degree-level courses. In Scotland, the public sector is made up of the central institutions (16) and the free-standing colleges of education (7) and a similar penumbra of other colleges (DES, 1985).

The institutions of higher education, as this brief catalogue implies, differ from each other in a whole variety of ways. One obvious difference, which is underlined in the chapters that follow, lies in the degree of freedom enjoyed by colleges in the two sectors. Another lies in the nature of their offerings. Many public sector institutions provide a range of non-advanced courses, and so have a relatively high proportion of part-time and mature students, and often only a handful of students taking degrees or equivalent qualifications – a pattern that is uncommon in the autonomous university sector. There is, by and large, a stronger emphasis on vocationally oriented courses in the polytechnics and colleges and a heavier concentration of research in the universities. There is also a considerable variation in size and age between the various institutions. London is the largest university, whose constituent colleges between them cater for some 49,000 full-time and part-time students; Oxford and Cambridge have slightly more than 26,000 between them; the smallest university, Keele, has around 3,000 students. In the public sector, Manchester is the largest polytechnic, with 10,000-plus full-time equivalent students; the smallest is Teesside, with some 3,600 students. The oldest university (Oxford) was founded in 1249; most universities are products of the early twentieth century; all the polytechnics and colleges of higher education were established in the late 1960s or 1970s.

Each university, college or polytechnic is divided into constituent elements. The smallest independent entities of this kind, each with its designated head, its own range of courses or programmes and (usually) its own territorial boundaries, constitute the fourth tier in the system – the basic academic units. For the most part, these are traditional departments, organized round academic disciplines (such as history, physics, economics and engineering). Some institutions, however (usually the more recently established ones), favour a form of organization – schools of study – based on a wider range of interrelated fields (environmental science, urban studies, African and Asian studies, and so on). Others, particularly those that have adopted a modular course structure, operate a more complex variant on these two systems – a 'matrix scheme' – in which academics from specific subject groups are allocated to interdisciplinary course teams as the need arises. A minority of units is concerned solely with research; a limited number solely with teaching; but the considerable majority combines both activities.

Where academic institutions tend to be large, diverse and pluralistic, basic units are relatively small and coherent. Each defines an area of expertise that is not usually shared by other parts of the institution, and is thus able to enjoy a reasonably high degree of independence. Looked at from the perspective of this fourth tier of organization, the universities, polytechnics and colleges that constitute the third tier may appear as little more than holding companies for their constituent elements: but, as is made clear in Chapters 5 and 6, the institutions themselves perform a multitude of functions, especially in relation to resource management and planning.

At the end point of this hierarchical chain come the individual members of the academic world – those who inhabit the basic units and their parent institutions, and who are ultimately subject to the controls exercised by the central bodies and by the relevant branches of government. How membership of the higher education system is to be defined is an arguable point. It clearly includes those members of staff of universities, polytechnics and colleges who are appointed to teach and do research. It must also, of course, embrace the senior academics whose current job descriptions require them to manage and administer all or part of their institutions on a full-time basis. The activities, values and ways of life of these groups of individuals form the main subject of Chapter 7.

It is less obvious that the professional administrators who act as the civil servants at the institutional level should be counted in, although there seems a reasonable case for this. There are also – as in most large organizations – several members of staff (technicians, clerks, secretaries and the like) who play important supporting roles, but who are not generally seen as direct constituents of the higher education system. Finally there are the students for whom (in very large degree) the whole enterprise exists. But they, too, in one important sense are outside the system as such, in that they are its clients rather than its members. In a comparable way, a study of the British National Health Service would be likely to include the doctors and nurses as well as the management hierarchy at local and national levels, but would regard the patients as being in the different category of those the system was designed to serve. In the pages that follow the students, therefore, feature only indirectly, in so far as attention is given in Chapters 8 and 9 to the types of courses on offer to them and the ways in which they are taught and examined.

THEMES AND CONTRIBUTORS

The five levels of the higher education system, as identified in the previous section, may be seen as resembling a series of Russian dolls: the most all-embracing level (that of national government) contains within it the next level down (the central agencies), which in its turn embraces the third (the individual institutions), and so on. It is basically on such a pattern that this book is constructed, although because of the many differences between the autonomous and public sectors – particularly at the level of the central bodies and the institutions themselves – it has been found necessary to look separately at the issues of governance and management in the two sectors. Moreover, because the relationships between the different tiers are important to an understanding of how the system works, the boundaries of the discussion are as a matter of policy not tightly defined between one chapter and another. The aim has been to achieve comprehensibility, clarity and coherence rather than an uninformative tidiness of design.

The book falls into two unequal parts, dealing respectively with what have been called the public and the private lives of higher education (Trow, 1975). Chapters 2 to 6 concentrate on such issues as management, control, policy and finance – on how the system works, what are the rules of the game, and who are the leading players. These constitute the publicly visible aspects of higher education, those that are most commonly discussed and written about and that relate to the structure and fabric of the system and its member institutions.

The substance of higher education – the activities that go on in private, behind the closed doors of committee rooms and classrooms – provides the theme for Chapters 7 to 9. Those aspects of the system that relate to the sub-institutional levels, to basic units and individuals, are less well documented than the ones at the institutional level and above. The arguments that go on about the shape and content of the curriculum or about learning methods or the nature of student assessment are predominantly seen as domestic arguments, even if their eventual outcome is a more formal and public process of external examination of course approval. Yet there is another sense in which such questions constitute the central core of the academic enterprise, the issues it is really about when the institutional superstructure has been stripped away. Research spans the borderline between private and public, in that both its genesis in outside funding and its outcome in a published product often entail some substantial degree of professional visibility, though its actual pursuit is seen as the personal business of the individual or team concerned.

Privacy is a problem for anyone seeking to give a reasonably comprehensive overview of higher education – that is, one that includes some account of what goes on inside universities, polytechnics and colleges as well as how they operate as institutions within the system as a whole. There seems no sensible substitute here for an ethnographic approach, based on informants who are themselves directly involved in the business of teaching and research. Such an approach does in fact provide the basis of the material in Chapters 7, 8 and 9, whose respective authors were earlier involved in the same wide-ranging study of new developments in undergraduate teaching.

The authors of the earlier chapters have similarly been invited to contribute in virtue of their specialist knowledge of the themes assigned to them. The brief notes on contributors at the end of the book testify to their expertise: although its exercise in practice is of course open both to public validation by reviewers and to private assessment by other readers.

The concern of contributors and editor alike has been to develop an approach that is scholarly in the sense of being well-informed and authoritative, offering critical analysis not mere facts. A second, related aim has been to strike a balance between an over-specialized and a too-superficial level of exposition, by restricting the annotation and the use of technical language to a level appropriate to the intended audience. And, finally, there is a shared emphasis on adopting a long-term, fundamental perspective as against a short-term, ephemeral one. This book accordingly makes no pretence of addressing all the problems that presently beset higher education: but if it succeeds in throwing light on some of the more deep-seated ones, it will have achieved its most important aim.

2

The Political Context of Higher Education

STUART MACLURE

INTRODUCTION

The decade of the 1970s can now be seen as a period of uncertainty and flux throughout English education when many policy assumptions were radically revised. It is important to see changes in the political context of higher education against this broader background.

At the level of primary and secondary education there was a sharp reaction against the liberal notions that had held sway in the 1950s and 1960s. In particular, there was a readiness to set aside conventions about the school curriculum which had all but ceded control and initiative to the teaching profession. The focus of policy debate moved away from organization and structure; the curriculum was taken back into the public policy domain and a process begun by which the powers and influences of central government with regard to content of study, examinations and teacher training were to be redefined and extended.

Economic recession, unemployment and restrictions on public expenditure – important factors in changing the political context of education at the school level – also brought a radical alteration in the framework for policy-making for higher education: a framework already shaken by politically damaging student unrest in the late 1960s. The arrival of a radical Conservative administration in 1979 under Margaret Thatcher intensified the will of central government to hold down public expenditure, and this provided a catalyst to precipitate changes that were already in train.

To make sense of the changes in political context it is necessary to examine the former assumptions about the relationships between the Government and higher education. In so doing, it is important to recognize that what can, for want of a better term, be described as conventions, were usually unstated: and the act of writing about them inevitably results in some degree of caricature. Behind the caricature remains a recognizable truth.

MINIMUM INTERVENTION

The limitations of British Government involvement in higher education policy for the first seventy years of this century were rooted in the social values of the time. Policy for the universities was obscure and ambiguous. For much of the time, over large areas, the policy was to have no formal policy at all, except to give autonomous institutions as much or as little money as the Government thought it could afford.

The idea that governments should interfere as little as possible in the universities was derived as much, one suspects, from the way in which the universities were founded, and the relatively late involvement of the Exchequer in their funding, as from any ideological commitment to the highly prized academic freedom that has been one of the beneficiaries of this benign neglect. Academic freedom, however, has become one of the cornerstones of higher education in the liberal, humanistic tradition, and its defence against subtle undermining will continue to figure in the politics of higher education.

An extension of this notion of academic freedom has been the idea that universities serve the body politic as repositories of independent criticism and non-partisan wisdom. This has appealed to the universities (for it flatters their aspirations and licenses their political judgements) and to governments (who have found it useful to use academic experts to defuse highly charged issues). But the more polarized politics becomes and the more extensive the intervention of government, the less welcome is the idea of licensed criticism from any source.

The general disposition not to interfere in higher education has not, of course, prevented governments from getting involved in questions relating to scientific research and the functions of the universities as suppliers of educated manpower to the nation.

The setting-up of the Department of Scientific and Industrial Research in 1916, leading to the creation of the Research Councils and to the present involvement of the Department of Education and Science in the funding and strategy of research, was an inevitable development – as, in the British context, were the elaborate mechanisms chosen for ensuring that the scientific community, not

11

the politicians, should play the leading part in formulating and executing the policies that resulted.

It was one thing, however, to recognize a public interest in ensuring a sufficient supply of qualified manpower: any general temptation to engage in detailed manpower planning was firmly resisted – except in regard to particular professional categories of public sector employment, such as teaching and the health services professions. Major decisions followed from the broad recommendations of the Barlow Committee in 1946 (whose arguments for doubling the output of scientists became the basis of a doubling of the rest of the university population). But attempts to make more specific estimates of demand by the Committee on Scientific Manpower under the chairmanship of the then Sir Solly Zuckerman (1954–62) came down firmly on the side of reasoned scepticism. The same conclusion was reached in 1963 by members of the Robbins Committee in Chapter VI of their report (Committee on Higher Education, 1963).

When a junior minister at the Department of Education and Science, Lord Crowther-Hunt, tried to take up the idea again in the mid-1970s, he was conspicuously unsuccessful. Lord Crowther-Hunt was influenced by the growing frustration among politicians of both parties, who regarded the universities as a great public resource that had not yet been effectively harnessed by the Government to the main social and economic purposes of the country.

Those who wanted a more interventionist policy in the 1960s and 1970s had only a limited success, because neither the politicians nor their senior civil servants could come up with a strategy that carried the conviction necessary to challenge the entrenched independence of the higher education community. But the absence of any clear strategy did not prevent successive governments from extending their commitments in relation to the finance of the universities. Nor did it prevent the growth of a public sector comprising a range of colleges administered by local authorities and voluntary bodies.

To cope with the obvious tensions arising from a policy of non-intervention in an area of activity that was increasingly dependent on public funds, governments had deliberately maintained an arms-length relationship in all their dealings with the universities. In the public sector, where, theoretically, the government could take more direct control, complex financial mechanisms were developed in conjunction with the local education authorities, which contrived to limit intervention. Moreover, there was a strong belief in the public mind, which the educational establishment shared, that status was directly linked to autonomy. This ensured not only that the

12

universities would, in general terms, continue to get the first pick of the students, but also that the conventional wisdom would search for ways of maximizing the autonomy of public sector colleges by giving them strong governing bodies and encouraging them to develop in their own ways.

PUBLIC FUNDS

The first funds from central government for the university sector, voted in 1889, were £15,000 for the university colleges, all of which 'with the possible exception of Owens College, Manchester', were said to be 'in pecuniary straits'. The grants had grown to £170,000 by 1914. After the First World War, they were extended to all the universities, rising from £779,000 in 1919 to £3.5 million in 1937–38. They then accounted for 51 per cent of total university expenditure on teaching and research.

After the Second World War, the trend of rising expenditure and increased dependence on public funds continued. The last figures available to the Robbins Committee (1962–63) showed the public contribution at £73 million, i.e. 88 per cent of total expenditure. By 1983 the UGC recurrent grant had risen to £1,225 million and the percentage of all university income flowing in one form or another from public funds was higher than ever.

Although fee income appears as a separate item in university accounts, in practice almost all students' fees are paid from public funds via the local education authorities.

STUDENT SUPPORT

A feature of the post-war period has been the way public funding for higher education institutions has been matched by increased support for student maintenance. After the Anderson Report (Ministry of Education, 1960), all state scholarships and county awards were consolidated into mandatory major awards paid, subject to a means test, to all home students admitted on the basis of a minimum of two A-levels, and subsequently to all students admitted to first degree courses or their equivalent.

A measure of the limitations on policy accepted till now has been the Government's reluctance to use the grant system to steer students into favoured courses. It would have been quite possible – though highly controversial – to weight the student grant in such a

13

way as to reflect the Government's assessment of national need. But here again, the absence of any clear manpower policies meant that there was no official will to impose, and given the great hostility such a measure would have aroused, the orthodox view was that it would be inappropriate to use the grant as a tool of policy in this way. What successive governments did have strong views about, however, was the overall cost: so the real value of the grant was allowed to fall as a result of a failure to make adequate allowances for inflation.

By the mid 1980s the grant system had come to occupy a central position in discussion about access to higher education and there was mounting pressure to introduce a more flexible system, which would include loans. Various attempts by ministers at the Department of Education and Science between 1980 and 1985 failed because of Cabinet opposition and fears of a political backlash. The issue turned on the possibility that the financial limitations imposed by the cost of mandatory student grants might have begun to restrict the opportunity that grants were expected to extend. It had long been recognized that the grant system was regressive – it takes resources from taxes paid by everybody and reallocates them to those whose expected earnings far exceed the average. Unfortunately student subsidies had not prevented the social mix of the student population from continuing to be skewed in favour of the well-to-do, and from becoming more so rather than less.

THE UNIVERSITY GRANTS COMMITTEE

From the start, when the first central government funds were paid to university colleges, the Government brought in people from the relevant institutions to help distribute the money. The Treasury Memorandum of 1 March 1889 (Sanderson, 1975), authorized the Lord President of the Council and the Chancellor of the Exchequer to nominate 'a small committee of men well-versed in academic questions, to elaborate a plan for the distribution of the grant'. As the size of the grant grew, the arrangements for its distribution continued to reflect the general principle that people from the universities should have the main responsibility for deciding how to share out the central government funds. All this was formalized and restated in the creation of the University Grants Committee in 1919 (reviewed again in 1946) when grants were extended beyond the limits of the university colleges to take in the rest of the universities, including Oxford and Cambridge.

14

The modern UGC, with responsibilities for universities in England, Wales and Scotland, has usually had a leading academic as its full-time chairman. For pay and rations he ranks as a second permanent secretary in the DES. The UGC has a small secretariat, drawn from the DES, which services the 20 members who, with the chairman, constitute the Committee and the sub-committees that it spawns. A considerable part of the membership was traditionally made up of academics (not vice-chancellors) with a few people from industry, a chief education officer, a couple of secondary school heads. The academics are not representative in any direct sense, but there is a spread of departmental expertise and they are chosen because they are among the 'best' in their fields.

Until 1972, the UGC funds were allocated on a quinquennial basis, to provide the universities with the maximum flexibility in working within the sums allocated to them. Quinquennial grants came to an end with the rapid rise of inflation, to be replaced by an annual grant with as much or as little allowance for inflation as the Government chooses to make, and a forecast of future intentions extending several years ahead. Since the creation of the Department of Education and Science in 1964, the UGC has reported to the DES and, in theory at least, it is the DES that should be the source of Government policy for higher education.

In what are now thought of as the palmy days of the 1960s, the University Grants Committee served as the long-term planning body for the autonomous sector of higher education and, although on various occasions its recommendations were turned down by the Treasury (before and after the creation of the DES), the UGC was seen as a resilient buffer between the universities on the one hand and the politicians on the other. Its chosen methods have been secretive and it has avoided public recriminations while being thought to represent the universities' point of view forcefully in confidential in-fighting. Such methods have become increasingly hard to sustain and came near to breaking-point in the early 1980s, when the UGC was required to execute a financial policy that imposed severe cuts on many institutions.

As recently as 1980 a memorandum submitted by the UGC to a House of Commons Select Committee could confidently assert: 'no attempt is made to lay down in detail from the centre how much of a university's grant should be spent on this or that ... activity ... [but] the freedom of discretion afforded to the universities by the block grant principle is qualified in practice by convention. Universities accept that it is the UGC's business to set the general strategy and that ... they have a responsibility for exercising this freedom

15

within the framework of national needs and priorities, and in the light of the guidance, general or particular, given to them by the UGC. This is a well-established convention and it is an essential part of the UGC system.' (House of Commons, 1980).

THE CRISIS IN 1981

After the 1981 crisis, in which university funds were subject to severe reduction, the UGC retained responsibility for the distribution of the global sum allocated to the universities by the Government, but the Government agreed to make its own priorities public by setting them out in letters of guidance to the UGC. The crisis demonstrated the strength and weakness of the arms-length approach.

On the one hand, it enabled the Government to make clean financial cuts without getting directly involved in the politics or the academic merits of the process by which these were enforced. The UGC's purse-strings are held by the Government; it has no other source of funds, so by drawing the strings tighter the Government can make certain that savings are actually made. In this, the universities are in a different situation from the polytechnics and other public sector colleges, whose funds are channelled through the local authorities and whose expenditure the central government has had much more difficulty in controlling. While the universities were trying to cope with harsh cuts, the public sector colleges enjoyed a brief boom.

On the other hand, the limitations of the arms-length approach (from the Government's point of view) became apparent in the manner in which the UGC applied the financial cuts, university by university. The UGC represented the 'best' conventional views of the British university establishment. Having decided not to make a cut evenly across the board, the Committee gave more to those universities and departments that stood high in the esteem of their colleagues and less to those that did not. The UGC priorities reflected the values of the international academic establishment, which were not necessarily the same as those of the Government. As a result, the politicians had to watch, with anguish, disproportionately large cuts falling on universities such as Salford and Aston, which were trying to develop close links with industry, in line with government policy.

The episode did not lead to the eclipse of Salford, whose vice-chancellor seized the opportunity that the crisis presented to shake up his university and redevelop it on a much more entrepreneurial model. He set out to market the university to industry, especially in the North-west of England, raising from business the funds that he could not raise from the University Grants Committee. In the process, he changed the reward structure, both in money and status, to encourage professors and lecturers to heed the needs of industry and commerce rather than the shibboleths of academe. All this – including those changes that were more apparent than real – can be seen as a consequence of the Government's original cuts and the UGC's response to them.

It can also be shown that, taking the universities as a whole, the cuts led to a fall in the number of university engineering students, which was not part of the Government's intention, and the loss through early retirement of irreplaceable university teachers in science and technology. The whole exercise was largely improvised; it was not a carefully thought out strategy for change devised by the DES, but a hasty response to a sudden demand for large savings. The fact that the DES had absolute control of the UGC's budget (unlike the budgets of the local authorities) made the universities a natural target.

The episode certainly dented the reputation of the UGC and called in question the wisdom of leaving to a body composed of the universities' own brightest and best the responsibility for carrying out policies with which they disagreed. The appointment in 1985 of a committee to review the UGC itself, chaired by Lord Croham, the former head of the Home Civil Service, was a delayed consequence of the 1981 episode. An arm's-length formula can only succeed where there is a high degree of mutual trust. The 1981 crisis showed that this had broken down: there was no longer a comfortable Establishment view shared by ministers and vice-chancellors alike. Nor was there indifference on the part of the Government about what happened an arm's-length away. The Government had begun to develop important political and economic aims that it wished to impress on the universities and these were not shared by the universities' own leaders.

In the aftermath of the 1981 crisis, the UGC and the DES were forced to adopt a more open style. It also became clear that the Department of Trade and Industry and the Department of Education and Science would in future try to channel money to chosen projects, such as information technology, by ways that would by-pass the UGC.

At the end of 1984 a scheme was announced for creating extra places in engineering and other vocational courses, including conversion courses for students who had previously studied in other disciplines. The novelty in this instance was that, although the money was formally allocated by the UGC, this allocation was made on the advice of a powerful inter-departmental committee, which canvassed the views of industrialists on the merits of particular universities and departments.

If the UGC were to lose its control of the allocation of funds – or if, say, individual universities were able to go behind the UGC to the minister and persuade him or her to 'second guess' the Committee's judgement – the threat to the arm's-length system would be obvious. Not surprisingly, in discussing Lord Croham's review in *The Times Higher Education Supplement*, Sir Edward Parkes, vice-chancellor of Leeds University (and incumbent chairman of the UGC during the 1981 crisis), saw the 'theft by Government of university funds for redistribution by an interdepartmental committee' as 'folly' and a form of 'depredation which, if it proved to be inevitable, given a change in the political climate, might have to take place before the block grant gets into the UGC hands and not after' (*THES*, 21 March 1986, p. 19).

It will be for the Universities Funding Council, the post-Croham replacement for the UGC, to function as the new instrument of external intervention. The Government guidelines will be clearer; university representation smaller; industry and business will have a bigger voice. The emphasis will be on accountable grants made against the promise of specific services. The more it is to be the vehicle for central control, the more staff it will need and the more bureaucratic it will become.

PUBLIC SECTOR HIGHER EDUCATION

Like Exchequer support for the universities, the public sector of higher education also goes back into nineteenth-century history, with the first grants going to church teacher-training colleges from the Committee of the Privy Council and, later, the Board of Education and, in due course, the local education authorities. Apart from teacher training, the larger towns also came to support a growing amount of technical education, including some of an advanced nature linked to the London University external degrees and other professional qualifications.

By 1945, when the Percy Committee came to report on 'higher technical education in England and Wales and the respective contribution to be made thereto by universities and technical colleges'

(Ministry of Education, 1945), more than half the national output of professionally qualified engineers was receiving education in the technical colleges, the majority attending part-time.

Early attempts to rationalize the higher education function of the technical college therefore revolved around the arrangements for engineering education. There were two requirements, which provided beacons for the policy-makers: advanced work had to be concentrated in a limited number of colleges, which could then be built up; and a recognized qualification had to be introduced that was less restrictive than the London external degree, while still providing an adequate guarantee of standards.

Various White Papers and policy statements have developed policy in both of these directions. The 1956 White Paper (Ministry of Education, 1956) ended the ten years of vacillation that followed the Percy Report by setting up a limited number of colleges of advanced technology (CATs) – eight were designated from among the major colleges – which were to concentrate on degree work. A special 75 per cent grant for advanced work and the elaboration of arrangements for pooling the local authority share of the costs marked the beginning of a phase of rapid development, in which these colleges shed their junior work and extended their range of higher education.

A year earlier the National Council for Technological Awards (NCTA) had been set up to devise a method of examination control that would leave the maximum scope for professional curricular initiative within the colleges, while exercising effective external monitoring of course content and the standard of institutional provision. After the Robbins Committee elevated the CATs to university status it was necessary to repeat the exercise in modified form. Anthony Crosland replaced the CATs by the polytechnics, as public sector colleges concentrating on advanced work (though not exclusively), while the Council for National Academic Awards took over from the NCTA, awarding degrees not diplomas.

The rationale had changed in one important respect, however. What had begun as a means of providing for more and better higher technological education rapidly turned into a second tier of higher education generally. The expansion outran the rise in the number of technology students. The growth of facilities for them in the universities had not been held back to make room for the polytechnics, there being little attempt to co-ordinate the two sectors. The polytechnics and the larger colleges of further education, which ran some advanced courses alongside less advanced work, filled up with social scientists and students of the humanities. When, as a result of the demographic trend, the bottom fell out of teacher training in the mid-1970s the process of change was speeded up. The former colleges of education fought for survival by putting on diversified social studies programmes, aimed at students who could not now expect to be teachers. Some of the colleges were merged with polytechnics, further diluting the higher technological element; others sought to become free-standing liberal arts colleges.

A NATIONAL ADVISORY BODY

By the end of the 1970s it had become clear that there had to be a more coherent and effective planning mechanism for public sector higher education. The main issue in contention was how this was to reflect the legitimate interests of central and local government. Most of the money came from the centre, yet most of the institutions were owned and administered by the local authorities. The National Advisory Body emerged as a device that left a large measure of initiative to local authority representatives, while reserving to the Secretary of State the right to accept or reject its advice. The political compromise accommodated a DES that was reluctant to part with the ultimate authority (or to connive in the establishment of conventions that would let this happen *faute de mieux*) and local authorities that wished to retain their formal role as owners and managers of higher education colleges, while being content to leave final decisions to the Secretary of State as a long-stop to save them from their own folly.

How permanent any set of arrangements for regulating public sector higher education can be, given the volatility of the relations between central and local government, is a matter for speculation. Paying for the public sector through the 'capped pool' (the technique improvized to impose financial discipline on local authority colleges whose organic growth threatened to defy national planning) can be likened to a form of specific grant, a mode of funding the DES would like to see extended in any reform of local government finance. One school of thought within the DES always favoured the nationalization of advanced and non-advanced further education with a more powerful input of planning advice from other government departments, such as Industry and Employment, with the DES as the co-ordinator and paymaster, taking over roles hitherto performed by the Manpower Services Commission and the local authorities.

The emergence of NAB put into sharper focus questions about

the wisdom or necessity of having two separate sectors of higher education, one public, one autonomous. The hackneyed arguments about the binary system look increasingly irrelevant if the Government intends to take a firmer hand in the running of both sets of institutions. In the Green Paper, *The Development of Higher Education into the 1990s* (DES, 1985a), the Government made it clear that it saw 'no need for a united planning body for higher education of the kind comprehended by the term "over-arching body" '. Significantly, the same paragraph (8.3) went on to insist on the Government's own responsibilities for policy and planning which would be 'enhanced by the absence of such a body'. The acknowledgement of such 'enhanced responsibilities' was a clear indication of the change in political context. The sequel – the 1987 White Paper (DES 1987) – was designed to remove public sector higher education from local control and to replace NAB with a new Polytechnics and Colleges Funding Council.

TACTICS OR STRATEGY?

The events that marked the start of this new era took place under the Conservative governments of the 1980s. But it would be naive and unhistorical to regard the revision of the ground rules as something linked in a singular fashion with any particular political party.

The area and extent of government interest having been broadened and a much greater degree of intervention having been legitimated, ministers and civil servants in at least four government departments – the Treasury, the Department of Trade and Industry, the Department of Employment (and its executive arm, the Manpower Services Commission) and the DES – now expect to address questions about higher education and to do so not as matters of armchair criticism, but as part of the regular pursuit of government policies and their stewardship of public funds.

The last factor – the stewardship of public funds in a period of acute financial constraints – has exercised a strong influence on the way the framework of policy-making has changed. To assess the value obtained for the money spent in higher education quickly leads into deep waters. Efficiency cannot be measured without a definition of aims and a method of assessing both inputs and outputs. There has been a notable increase of interest in 'output' measures and other ways of comparing efficiency of higher education institutions and departments, even if (as witness the scant regard paid to the relevant appendices to the Green Paper of 1985) people will only pay attention to the evidence that suits them. When the paymasters start asking why this or that programme is being supported by public funds, or why it requires so much money to provide this or that service, the pressure to intervene mounts and with it the urge to develop public policies in areas hitherto left to institutions on the periphery of the public domain. Governments are always tempted to attack wasteful public spending by cutting the money first and asking questions afterwards – reducing the level of funding and using the threat of imminent insolvency to concentrate minds on unwelcome forms of cost-saving.

In many universities the crisis measures of 1981 led to false economies, including those later criticized by the Comptroller and Auditor General (National Audit Office, 1985). In others, necessity proved the mother of inventive administration and imaginative finance. By positing a continuing reduction in real resources as part of its plan for the pursuit of efficiency in the universities, and attempting to force a similar, though even more severe, regime on public sector higher education, the architects of public expenditure policy were imposing their own terms on the higher education policy debate. Privatization of one or more universities appeared at one time to be high on the agenda, but the 1985 Green Paper regretfully concluded that, although various less than satisfactory schemes for raising private funds had been put forward, 'no substantial part of established public funding responsibilities can be shed'.

What can be done, however, is to put predetermined limits on funding and then tell the policy-makers that all their plans must be accommodated within these limits. Again, the 1985 Green Paper was blunt about the limited planning horizon imposed on higher education by the conventions of public financial planning. Writing in 1985, the authors of the Green Paper declared that 'Cmnd 9428 [*The Government's Expenditure Plans 1985–86 to 1987–88*] provides the best indication that the Government can give of the public funding likely to be made available for higher education up to 1987–88. Beyond this there are the same difficulties about providing financial projections for the funding of higher education as for other public expenditure programmes . . . Planning must proceed on the basis that the policies underlying the Government's expenditure plans will be sustained beyond the immediate planning horizon, in the light of the guidance that the Government is able to give from time to time about its longer term policy intentions' (DES, 1985a, paragraph 9.10, p. 41).

The long-term financial plans (in so far as they could be relied upon) as propounded in 1985 implied the cuts of 2 per cent per year, which the UGC warned the universities to expect for the rest of the decade, and larger cuts for the 1990s. Moreover, although the Green Paper recognized the tentative nature of its forecasts of student demand and student numbers – and therefore, that these might have to be revised upwards in certain circumstances – the implication of what it had to say about finance was that the universities could not rely on any more money even if the planned numbers of students were to rise. When the Vice-Chancellor of the University of Oxford, in presenting the University's response to the Green Paper, questioned 'whether the policies indeed underlie the expenditure plans, or whether the expenditure plans do not in fact underlie the policies', he was not simply indulging in forensic licence. 'We fear', he said, 'the cart has preceded the horse.'

Tighter financial controls will certainly lead to more bureaucratic controls in the DES's relationship with the reconstituted Universities Funding Council and the UFC's own working methods and staffing requirements. Indeed, if there is no larger strategy for shaping higher education to serve more clearly articulated national aims, then an increase in bureaucracy could well turn out to be the main outcome. The managers would take over – centrally in Government and locally in the individual institutions.

NEW HIERARCHIES

The pattern of university provision would change in predictable ways if a combination of restrictive policies on student entry numbers and limited research funds forced a reduction in the number of universities that could be resourced to compete at the highest level. A more hierarchical structure would be created, which would bridge both sectors of higher education and replace the present clearly differentiated university and college networks with institutions of unequal status ranged in a pecking order. Such a hierarchy, which, ideally, would reflect transient differences of merit between institutions, would in reality be crude and dubious but would be given authority by being used as the basis for bureaucratic decisions about the allocation of funds. If the unequal distribution of funds were taken to its logical conclusion, it would turn peer-group impressions into self-fulfilling prophecies. The result would be a much more frank recognition of the differences in quality and status that already exist between universities and university departments, with a few awarded a special accolade as

23

international research universities while the remainder competed for promotion or relegation among the lower divisions.

In 1986 the UGC took the first steps along such a road, believing rationalization was necessary if the high quality research potential of the best places were to be protected in circumstances where there was not enough money to go round.

The first chapter of the 1985 Green Paper, which set out 'The Government's main concerns', put at the forefront of the discussion 'the economic performances of the United Kingdom since 1945' and the vital need for the universities and colleges 'to contribute more effectively to the improvement of the performance of the economy' in competition with other countries. The need for more scientists, engineers, technicians and technologists is taken as axiomatic in the light of modern industrial trends. 'A thriving economy needs these skills both to develop the talents of entrepreneurs and to support their achievements: if the present trends continue, the result seems likely to be a further fall in our relative standard of living and our ability to sustain our cultural heritage' (DES, 1985a, paragraphs 1.2–1.3, p. 3).

The Green Paper went on to itemize the responses required from higher education in implementing the 'switch', that is, increasing the output of scientists and engineers in a period when overall numbers would tend to fall rather than rise. 'Flexibility' (linked in this context to managerial streamlining) headed the list. In addition, higher education establishments were enjoined to 'be concerned with attitudes to the world outside higher education, and in particular industry and commerce, and to beware of anti-business snobbery' (ibid., paragraph 1.6, p. 4).

In this statement of its main concerns, the Government was following up a line of reasoning that had been pushed hard by the Department of Industry from the period in the mid-1970s when the notion of a national industrial strategy was in vogue. In fairly bland form, it emerges in a Department of Trade and Industry discussion paper on 'Industry, education and management' (July, 1977) and in the Central Policy Review Staff's report, *Education, Training and Industrial Performance* (1980). More explicitly, the DTI committee chaired by John Butcher, produced a series of initiatives with regard to information technology.

A similar 'switch' had been attempted after the Robbins Report (Committee on Higher Education, 1963), and the result within a few years was empty laboratories and workshops because student-demand failed to follow the top-down orders of the Government. The attempt to do the same trick with greater success in the 1980s and 1990s would clearly depend on how successfully the Government could change the schools and their curricula, and this in turn would depend on the recruitment and training of science teachers. As many of the science teachers are themselves trained in universities, the circular nature of the argument (and the difficulty of breaking it) become obvious. Ironies abound. The more Government urges graduates – especially maths and science graduates – to look to industry, the harder it becomes to get them to enrol for teacher training.

The intervention of the DTI has stepped up the pressure on the universities (in particular) and on students to distinguish between 'useful' and 'useless' studies, albeit in a highly simplistic manner, and to challenge the casual manifestation of prejudice against 'trade' and in favour of the professions. Ironically, the drive to combat anti-industry sentiment coincided with 'deregulation' in the City of London and the rocketing salaries offered to young graduates by merchant banks and stockbrokers, which reinforced prejudices against manufacturing industry.

The 'switch' represented an attempt to impose public policy constraints on students' choice of course on the basis of manpower-planning assumptions, but without any of the paraphernalia of scientific manpower-planning. The market mechanisms that might be expected to direct students' eyes away from law, accountancy and merchant banking had failed to exert themselves, so additional measures were deemed to be necessary. 'The 'switch' was based on a belief that industry's needs could be anticipated – that young people could be trained for the high-tech jobs in industry that would become available if and when employers came to understand their own best interests.

The thinking behind the 'switch' goes beyond the specifics of manpower-planning, with related reforms of secondary and further education, and industrial training. It aims at deeper cultural changes – changes in popular values sufficient to alter Britain's whole attitude to wealth creation. In essence, this amounts to an acceptance of the persuasive thesis put forward by Martin Wiener in his study, *English Culture and the Decline of the Industrial Spirit* (1981), echoed and brought up to date by Correlli Barnett in *The Audit of War* (1986), in which he, too, sought to spell out the links between the decline and fall of Britain's manufacturing industry and the inherited humanistic values of English higher education.

If the shortcomings of British industry, its low productivity, poor standards of training and the shortage of educated manpower at every level are to be blamed on a set of cultural values that embodies an out-moded world view and an unserviceable reluctance to make earning a good living a high priority, then the implications are likely to extend to every aspect of educational policy, and this would hold good whichever political party held power at Westminster. Higher education would be judged against criteria of national economic need. The outcomes would be different in an 'enterprise' society from those in a 'socialist' society, but in their different ways all the main political parties have come to put higher education's obligations towards national economic renewal at the centre of the debate about the future of the universities and polytechnics. The content and organization of higher education is now squarely within the arena of political debate.

To the best of their limited abilities, the politicians will not hesitate to make their demands on the universities and polytechnics and to use all available bureaucratic means to make them follow their wishes. They will do so with new vigour if they believe they have identified higher education as part of the problem as well as the solution.

It would be naive to suppose this has no implication for academic freedom. When higher education was seen as a self-justifying good, access to which governments would like to see extended as widely as possible, it was convenient as well as intellectually desirable for academics to be left alone. When, on the other hand, universities and polytechnics are to be used as part of the armoury of weapons deployed to dislodge one set of cultural values from their stronghold in order to install another, governments will not find it easy to live with dissidence in the academic world.

It is ironical that the argument about the purpose and public responsibilities of higher education should thus be led into more and more far-reaching realms of policy at a moment when the scope for expansion is eliminated and the prospect that the paymasters hold out is one of contraction. It seems reasonable, however, to expect that real demand (whatever that is) will continue to increase and that the more pessimistic projections of student numbers will only prove accurate if the relative decline of the British economy continues without remission. In the long run, it must be likely that liberal arguments in favour of wider access will march hand-in-hand with instrumental demands for an increase in trained manpower as essential to economic revival. They are complementary, not con-flicting, provided the actual experience that higher education offers is deemed to increase (not diminish) competence in a competitive world. But it is a measure of how acclimatized the British higher education community has become to the end of an expansionist

26

era – and a measure, too, of the changed political framework for higher education – that 'level funding', i.e. no actual reduction in resources, has become the slogan of the optimists.

CONCLUSION

To sum up, therefore:

- The political context of higher education changed during the decade from 1976–85.
- A combination of reasons (budgetary, economic, managerial) heightened Government interest in the value to the nation of the money spent on higher education.
- This has affected the arm's-length techniques for the management of Exchequer support for the universities, and caused the introduction of a new policy-making body for public sector higher education, which is subordinate to the ultimate authority of the Secretary of State.
- The range of public concerns about ends and means in higher education has been extended. The long-standing concern for qualified manpower (but not, generally, for manpower-planning) has been heightened. In particular, there has been a new interest in qualified manpower questions on the part of the Department of Trade and Industry, which has been fed into government thinking. This is manifest in the policy that the Government has conveyed to the University Grants Committee in the form of a request for more scientists and engineers and for fewer students of the humanities. The limits of acceptable intervention, and in particular of financial pressure, in support of this (or any other) policy have yet to be explored, but such exploration is now part of the political context of higher education – the UGC has always seen earmarked grants as the device by which pressure might be stepped up, and has therefore resisted them. Earmarked grants for universities, specific grants for polytechnics, 'education support grants' – the names vary from one generation to the next: but increasingly the policy argument will focus on the willingness of the universities (in particular) to accept tied money. The consequences of earmarked funding will not stop at the universities; if this is how money is to be paid out, it will put pressure on the DES to develop coherent long-term strategies, to which ministers would be held accountable in administering a specific funding programme.

27

- So far, any such long-term strategy has proved elusive for two reasons. First, the planning mechanisms inside the DES and in the UGC are inadequate for the task and the management of the system as a whole has so far been on a hand-to-mouth basis. Secondly, an adequate strategy depends on a coherent and intellectually respectable theory of the relationship between higher education policy and national economic management. In the absence of a working manpower-planning model, there is a long way to go before a serviceable strategy can be evolved. In the absence of such a strategy, the tendency is to fall back on more and more fussy, bureaucratic intervention and financial control.

- The other major change affecting the political framework within which plans for higher education will be considered relates to the wider cultural climate of Britain and whether or not this is dominated by 'anti-industrial' values. The suspicion – that the universities and colleges (with other social institutions) may perpetuate cultural assumptions that are deemed to be hostile to the 'enterprise culture' needed for an economic revival – lies at the centre of a debate that is far from finished.

- It is easy to see how quickly this could lead to classical questions relating to academic freedom and the limits of legitimate state intervention, but easy, also, to see how these issues extend the framework within which policy studies in higher education have to be conducted.

NOTE

In preparing this essay I have drawn, with permission, on an article on British higher education policy, which I contributed to the *Political Quarterly*, vol. 53, no. 3, July–September 1982. The text was written in 1986, and was set in type before the publication of the White Paper on Higher Education (DES 1987). Only minor amendments have been possible to take account of the proposed structural changes.

3

Central Control of the University Sector

JOHN H. FARRANT

INTRODUCTION

The universities are often called the 'autonomous sector' of British higher education, as distinct from the 'public sector'. However, British universities, in modern times at least, have always been beholden in some degree to other institutions or persons. The public sector institutions are less autonomous because, among other reasons and with some significant exceptions, they are each an establishment of a local government authority. They are firmly within a framework of statute law which places powers of direction, legitimated ultimately through the ballot box, with the local authority and the relevant Secretary of State. The universities, like the public sector institutions, are financed mainly from public funds, but their legal constitutions do not specify how they are subject to the public authorities, which (on behalf of the electorate) provide the funds. In the 1980s, the universities' autonomy is perceived as eroded, as those to whom the universities stand accountable seek or exact greater accountability.

This chapter is concerned primarily with the relations between universities and Government, represented by ministers, departments of state and agencies directed or funded by them. The main structural elements of those relations have remained remarkably constant and put the two parties at arm's length. They are without close parallel among other major social institutions that are dependent mainly on public funds. But British government customarily provides the services of the welfare state through intermediary bodies. The universities are among the suppliers of those services, and the distinctiveness of their relationship with Government is a matter of degree: they lie at the extreme of the spectrum. Unlike many other aspects of social provision as the functions of the State

29

have expanded, though, university education has not been the object of systematic reorganization embodied in legislation. R. A. Butler, the architect of the 1944 Education Act, did not press his preference for bringing universities within the scope of the public educational system that the Act established, and outside it they have remained (Gosden, 1976, pp. 422–30).

The sections that follow examine first the legal embodiment of the universities' autonomy, then the government agencies through which public funds are provided, next the mechanisms of voluntary co-ordination, and finally the constituents of university autonomy.

THE LEGAL CONSTITITION OF THE UNIVERSITIES

'The universities' are here defined as those teaching institutions that are acknowledged by the Government as empowered to award degrees. There are four groups of institutions, not all of which have 'university' in their title. The first and largest are the institutions in receipt of government grant from the Department of Education and Science (DES) on the advice of the University Grants Committee: 53 in England, Wales and Scotland comprising 42 universities and 11 institutions which for various historical reasons receive their UGC grant direct and which have their own governing bodies but which for certain purposes, most particularly the award of degrees, are constituent parts of a university. Secondly, there are three institutions that are constituted similarly to the universities on the UGC's list and receive government grant from the DES, but not on the advice of the UGC. They are the Royal College of Art, the Cranfield Institute of Technology and the Open University. In 1965 the UGC recommended against the first two being taken on to its list; the foundation of the third was not handled by the UGC or even by the DES's Universities' Branch, and its transfer to the UGC was rejected in 1981 mainly because (like the other two) it was so dissimilar to those already on the list and because it did see advantages in direct funding (UGC, 1968, pp. 77–8; Carswell, 1985, pp. 68–9; Open University, 1982, pp. 10–11). Thirdly, Northern Ireland has two universities, on whose grants the UGC advises the Government of the Province. The fourth group comprises only of the University of Buckingham, which has eschewed acceptance of institutional grant-aid from the Government (though it receives public funds through other channels). The definition excludes the

Council for National Academic Awards, which confers degrees but does not teach, and the legally independent colleges of Oxford, Cambridge and Durham, which do not award degrees. With the exception of the London and Manchester Business Schools and the Royal College of Art, the executive heads of the institutions in these four groups plus principals of six Schools of the University of London and the Registrars of Oxford and Cambridge comprise the members of the Committee of Vice-Chancellors and Principals of the Universities of the United Kingdom (CVCP).

In Britain, in contrast to other major European countries, there is no specific act of the democratic legislature that constitutes universities as a class of institutions within the nation or regulates their general character. All British universities created since 1900 – which is all bar eight – were established as legal entities by Royal charter. With the exception of the University of Wales they were to be unitary rather than federal, with each institution having extensive rights of internal self-government as well as the power to award degrees. Most of the older foundations are now constituted under special Act of Parliament, or a combination of Act and charter. Under the authority of charter or Act, all universities have statutes that set out the main elements of their internal organization.

The grant of a charter to a university is regarded as a matter of public concern. First, the promoters of a new college or university apply to the Privy Council for a charter. A copy of the draft charter and statutes is laid before both Houses of Parliament for at least thirty days. Lords or Commons, their members lobbied by interested parties, can then resolve to ask the Queen not to grant the charter, as happened once in 1892 (Berdahl, 1959, p. 43). Supporters and opponents may be heard before a committee of the Privy Council (Ashby and Anderson, 1974, pp. 64–70). Secondly, where the Privy Council's business concerns the activity of a department of state, that department's minister bears responsibility for it. So 'the Secretary of State for Education and Science is responsible for decisions of the Privy Council regarding university charters, although this responsibility tends to be obscured by the dignified facade of Privy Council formality' (Wade and Bradley, 1985, p. 245).

The Secretary of State in turn looks to the UGC for advice; and the petition for a charter may be only a late stage of lengthy discussions between the institution and the UGC on the former's development. The granting of charters to university colleges from the 1920s onwards was closely considered by the UGC, which prevented Nottingham's elevation until the academic staff had an adequate role in governance (Shinn, 1986, ch. 2 and pp. 119–29). The UGC was not involved to the same extent in the chartering of the colleges of advanced technology, because both chartering and transfer to the UGC list (in 1964–65) were recommended by the Robbins Committee. The only newly chartered institutions since the establishment in 1966 of a binary system of higher education have been the Open University (1969) and the University of Buckingham (1983), both unambiguously political decisions, outside the ambit of the UGC. Nevertheless, the UGC still maintains an important role in the institutional shape of the universities, ultimately embodied in charters and legislation: for instance, during the 1980s, by encouraging reorganization within the University of London and the merger of two of the University of Wales's colleges in Cardiff.

Involvement of the Privy Council and, through it, other government departments extends beyond the initial grant to amendments both to the charter and also, when the university is constituted by Act, of the statutes. Although amendments can normally be initiated only by the university, the need for amendment may have been indicated informally by the Privy Council, and informal discussion is likely to have taken place on what would be acceptable. The Privy Council Office consults the DES and the UGC. It clearly has guidelines on matters of internal government, such as the proportion of seats in the Senate that may be occupied by constituencies other than professors and other senior staff. Indeed the Privy Council Office revealed in 1982 that ministers had concluded that all new and supplementary charters that contained provisions on the tenure of staff must include explicit mention of redundancy as a reason for dismissal (*THES*, 11 February 1983, p. 5). The means for imposing amendments to statutes is the appointment by special Act of Parliament of 'statutory commissioners'. This mechanism was first used to reform recalcitrant 'Oxbridge' colleges following the Royal Commissions established in 1850, but was also invoked in the twentieth century to resolve constitutional disputes within the older universities (Berdahl, 1959, pp. 32–46). It was only want of parliamentary time that obliged the Secretary of State for Education and Science, in 1986, to abandon seeking legislation to amend charters and statutes in order to restrict tenure (*THES*, 28 March 1986, p. 1).

Two aspects of universities' internal constitutions that are inherent in their charters represent forms of external control. First, all the charters appoint (or provide for the appointment of) a 'visitor' (Smith, 1981, 1986). The concept of the visitor comes originally

from the ancient ecclesiastical law through the colleges of Oxford
and Cambridge. The visitor's duty is:

> to supervise the government and regulation of the foundation
> of which he [is] visitor, on behalf of the founder, to see that the
> private laws given in the form of statutes, ordinances, regula-
> tions, etc. by the founder to his foundation [are] observed, and
> out of this supervisory role [has come] a jurisdiction to hear and
> determine any disputes within the foundation concerning the
> enforcement or interpretation of those private laws.

The general courts of law have long declined jurisdiction in matters
that fall within the visitor's province. As academic staff are normally
appointed by a contract of employment to a position in the
university that carries with it membership of the foundation, the
increased statutory protection afforded to employees has brought a
rash of cases in which the courts have had to determine whether, or
which parts of, a dispute should fall to the visitor (Smith, 1986,
p. 484). They have tended to give primacy to the contract of
employment. For a student, the courts have found a contract of
membership by which the university undertakes to treat him or her
fairly and in accordance with the rules; they have therefore required
the observance of the principles of natural justice in the imposition
of academic discipline but have not ruled on the merits of the case
(Wade, 1982, pp. 418, 501–3, 566–7).

For the great majority of universities the visitor is the Queen or
the Queen in Council, so the visitatorial authority is exercised
through the Lord President of the (Privy) Council or (if a visitor has
not been appointed) the Lord Chancellor. Although this side of the
Privy Council's business is not subject to political influence in the
way that the granting of charters is, the aggrieved party may see it as
a means of appeal outside the university rather than as a domestic
tribunal. As an example of a collective dispute, Hull's Students'
Union claimed in 1984 that the University's Council acted ultra
vires in disregarding a resolution of its Court. Most appeals probably concern individual students' examination results and have
increased significantly in number since the mid-1970s. Although the
Privy Council has not interfered in matters of academic judgement
and seems rarely to have found in favour of appellants on grounds of
irregularities of procedure, the burden of work on its officers and
members has led to informal encouragement to the universities to
extend the appeal procedures that operate under the Senate and the
Council. It may have thus prompted the CVCP code of practice on
appeals against the results of examinations for research degrees

(CVCP, 1986, pp. 28–30). The decision in a successful appeal is likely to be circulated by the university concerned to other universities, which may review their procedures in consequence.

The second form of external control inherent in a university's statutes is the membership of its executive governing body. Most universities' constitutions provide for a large, inert body which receives an annual report and elects honorary officers and which is usually called the Court (or, in Scotland, the General Council). The executive body entrusted with the overall management of the university is the Council (or, in Scotland, the Court). Most members of the Council are 'lay', in that they are not drawn from the body of staff and students. Typically, one-third may be nominees of local government authorities, one-third nominees of the Court or co-options, and one-third academic staff and students. Only Oxford and Cambridge have no lay members on their governing bodies. The local government representation is a relic of the times when local authorities contributed substantial funds, in part for education not of a university standard and therefore not supported by the UGC. The lay membership of Council now embodies what Clark (1983a, p. 29) calls trustee authority 'in which there is some supervision by outsiders who are part-time, unpaid, and have primary commitments elsewhere. Trusteeship is a form of public influence effected without going through governmental channels'. The statutes usually constitute the Council as the effective internal governing and managerial body, subject only to visitatorial authority, some supervision by the Court and the right of the Senate to be consulted on academic matters generally and to be the final authority in some of them. The Jarratt Committee (CVCP, 1985, pp. 23, 36) has emphasized the internal managerial role of the Council in recommending that it should assert its responsibilities, particularly in strategic planning.

The form of the modern university's constitution was established, with the concurrence of politicians and other representatives of the public interest, in the early years of the present century, when charters were granted to the first generation of civic universities (Ashby and Anderson, 1974). It was refined by the University Grants Committee in its sponsorship of the university colleges (Shinn, 1986). It permeated the thinking and conclusions of the Robbins Committee: 'the pattern [of institutions] must provide for organic growth not only in total but for individual institutions. It must neither force their development at an intolerable pace nor leave them undisturbed when foresight would indicate the need for action' (Committee on Higher Education, 1963, p. 150). The

34

emphasis was on the free development of individual institutions rather than on the formation of a 'system' of higher education.

CONTROL THROUGH THE PURSE

Because British universities are neither public corporations nor establishments of central or local government, the Government does not have direct control over their activities. Its principal means of influence lies in the provision of finance – an influence exercised mainly through intermediary bodies of which politicians are not members. These bodies are permeated by people who are academics by profession, even if, for the time being, they have mainly administrative responsibilities. From the senior academic staff of the universities are recruited most members of the UGC, a sizeable fraction of the research councils, and most of the vice-chancellors and principals. There is in consequence much informal interaction between universities and paymasters, which the following description of relations between formally constituted bodies understates.

The institutions on the UGC list had an income of 1983–84 of about £2,000 million for recurrent expenses and about £100 million for capital, excluding the receipts of their ancillary enterprises financed mainly by charges to consumers (catering, student residences and the like) or conducted through subsidiary companies (such as publishing and industrial consultancy), and also excluding capital receipts other than through the UGC. Of this total, 79 per cent can be classified as 'general' income, as distinct from 21 per cent 'specific' income which was received only because a fairly closely defined activity was undertaken and which was related to the estimated cost of the activity (often the marginal cost, on the assumption that basic facilities were provided from general funds). The single largest source of income was the UGC, through which came 63 per cent. But the UGC was only one of several channels flowing from the DES (and, in small degree, the SED) whose parliamentary votes provided 78 per cent of all income, the other channels being the research councils, the Computer Board for Universities and the Research Councils, and tuition fees for home undergraduates (these being at rates determined by the Education Departments, paid mainly through local education authorities but largely reimbursed by DES). As a proportion of general, or core, funding, that from DES votes amounted to 87 per cent. The proportion of total income from all types of British public funds was about 84 per cent (estimated from UGC, 1985a, pp. 9–11).

These proportions are very much greater than when the modern chartered university first emerged at the turn of the century or when the UGC was established in 1919. In the 1920s and 1930s, the UGC worried when its grant constituted more than half a university's income. It repeatedly urged universities to diversify their sources of income as a buttress of independence, and offered extra grant to match extra locally raised money; it even reduced its grant in response to a local authority so doing (Shinn, 1986, pp. 155–67). General endowments were the most desirable form of income, and indeed the early arrangements for grants through the UGC have been characterized as simulating private funds: 'in the golden age of the UGC it acted rather like a board of governors of a system of private universities managing an enormous and growing corporate endowment; the Treasury's annual subvention simulated this phantom endowment's annual return' (Trow, 1983, p. 117). In 1983, the Secretary of State emphasized the advantages of diverse funding and encouraged suggestions that some universities might be bought off the UGC list by being given a lump sum as capital endowment and the freedom to fix rates of tuition fees (UGC, 1984a, pp. 34, 37–8).

The dominance of UGC grants dates from the late 1940s, as local authority funding declined in real terms and as private philanthropy did not keep pace with the expansion of the universities. It was reinforced by the extension of the grant list in the 1960s. Despite the crucial importance of the grants, their only statutory authority lies in a line item in each annual Appropriation Act (Class XII, Vote 3, Universities, etc.: 'expenditure by the Department of Education and Science on universities and certain other institutions, grants for further and higher education, grants in aid and a subscription to an international organisation'). The same vote includes grant to the Open University; vote 1 includes the grants to the RCA and Cranfield. The monies for all these institutions' recurrent expenditure and equipment are grants in aid, meaning that DES does not have to account for them in detail to the Comptroller and Auditor General, and that unexpended balances are not liable to surrender to the Consolidated Fund at the end of the financial year (HM Treasury, 1986, pp. iv, 15).

At his discretion, the Secretary of State for Education and Science takes advice on how much of the grants should go to each institution. For this purpose, individual Visiting Committees are appointed for the Open University, the RCA and Cranfield. For the bulk of the universities, the University Grants Committee is consulted. The UGC was established in 1919, but committees had been set up temporarily several times in the previous thirty years to advise the Chancellor of the Exchequer or the President of the Board of Education on specific issues or distributions of grant. The UGC has existed continuously since 1919, although always at ministerial pleasure. All its members are appointed by the Secretary of State (after consultation with the Secretaries of State for Scotland, Wales and Northern Ireland) and the scale of its administrative support is also determined by the Secretary of State. Thus far, the UGC is not greatly different from many other bodies advisory to ministers. What is distinctive is the combination of nearly a century's existence in various forms, although without statutory or chartered embodiment, of advising on the disbursement of so large a sum of money (about 1 per cent of central Government expenditure), and of the convention that ministers always accept its advice on the distribution between universities.

The UGC's nature and functions have been discussed in general terms in Chapter 2. In the rest of this chapter, a more detailed account will be given of the degree to which it operates as an instrument of central control. The UGC's terms of reference have been unchanged since 1946 except for an extension of its role in relation to Northern Ireland:

> To enquire into the financial needs of university education in the United Kingdom [in Great Britain, until 1983]; to advise the Government as to the application of any grants made by Parliament towards meeting them; to collect, examine, and make available information relating to university education throughout the United Kingdom [at home and abroad, until 1952]; and to assist, in consultation with the universities and other bodies concerned, the preparation and execution of such plans for the development of the universities as may from time to time be required in order to ensure that they are fully adequate to national needs (UGC, 1984a, p. 42).

Between 1919 and 1964, the UGC advised the Chancellor of the Exchequer, who was accountable for the universities' vote. Although this arrangement seems not to have originated in considered judgement that the universities' grants should be detached from the department responsible for education, it was soon elevated into a matter of high principle, a proper buttress to university autonomy: the Chancellor was less likely than the Education Minister to seek to impose on universities (Ashby and Anderson, 1974, pp. 93–101, 150–2; Gosden, 1976, p. 423).

The transfer of the UGC to the newly formed DES in 1964 was in part for administrative reasons. The Public Expenditure Survey, introduced in the early 1960s, required that the Treasury's role should be distinct from that of spending departments and that therefore the Treasury should shed its spending responsibilities – of which the universities were the largest, but which also included civil science, museums and galleries and the Arts Council (Carswell, 1985, pp. 10, 17, 55–6). In turn, the application of the prevailing rules of the public expenditure survey contributed to the abandonment (in the early 1970s) of the system whereby universities' grants were settled for five years at a time. Until 1967, the principle of grant in aid was interpreted so that only the DES's books and accounts were open to the Comptroller and Auditor General's inspection – which stopped at the issue by the DES of money to a deposit account from which payments were made, on the UGC's recommendation, to individual universities (UGC, 1968, pp. 186–9). Since then, inspection has extended to the universities as the effective spenders of the grant. The opening of the universities' books to inspection was the inevitable application of a general rule for all bodies receiving more than half their funds from Government; but its application to the universities was delayed for twenty years owing to the benevolent protection of the Treasury (Carswell, 1985, pp. 48, 86–7). Although the CAG's inspections have not intruded into matters of academic policy and have concentrated on 'housekeeping' and non-academic services, the long arm of the Public Accounts Committee is evident in the Permanent Secretary of the DES, as Accounting Officer, commissioning chartered accountants to investigate the financial affairs of University College, Cardiff (*THES*, 6 June 1986, pp. 1, 6). Also, the first report of the CAG's strengthened department, the National Audit Office (1985, pp. 3, 4), bearing on universities, was critical of which academic staff the UGC enabled to take voluntary redundancy in 1981–84 and endorsed the need for a fundamental review of the UGC's role and responsibilities.

The UGC's affiliation to the same department as is responsible for the rest of education in England has shortened the line between ministers and universities. Normally a minister of state at DES is responsible for higher and further education and civil science, and the Deputy Secretary in charge of the higher and further education branches attends meetings of the UGC. The UGC has to make its case annually for funds, like any other interest represented in DES, and to see its recommendations pass through several levels of competition and aggregation before the proposed vote (often not separately identified for more than a year ahead) appears in the

Public Expenditure White Paper early in the calendar year. Ministers' influence lies in their decisions on which of the DES's priorities to argue in Cabinet committee, in the allocation between the DES's votes of whatever funds become available, and in their responses to reports from the UGC, and their guidance transmitted to it through its chairman. The UGC's allocation between universities is formally a recommendation to the Secretary of State, but ministers have always accepted the UGC's advice and have never publicly questioned it afterwards. For instance, they made no concession to parliamentary pressure in the wake of the large cuts in some universities' grants recommended by the UGC in 1981.

The composition of the UGC (see Chapter 2) has been broadly consistent for forty years: a full-time chairman, usually a former vice-chancellor, who is appointed to the civil service as a Second Permanent Secretary, and unpaid members, a dozen from the ranks of senior university academic staff, four from other sectors of education and four from industry and commerce. They are appointed for five years; some academic members serve second terms. Selection has to ensure adequate representation of the major groups of academic disciplines and of the countries of the United Kingdom. Assessors or observers from the Education Departments, the research councils and the National Advisory Body are invited to meetings of the Committee for business not concerned with individual universities. The UGC's secretariat is part of the establishment of the Department of Education and Science, with almost entirely career civil servants posted to it.

The academic members are the most active in the UGC's business. Their universities willingly release them for service, in a way that the employers of the other members are unable to. It is the academic members who chair the sub-committees and are more likely to be appointed from the UGC to other bodies. The chairman is the dominant figure because he is full-time, has Civil Service status, has the secretariat at his command, is the public spokesman (although other members have been more conspicuous since 1981) and meets frequently with the DES ministers and officials.

The sub-committees relate to groups of academic disciplines, plus one concerned with scientific equipment. Most of their members are academics not on the Committee. The more detailed and sophisticated the Committee's distribution of grant becomes, the greater the workload and influence of the sub-committees. Sub-committees make visits to universities with the relevant disciplines, but a full programme now takes eight or more years to complete. One sub-committee that covers a large section of the universities' activity, physical sciences, makes few visits, apparently relying heavily on the research councils in framing its judgements of university departments. The Committee makes one-day 'visitations' on a similarly long cycle. Communication with the universities is otherwise through informal contact with their senior officers, ad hoc enquiries, and periodical major planning submissions. Most requirements for statistics on staff and students are met through the Universities Statistical Record.

The UGC's advice became more public from around 1980. The greater openness is largely a result of the changing way in which public affairs are conducted, but contributory factors are the widened participation in universities' internal governance, increased unionization of staff, the establishment in 1971 of a specialist weekly journal – *The Times Higher Education Supplement* – and the open style adopted by the UGC's public sector counterpart in England, the National Advisory Body, from its inception. UGC circular letters to universities seem regularly to have been released to the *THES* since the late 1970s; its 'strategy advice' (UGC, 1984a) was the first submission to the Secretary of State drafted with the intention of publication.

Whatever criteria the UGC may use to determine each university's share of the grant available, most of what the university receives is as a block recurrent grant. Less than 6 per cent (in 1983–84) of recurrent grant was 'earmarked' for closely specified expenditure, a proportion which had risen during the preceding few years but which was still small. There is no specification of how the rest of the recurrent grant (or of general income) should be spent between different types of resource (academic salaries, building maintenance, etc.) or between constituent parts of the university (e.g., the Faculty of Arts, the Library, etc.). What has increasingly been specified is the assumed programme of activity (the number of science under graduates, the discontinuance of teaching of Russian, etc.). The main constraints on the university's spending of the block grant are, first, what activities are deemed to fall within the scope of general income, defined mainly by exceptions (thus major capital projects may not be funded from general income) and additions (for instance, grants for vacation study and subscriptions to students' unions, for home students holding maintenance awards, were added in 1971 and 1981). Secondly, the UGC has stated the permitted subsidy to student services, such as catering, residences and creches, the proportion of the academic staff who may be in the senior grades, and the proportion of the recurrent grant that may be spent on minor capital projects. Thirdly, there is a distinct block grant for scientific equipment and for furniture. Fourthly, grants for major capital works (costing £1 million or more) are made only for specified projects.

The DES may make some money available to the UGC on condition that it is used for specific purposes and not for the block recurrent grant; the UGC may decide to hold back money for specific allocation. For instance, the DES allocated money specifically for redundancy payments in 1982–84, for 'new blood' and information technology posts in 1983–85, and for additional engineering places in 1985–87. The UGC has usually held back money to stimulate new developments by 'pump-priming' funding. The detailed supervision of which the DES is capable is illustrated by its grants to extramural departments of English and Welsh universities for liberal non-vocational adult education. These grants (amounting to only £5 million) have not been amalgamated with the UGC grant, though they assume contributions from general funds. The schedule of classes to be offered has to be approved by HM Inspectors if they are to rank for grant; the grant is related to the number of hours attended by enrolled students, the location of the class relative to the university and the status of the tutor.

The mechanism of the UGC relies on the restraint of Government in not seeking to impose its will directly through the purse on individual universities – and also on the compliance of the universities in adapting to national needs as perceived by Government and in not provoking Government to abandon its restraint. Vice-Chancellors have always known that the DES and the UGC can apply financial sanctions and have had to weigh very carefully whether or not to follow UGC advice. No one has put to the test what would happen if a university ignored repeated advice to discontinue a particular subject. There has long been unpalatable advice and unwelcome decisions (e.g. not to finance building projects); there has been an increasing amount of this in the past decade. The mediating role of the UGC between the DES and the universities has remained superficially the same, but the degree of direction delivered through it has increased. The conventional metaphor of the UGC as a buffer between Government and universities carries perhaps too much the connotation of collision and shock absorber. The metaphor of the coupling between locomotive and truck may now be more accurate: the coupling causes the following truck to move in the same direction as the leading one, but allows some differential movement and may vary in length and looseness; the power of the locomotive may be great or small relative to the weight of the truck.

A significant illustration of the changed relationship is the UGC's recommendation of 1984 that the Government explicitly revoke the principle of deficiency funding (UGC, 1984a, p. 35). The criteria laid down in 1889 for the committee to distribute the first government grant to the universities included 'the income of the institution, from whatever source derived, and the amount by which it falls short of its necessary expenditure, or would fall short of it, if the fees charged were such as the class of students who were likely to belong to it might reasonably be expected to pay' (Shinn, 1986, p. 24). The principle implied that the unit for consideration was solely the institution and its programme. Progressively, the UGC has become concerned with the pattern formed by all the institutions. One stage was marked by the extension of its terms of reference in 1946 to include a planning function – which until the early 1970s was expressed particularly through detailed control of the building programme, i.e. through the provision of additional student places necessarily specified by subject groupings. The need for additional recurrent grant followed fairly automatically from the capital allocations. With the virtual cessation of new building and the reduction of recurrent grant in real terms, the recurrent grant became the essential instrument of planning and the question of what was being bought with it was inevitably posed. In these circumstances, the fiction implied in the deficiency grant principle that the UGC acted only in response to universities' plans could not be sustained.

Having extracted from Government an assurance that universities' success in raising funds from other sources would not lead to reduction in recurrent grant, the UGC adopted thoroughgoing formula funding for its distribution to the universities in 1986. Some elements of formula funding had probably long been present, but with a large margin of moderation by judgement (e.g. UGC, 1982, pp. 24–7). For 1986–90, the framework of allocation was provided by formulae that differentiated research from teaching, and that allocated a uniform sum to each university for teaching a unit of 'student load' in a given group of disciplines. Judgement was applied to the planned distribution of home student numbers by twenty categories and three levels of subject studied, and to the relative research standing of universities in at least thirty-seven fields. Additions were made for 'special factors' not adequately covered by the formulae, such as copyright libraries and major museums. The resulting sums were then reduced by the fee income accruing from the planned number of home students and by other public funding considered to be for purposes otherwise covered by UGC grant. The grant for each university was nevertheless still announced and paid as a block grant. The planned student numbers and, in very summary form, the assessments of research standing were published, but not the money values used in the formulae (UGC, 1985c; 1986).

The reduction of recurrent grant has obliged the UGC to be much more concerned with the spread of subject provision across institutions. For medicine and schoolteaching, the total number of entrants each year has long been determined by Government, the UGC's role being to ensure a sensible apportionment of the total among the universities. 'Rationalization' is not a new term in the UGC's vocabulary. In 1966, at the height of the general expansion, the UGC advised three universities, Cambridge, Glasgow and Leeds, to discontinue undergraduate teaching of agriculture (UGC, 1968, pp. 109–10). A report to rationalize Russian and Russian studies was novel for being concerned not with an excess or deficit of graduates in relation to manpower needs, but rather with the shortage of applicants in relation to the teaching capacity (UGC, 1979). The 1981 grant settlement was accompanied by advice to discontinue named subjects, but probably not as a result of systematic review across all institutions. Systematic studies between then and the 1986 settlement were in fields in which manpower planning can be attempted (since 1983 in conjunction with the NAB). In other fields, from 1985 particularly, the UGC provided informal brokerage for universities bilaterally transferring staff, so closing a subject in one and strengthening it at the other, standard arrangements being made for adjusting grant and meeting expenses (UGC, 1985b). Recommendations to close provision sometimes led to political lobbying on a scale not previously known, by affected institutions as well as professional bodies and individuals, with, for example, debates in the House of Commons in 1984 on the future of pharmacy at Heriot-Watt.

Professional bodies have had a significant role in rationalization exercises, although it is only one aspect of their influence on universities. With the increasing number of generally recognized professional bodies and the steady assimilation over the years of professional training (at least in its theoretical aspects) into higher education institutions, the points of pressure on the universities have multiplied, mainly through the accreditation of courses. In some cases, accreditation is based on statutory authority, e.g. that held by the General Medical Council and (since 1984) by the Council for the Accreditation of Teacher Education in England and Wales. The latter is appointed by and advisory to the Secretary of State for Education and Science, who under his specific responsibilities for teacher training has opened relevant courses in the universities to HM Inspectors.

The distinction between teaching and research made in the 1986 grant settlement was highly significant, and reflected the influence of the research councils on the UGC and the universities. The five research councils (Agricultural and Food, Economic and Social, Medical, Natural Environment, Science and Engineering) are each a chartered body under the Science and Technology Act 1965, receiving most of their income under DES votes. These votes, with grants to a couple of other bodies, collectively form the Science Budget, on the distribution of which the Secretary of State is advised by the Advisory Board for the Research Councils. The councils support research by paying contributions to international facilities (such as CERN), maintaining their own research establishments (such as the Rutherford Appleton Laboratory) and making grants to researchers in other institutions, principally the universities. Although the councils provide only some 6.5 per cent of the universities' income, their influence is proportionately much greater. Their grants are not intended to meet the full cost of the research: they are made on the presumption that general income pays for the investigator, a 'well-found laboratory' and indirect support such as library, computer and administrative services. This division of responsibility is the 'dual-support system', which has repeatedly been reaffirmed by official committees because it provides alternative channels of funding for research, allowing the university to finance projects until they are sufficiently developed to be subjected to peer review in seeking council grants. The councils, particularly Science and Engineering, have argued since the mid-1970s that universities (and by implication the UGC) spread their general income too thinly, forcing the councils to bear more than their proper share of costs and to duplicate facilities; the universities should allocate more selectively to underwrite those projects that the councils would also support. In 1982, a joint UGC and ABRC working party recommended that each university should have a research committee to identify projects for support, to ensure that general funds were allocated to them and to monitor their progress (ABRC and UGC, 1982). Universities in their 1985 planning submissions were required to describe their machinery for the planning of, and resource allocation to, research. This was a novel incursion into the details of universities' internal management.

COLLECTIVE ACTION

Intrusion by the UGC or other government agencies into university affairs has been contained by the universities acting together to set up arrangements that satisfy the outsiders' legitimate requirements. These forms of collective action bring constraints, albeit more acceptable than those avoided, on universities' freedom. The key agency is the Committee of Vice-Chancellors and Principals of the Universities of the United Kingdom, chaired by a member usually for a two-year term; subscriptions from members' institutions finance a sizeable secretariat in London. The CVCP is criticized for not being a sufficiently forceful advocate and lobbyist for the universities' interests, but it is unable to take up positions that would be damaging to the interests of any one university. The connections between it and the UGC and the DES are continuous, multifarious and now indispensable. It plays a crucial role in representing the universities' interests to other official bodies, whether in evidence to parliamentary select committees, negotiations with HM Customs and Excise on the application of VAT, or a test case on valuation for rating. The flow of information and opinion through meetings of the full committee, standing committees and working groups, and through its distribution of documents, has a profound and probably underrated impact on the actions of senior administrators in the universities.

CVCP has spawned operational agencies to which each university has voluntarily surrendered some part of its autonomy. The best known is the Universities Central Council on Admissions, which since 1961 has operated a centralized applications system for admissions to full-time undergraduate courses at the UK universities whose grants are made on the advice of the UGC. The scheme specifies the number of applications that the candidate can make, the timetable for both candidates and universities and the form of universities' offers; but the decision whether or not to offer a place rests solely with the university (Kay, 1985). The limits of UCCA's role are emphasized by the parallel existence of the Standing Conference on University Entrance, a delegate body set up in 1965 and deriving its authority from all the universities. It formulates advice on behalf of the universities to government bodies about changes in the school curriculum and the public examinations system, and conversely proffers advice to the universities. It has been increasingly concerned with the presentation of information about preparing for university entrance aimed at schools, parents, teachers and advisers, as well as at mature students.

The Universities Statistical Record maintains, with information supplied by universities, an individual record for every student on a full-time course of a year's duration or the part-time equivalent, and for every member of staff on academic and related salary scales. Progressively from 1970, it has supplied statistics from these records and from other returns by universities (continuing education courses, student load, annual financial return) to the UGC and many other bodies, and has thereby eliminated most of the annual returns made by each university to the UGC. The imposition of more and more standard definitions has had an indirect but important impact on the ways in which universities perceive themselves and are perceived by others.

The University Authorities Panel and the Universities Committee for Non-Teaching Staffs have a more managerial role, acting as employers' associations for the purposes of negotiations at national level with trade unions on salaries – and, in the case of UCNS only, conditions of service (Bosworth, 1985). UAP is concerned with non-clinical academic and academic-related staff, within a negotiating framework established in 1970 by the DES which, with the Association of University Teachers, are the other parties. The involvement of the DES stems from (a) the decision of the UGC in 1946 no longer to recognize in its grant distribution the wide variations in universities' salary scales; (b) the imposition by the Treasury in 1949 of uniform scales; and (c) the practice, until 1976, of universities' UGC grants being supplemented for increases in academic salaries (Perkin, 1969, pp. 135–41). The UGC is involved only as the confidential adviser to the Government, and indeed its role in salary negotiations was reduced in 1970 to enable it to continue as such. Since 1979 there has been a separate Clinical Academic Staff Salaries Committee. UCNS dates from 1970, succeeding a body established in 1952, and conducts negotiations with the relevant trade unions through a Central Council and joint committees for different groups of staff. The broad policies within which all three bodies conduct detailed negotiations have, since 1980, been determined by the CVCP's General Purposes Committee.

These inter-university bodies were set up in response more to pressures external to the universities than to pressures from within them. The essentially reactive role of the CVCP – which nevertheless can lead to curtailed freedom for the individual university – can be readily illustrated. For example, in 1983 ministers wanted to subject universities to an efficiency scrutiny of the type that had been introduced in the Civil Service by Lord Rayner, the Prime

Minister's special adviser on efficiency. The CVCP negotiated for the DES to pay for independent management consultants to conduct, with university staff, efficiency studies in six universities, under the guidance of a steering committee that produced a general report, known after the chairman as the Jarratt Report (CVCP, 1985). Although the immunity of the universities from 'inspection' by Government was upheld, the report was critical of the prevalent management style and practices, and the DES looked for evidence of action on it as a condition of future enhancement of funding (see Chapter 5 for a more detailed account). Again, the interest of the Secretary of State in the maintenance of standards in education, which had led to the Lindop Report on validation in the public sector, moved the CVCP to set up in 1983 a group to study universities' methods and procedures for maintaining academic quality and standards. This group published discussion drafts and then final 'codes of practice' on the external examiner system, other forms of external involvement in maintaining and monitoring standards, internal procedures for the same, postgraduate training and research, and appeals against decisions of examiners for research degrees (CVCP, 1986).

The CVCP has sponsored many statements akin to codes of practice, as various as a concordat with the National Union of Students in the wake of student unrest in the late 1960s and 'Guidance on recommended accounting practices in UK universities' in 1985. The codes on academic standards broke new ground in advancing to the heartland of academic affairs. That this should happen reflects the absence of a single and strong professional organization among academics. Had there been such an organization, the codes of practice might have emerged from it rather than from a body representing senior management. There is in Britain no organized profession of scholars or researchers or scientists or even teachers of higher learning. The Association of University Teachers chose the road of trade unionism, symbolized by its affiliation to the Trades Union Congress in the 1970s. Most academics identify more strongly with 'invisible colleges' for their discipline or with professional bodies that embrace practitioners as well as teachers and researchers.

THE CONSTITUENTS OF UNIVERSITY AUTONOMY

That university autonomy and academic freedom are being threatened or eroded has provided a common source of concern in recent years, in response to this or that policy of Government or other body. Of what that autonomy and that freedom consist is less often stated. The autonomy of institutions is distinct from the 'academic freedom' of the individual scholar – which may serve as a protection against his or her university as much as against outsiders (Tight, 1985). The Robbins Committee (Committee on Higher Education, 1963, pp. 229–34) identified five desirable constituents of institutional autonomy. It saw that a nice balance had to be kept between two necessities:

> the necessity of freedom for academic institutions and the necessity that they should serve the nation's needs ... The urgent question is whether in the conditions of today the freedom from control that the universities have enjoyed in the past, and to which such importance has been attached, can be expected to persist unchanged ... When an autonomous institution is mainly dependent for its income not on the fees of the pupils, or on private endowments, but on subventions from the State, how far should it have completely independent powers of initiative and final decision? ... We believe that a system that aims at the maximum of independence compatible with the necessary degree of public control is good in itself, as reflecting the ultimate values of a free society. We believe that a multiplicity of centres of initiative safeguards spontaneity and variety, and therefore provides the surest guarantee of intellectual progress and moral responsibility. We do not regard such freedom as a privilege but rather as a necessary condition for the proper discharge of the higher academic functions as we conceive them.

The five constituents of the freedom that it identified were: freedom of appointment; freedom to determine curricula and standards; freedom of admission of students; freedom to determine the balance between teaching and research; freedom to determine the shape of development. To what extent do these freedoms exist in the late 1980s?

Freedom of appointment of academic staff remains, in that appointments financed from general funds are not referred to outside bodies, with a few exceptions of long standing (e.g. Regius Professorships). For appointment to 'new blood' lectureships in 1983–85, universities were expected to include on appointing committees a nominee of the relevant research council, who did not have a veto, however. Ability to attract the most suitable candidate is constrained by national salary scales, though the university is free to determine the grade and position on a scale.

Universities, broadly speaking, determine the content of their curricula and, subject to the involvement of external examiners, set the standards of competence. If a given course is to attract professional recognition, the curriculum has to be subjected to external scrutiny. Rarely can a university afford to forgo that recognition if it is to attract students (especially as, for home students, there is no competition on fees). The means of maintaining standards were openly questioned around 1983, with the suggestion even of a national accreditation agency (UGC, 1984a, p. 21). The CVCP's response was to set up the committee on academic standards (CVCP, 1986), which may for the time being have secured the freedom of the universities collectively at the expense of local diversity and discretion.

Robbins believed that a university should not be forced to accept or reject any particular student. Criteria and methods of selection have been the subject of continuous public concern, in relation to the impact on the school curriculum and, as regards Oxford's and Cambridge's practices, the apparent bias in favour of applicants from independent schools. Universities nevertheless have full discretion in selecting between applicants. The ability of any student to take up the offer of admission is most commonly constrained by finance. On this the university cannot help, except through private endowments. Universities may not use general income for the maintenance of students; statutory regulations determine who is eligible for payment of fees and maintenance from public funds; subsidy in the UGC grant for teaching overseas students was withdrawn in 1980.

The freedom to determine the balance between teaching and research was challenged by the UGC's explicitly selective distribution of recurrent grant in 1986. The principle of a block grant meant that a university could still vary the balance in any given subject from that predicated in the calculation of the grant. It had incentives to reduce the cost of teaching, without reducing the standard, in order to free resources for research for which it could also seek specific funding. Nevertheless, the university could expect to be judged in the next distribution on the results of the deviations it made.

Finally, the Robbins Committee wished for each institution the freedom to determine the shape of its development. It acknowledged that the resulting pattern would be unlikely always to be appropriate to the needs of society and the demands of the national economy, and that the high cost of supporting some subjects obliged those responsible to choose between some centres and others. A quarter of a century later, a university is free not to co-operate with national policies, but it would be likely to suffer punitive financial reductions if it significantly failed to do so. In general, the connection between outputs desired by the state and the financial inputs provided has become so close that the university's freedom to determine its own development is limited to what it can negotiate with the UGC. The University of Buckingham makes too small a contribution to the nation's needs for educated people and for research, in too narrow a range of subjects, to provide an appropriate model for funding less dependent on the state. Each university none the less retains some scope for promoting new activities on a modest scale, and cumulatively these may modify its character.

If it were reconvened today, the Robbins Committee would almost certainly judge that the autonomy of each university on the UGC list was both less than it had been in the early 1960s and less than the Committee intended by its recommendations. Many changes, often ostensibly of administrative practice or procedure, and each usually small in itself, have been cited above, which nevertheless entail diminution of every university's discretion and freedom of action. 'Central control' of the universities has undoubtedly grown in recent decades. The mould that was formed for the modern university in the early years of the century and which emphasized the development of the individual institutions under the benevolent eye of the state has been broken, not only because no more universities are likely to be cast in it, but because the changes have tended to form instead a 'university system'. Perhaps there is now a 'system' as much as is possible without fundamental change in the legal constitution of the universities.

Three points can be made to moderate a picture of remorseless erosion of autonomy, extending from the recent past through to the future. First, many characteristics of that autonomy were established only from the second half of the nineteenth century, as the older universities were reformed and, for instance, the hold of the Anglican Church on Oxford and Cambridge weakened. Secondly, the number and size of universities have greatly increased and most of these institutions have enhanced their autonomy by advancement to university status, shedding the tutelage variously of benefactors, local government, Ministry of Education and other universities. Thirdly, the firm establishment of a binary system of higher education and the rejection of the Robbins model of continuing progression to university status has probably enabled the universities to retain an extent of autonomy that Government would not otherwise have tolerated.

A strong public sector, which is not comprised of 'universities in waiting' and which has proliferated the activities in which the universities do not have a monopoly, has contributed to reducing the distinctiveness of the universities' relationship to Government. That reduction can be seen in the change in working mode portrayed by a former Secretary of the UGC: fifty years ago 'the universities and the machinery of Government in both its political and social aspects formed a kind of continuum, in which only the sketchiest of formality was either expected or required to maintain relationships . . . Gradually the social continuum between the state and the universities which had been the original basis of their financial relationship was replaced by an official system' (Carswell, 1985, p. 159). The change to an official system has as much to do with the changing character and role of Government as with the universities specifically. By the same token, speculation about the future form of relations between universities and Government must in large part be speculation about the future conduct of Government.

The Conservative administration elected in 1979 and again in 1983 was committed to reducing public expenditure, a commitment that lay uneasily with 'rolling back the frontiers of the State' because in its nature it required interventionist policies. If the resources of the community are seen as limited, then their utilization must be optimized by the careful determination of priorities. The emerging compromise is that the universities are taken at their word in their claim to autonomy and required to bear more fully the consequences of their actions. The Government, for its part, does not underwrite institutional ambitions but buys services in the market place. This implies the formal abandonment of deficiency funding and the explicit adoption of formula funding. In the 1986 grant distribution, funding for research was clearly guided by assessment of the likely quality of output. Although the UGC gave the same grant for teaching a unit of student load in each subject, irrespective of university, and although there was little redistribution of student numbers between universities, a predictable development, particularly if the demand for higher education falls in the 1990s, is that funded places will be allocated with regard to the quality of teaching and to the price at which each university offers them. Already, in 1984, universities were invited to tender for the additional places in engineering and technology for which the Government was willing to provide funds above the UGC grant already available. In reaching these allocatory decisions, Government will want advice that is more broadly based than that given by the UGC as currently constituted: a UGC on which academics were not in a majority might result. That might also come under a Socialist Government, on the grounds that the UGC should be representative, with its membership appointed by different interest groups – similar democratization being extended to university councils or regional authorities for all higher education.

The long tradition of evolutionary change in the relations of the Government and universities suggests that the structure of universities at the end of the century will be recognizable against that of the 1980s. However, the pressures of the 1980s and those predictable for the 1990s make it equally likely that the structure will be significantly different.

4

Central Control of the Public Sector

NIGEL NIXON

INTRODUCTION

Fundamental to the report of the Robbins Committee (Committee on Higher Education, 1963) was the principle of social demand, that expansion would continue consonant with the burgeoning qualified demand for places: 'Courses of higher education should be available for all those who are qualified by ability and attainment to pursue them and who wish to do so' (paragraph 31). Indeed, it was in no small measure due to the high quality of the evidence accumulated by the committee, and the debates which this initiated, that the Malthusian conception of a fixed 'pool of ability', hitherto a shibboleth of educated opinion, not least within the Ministry of Education itself, went into retreat. The expansion envisaged was massive. The age participation rate in full-time higher education (HE) was projected to rise from 8 to 17 per cent by 1981, entailing an increase in student numbers of approximately 350,000 from the 1963 figure of 216,000.

The report, which was university oriented, implied that most of this expansion would be accommodated within a unitary system of HE, consisting of autonomous institutions drawing the government's support through an independent grants body constituted on similar lines to the existing University Grants Committee. It was envisaged that most institutions offering predominantly degree-level courses would eventually attain university status, so that, by 1980, only a 'rump' of about 12 per cent of HE would remain outside the universities. In particular, according to Robbins (1980), it had been the committee's intention that the colleges of education and the regional colleges would ultimately cease to be either under local authority (LA) control or directly funded and become 'quasi-autonomous corporations coming under the University Grants Committee' (p. 99).

In short, the pattern of development as envisaged by Robbins, and enthusiastically endorsed by the government of the day, was that of a university system, vastly expanded in numbers and scope, within which a *single* hierarchy of self-governing and self-validating institutions would offer mainly full-time courses of a predominantly academic orientation to qualified school-leavers.

Despite a number of vicissitudes en route,[1] the Robbins projection of some 560,000 full-time students in HE by 1981 was to prove uncannily accurate. In 1981–82 there were already about 555,000 students enrolled on full-time courses of HE, although only slightly more than half (308,000) were pursuing courses of study in universities. The rest were enrolled in publicly funded non-university institutions of HE, offering courses leading to qualifications of a standard higher than GCE A-level (or Ordinary National Certificate). These courses of study, which include diploma and professional as well as degree-level courses, are currently distributed throughout the UK among more than 400 LA-maintained establishments (including the thirty polytechnics), some forty direct-grant, voluntary and jointly maintained colleges and, in Scotland, a number of central institutions and colleges of education, the latter restricted by regulation to professional training for teachers, social workers and workers in community education. It is with this large and disparate sector – the so-called public sector of higher education (PSHE) – that this and Chapter 6 are concerned. Though the detailed description and discussions presented are focused upon arrangements in England, it should be noted that they have their parallel in Wales, and (albeit to a lesser extent) in Scotland. In Wales, the Secretary of State for Wales is responsible for all further and higher education (FHE) in the Principality, with the exception of universities, mandatory student awards and matters relating to the pay, pensions and qualifications of teaching staff. In Scotland, the Secretary of State for Scotland has responsibility for all FHE outside the universities, most of which is located in institutions directly funded by central government (the central institutions and the colleges of education).

In marked contrast to the situation obtaining in the universities, PSHE is exposed to a significant degree of external control. Administrative oversight of course approvals has, in England and Wales, been exercised through a complex system involving Regional Advisory Councils and Regional Staff Inspectors acting on behalf of the relevant Secretary of State, while in Scotland administrative approval rests with the Secretary of State for Scotland acting on the advice of the Inspectorate and the Scottish Education

Department. In most cases, responsibility for the academic approval of courses is vested in one of the national validating bodies, principally the Council for National Academic Awards in respect of degree-level work and the Business and Technician Education Council in relation to sub-degree courses of HE. Nor are the validating bodies the only external agencies concerned with quality control. Her Majesty's Inspectorate, which although formally autonomous is, none the less, financially, geographically and, in many respects, administratively part of the Department of Education and Science, has in recent years come to play a more visible and proactive role in relation to PSHE, not least since its decision to make its reports publicly available. Finally, and, perhaps, most conspicuously, control over strategy, finance and administration rests ultimately with the local education authorities as owners of the institutions (or with the DES and denominational bodies in respect of the voluntary college sector).

The existence of external control mechanisms on this scale has elicited considerable, and mixed, comment over the years. For some the guidance and protection (both for providers and consumers) afforded by such controls encapsulate the essence of PSHE and are its major distinguishing trait. Without them, it is asserted, other objectives such as diversity, access and vocationalism would not have been achieved. On the other hand, it is argued that the various layers of control imposed on public sector institutions have had a negative effect, stultifying initiative and reinforcing a widely-held perception that they are of second-class status. From this viewpoint, the autonomous university model remains the only valid one and all mature higher education institutions should aspire to achieve university status.

THE DEVELOPMENT OF A PUBLIC SECTOR ALTERNATIVE TO THE UNIVERSITIES

The continuous system advocated by Robbins, which offered further education institutions the prospect of ultimate elevation to university status, was to be short-lived. Already, at the time of the report's publication, Sir Toby Weaver, then Deputy Secretary in the Ministry of Education, had questioned the report's tendency to underrate the claims that the community should rightfully have on the universities to promote its own well-being.[2]

This observation was to prove prescient: in April 1965, less than two years after the report's publication, Anthony Crosland delivered his Woolwich speech. In this, he acknowledged that the government concurred with Robbins on the need for a *system* of higher education with 'co-ordinating principles and a general conception of objectives', but, in contradistinction to the committee's recommendations, he emphasized that such a system 'must be based on the twin traditions which have created our present higher education institutions'. These two traditions were represented by an autonomous university sector (including the recently elevated Colleges of Advanced Technology), on the one hand, and by a more service-oriented public sector, comprising the leading technical colleges and the colleges of education, on the other. The government's preference for a dichotomous system was unequivocally asserted:

> The Government accepts this dual system as being fundamentally the right one, with each sector making its own distinctive contribution to the whole. We infinitely prefer it to the alternative concept of a unitary system, hierarchically arranged on the 'ladder' principle, with the Universities at the top and the other institutions down below (Crosland, 1965).

Based then on the leading further education colleges, the binary approach would aim to develop a sizeable, more accessible and more accountable alternative to the autonomous university sector.

Among the arguments advanced in support of the new policy were the following. First, there was a growing demand and need for innovatory vocational, professional and industrially based courses which, it was alleged, the universities were ill-equipped or unwilling to provide. Secondly, it was presumed that a system based on a 'ladder' concept 'must invariably depress and downgrade both morale and standards in the non-university sector' and, moreover, Britain could not survive in an increasingly competitive world 'if we . . . alone downgrade the non-university professional and technical sector'. Thirdly, and most controversially, it was asserted that 'a substantial part of the higher education system should be under social control, and directly responsive to social needs' and that, in furtherance of this end, the continued participation of local government in higher education would be advantageous since it was 'responsible for the schools and having started and built up so many institutions of higher education, should maintain a reasonable stake in higher education' (Crosland, 1965).

Social responsiveness was construed to mean a commitment to teaching rather than to research, the primacy of vocational and applied studies – often instituted in response to the demands of local and regional industry and commerce – over academic and theoretical courses and, finally, the provision of flexible modes of study and increased possibilities of access for students from manual working-class backgrounds. Social control implied according ultimate power over institutions to democratically elected representatives of society. Not surprisingly, the universities reacted with hostility to the implication that their autonomous status rendered them unaccountable and insufficiently responsive to national and other needs, and they evinced powerful arguments to counter what they regarded as highly tendentious and spurious reasoning.[3]

There were, in addition, more pragmatic and expedient reasons for the promulgation of a binary policy of this type. In the first place, given the context of rapidly expanding demand, it was not feasible to accommodate all advanced-level work in the universities except at the cost of massive upheaval. Consequently, it was judged preferable to develop provision by a process of accretion, supplementing and enhancing what already existed. And secondly, in view of the long-standing tradition of local authorities assuming responsibility for further education, LEAs were regarded as appropriate bodies to exercise the social control function over the emergent institutions, particularly as granting them a significant stake in HE could have political advantages in terms of central/local relations. On the one hand, it would provide compensation for the removal of the CATs from LEA control. And, on the other, it might help to attenuate the anticipated controversy between some LEAs and the DES once the Department had issued its Circular requesting LEAs to submit plans for the comprehensive reorganization of secondary education (DES Circular 10/65).

In furtherance of this policy, the Labour Government issued in 1966 a White Paper, *A Plan for Polytechnics and Other Colleges* (DES, 1966a), in which it stated its intention 'to designate a limited number of major centres in which a wide range of both full-time and part-time courses can be developed' (paragraph 11). No more new universities were to be created and there were to be no further promotions by merit to university status. Henceforth, the projected expansion in provision of advanced courses (that is, courses leading to qualifications higher than GCE A-level) was to be concentrated, under local authority control, in a limited number of specific institutions to be known as polytechnics, which, none the less, would remain 'comprehensive academic communities', retaining a substantial amount of full-time work at below degree-level and continuing to cater for part-time students at all levels. These institutions, which would have a strong applied science emphasis, were to be formed by the amalgamation of existing colleges of technology, building, art and commerce, mainly the twenty-four Regional and thirty Area Colleges and Colleges of Commerce, many of which had a long history of advanced work. Between 1968 and 1973 thirty such polytechnics were designated.

The 1966 White Paper, however, with Crosland's two major speeches (see Crosland, 1965, 1967), provided little more than a statement of intention and was inadequate in both educational and organizational terms. The main educational rationale for a binary policy rested on what was subsequently to be described as 'a doubtful dichotomy between the academic education of the universities and the vocational education of the colleges in the public sector' (Robinson, 1968, pp. 35–6). At the same time, little attempt was made to elaborate appropriate management and funding mechanisms to facilitate the co-ordination and planning of provision in the fledgling polytechnic sector and to ensure that stated objectives would be achieved.

This absence of an adequate framework for co-ordination from the centre was to make it difficult to ensure an equitable regional distribution of advanced further education (AFE) as well as co-operation between institutions across the binary line. In consequence, the development of 'collaboration on a regional basis to ensure that costly resources are used in the most rational manner' (Crosland, 1967) was to be limited from the outset. Again, scant attention was paid to specifying the roles and relationships of the DES, LEAs and the new institutions. The development of the polytechnics was, therefore, to depend primarily on the expansionary thrust of the individual institutions and their maintaining authorities. As a result, the emergent sector was to acquire less coherence than might otherwise have been the case.

Just as Crosland's advocacy of a binary approach to HE was to lead to developments that did not accord with those envisaged by Robbins, so the policy of concentrating public sector AFE in polytechnics was to be distorted by the wholesale reorganization of teacher education in the mid-1970s. The 1972 White Paper, *Education: a Framework for Expansion* (DES, 1972), made it clear that teacher education capacity would need to be reduced, given the demographic downturn from 1965 onwards, and hinted at possible developments. More details of the Department's intentions in this respect were to be provided in Circular 7/73, *Development of Higher Education in the Non-University Sector*, the publication of which, in March 1973, was impeccably timed to coincide with a period of maximum weakness for local authorities, who were preoccupied with the all-pervasive problems attendant upon reorganization. A major reappraisal of the future role of the colleges of education was called for, involving rationalization and contraction of the system. Within two years – and notwithstanding a change of government in 1974 – plans had been formulated and, in many cases, agreed with the maintaining authorities. These implied closures, mergers with polytechnics and, to a lesser degree, universities, and the establishment of a new kind of institution, the college or institute of HE, with only a minority of colleges remaining as monotechnic colleges of teacher education.

By the end of the decade twelve colleges had integrated with universities, thirty-seven had been absorbed into polytechnics, twenty-four had amalgamated with colleges of further education, twenty-six had merged and diversified with other colleges of education, twenty-five had been closed, and a 'rump' of twenty-eight remained as free-standing colleges. A mere nine years after the White Paper proposals had first been adumbrated in 1972, not a single former college of education offered the same pattern of courses as it had then.

Largely as a consequence of this reorganization of teacher education it became less and less meaningful to describe higher education in terms of a binary system. A 'third force' of predominantly HE institutions, neither universities nor polytechnics, had evolved, thereby distorting the original policy of concentrating PSHE provision in the polytechnics. These colleges and institutes of HE of widely divergent traditions and ethos have come to offer a range of courses, many at degree-level, and principally in the humanities and social studies and, in so doing, have made possible a more equitable regional distribution of HE.

At the same time, the absorption of as many as thirty-seven of the colleges of education into the polytechnics led to a broadening of the subject range offered by many polytechnics at degree-level, with a consequent diminution of their technical emphasis. Thus, the non-university public sector, which from its inception was always extremely diverse, has become increasingly so. Scott (1984) sums up the situation aptly:

> a system neatly and symmetrically divided into two homo-
> geneous sectors . . . was not an accurate description in 1965 and
> is even less accurate in 1983. The non-university sector . . . is
> a heterogeneous collection of institutions which have little
> in common with each other except the fact that none is a

university in the rather precise constitutional sense which we have adopted in Britain (Scott, 1984, p. 165).

Yet, despite this apparent diversity, certain broad emphases can be discerned, serving to mark off PSHE from the university sector. Nowhere is the divergence more evident than in the types of students who, in each sector, form the substantial minority not on full-time first degree courses. Whereas in the universities these students are mainly postgraduates, in the public sector most are following sub-degree diploma and technician-level courses, often on a part-time basis. In other words, among the salient character-istics of PSHE provision is its comprehensive range in terms of level of course and mode of study.

THE DEVELOPMENT OF MACHINERY
FOR FINANCING AND PLANNING PSHE PROVISION

The need to relate the financial and planning systems of HE through the establishment of some authoritative central body received wide-spread recognition in the decade following the formulation of the binary policy. Various solutions were proposed. These ranged from suggestions for some kind of overarching body with responsibilities extending to the whole of HE – generally viewed as an antidote to the separatism implicit in the binary policy – to proposals, in various guises, for the establishment of a body paralleling the UGC, and enjoying parity of esteem with it, having responsibility, initially, for co-ordinating provision within the public sector and, subsequently, for facilitating co-operation between the two sectors.

However, little headway was made at the time, due mainly to pressures deriving from the reorganization of local government and the decision to establish the Layfield Committee of Enquiry on Local Government Finance. As long as these were pending, it was unlikely that any major initiative in respect of PSHE would be to the forefront of the political agenda. Indeed, it was only after the Layfield Committee had reported in 1976 that the long-anticipated major review of the system was set in train, with the establishment, in February 1977, of a working group, under the chairmanship of Gordon Oakes, Minister of State for Higher Education, with the following terms of reference:

> To consider measures to improve the system of management
> and control of higher education in the maintained sector in
> England and Wales and its better coordination with higher

education in the universities and, in the light of developments in relation to devolution and local authority finance, what regional and national machinery might be established for these purposes. (DES, 1978, p. 1).

Its membership of twenty-nine was drawn predominantly from representatives of the local authority associations, the institutions and the teacher associations. It was assumed from the outset that LEAs would continue to be the major providers of HE, and so the possibility of the wholesale transfer of institutions to other management was not considered. None the less, the working group did address itself to what were perceived to be the more glaring inadequacies of the existing arrangements. These were that management responsibility for what was essentially national or regional provision lay locally, that maintaining authorities did not pay *directly* for the HE courses run in their colleges, that the pooling formula contained weaknesses, that the means of ensuring co-ordination of AFE at regional level were inadequate, and that existing course control mechanisms were unsatisfactory.

The group completed its deliberations within a year, thereby demonstrating that the necessary machinery could be devised to manage what had become a huge and complex sector, whose development to date had been largely uncoordinated and demand-led. Its report was published in March 1978, and, despite being the object of considerable obloquy from Conservative educational spokesmen at the time, was to provide a fixed reference point for policy-makers throughout the ensuing period.

The report's principal recommendation was for the establishment of a national body comprising twenty-five to twenty-eight members (one-third of whom would be nominated by the local authority associations) to advise the Secretary of State and the local authority associations on the provision of HE in the maintained sector and to allocate funds to it, having regard to its development and cost-effectiveness. By November 1978 a proposal to establish two Advanced Further Education Councils (as the Oakes 'National Body' came to be known), one for England and one for Wales, had been included as clauses 20 and 21 of an Education (Miscellaneous Provisions) Bill and introduced into Parliament. By April 1979 the Bill had reached its committee stage and the committee in question had just directed its attention to the relevant clauses when a general election was announced. As a consequence, this Bill, like all others before the House, fell on the instant.

With the election of a Conservative government publicly committed to quango-culling and the appointment to the higher education portfolio of Rhodes Boyson, who had been a particularly astringent Opposition spokesman on the Bill, there was scant immediate prospect of the Oakes prescriptions for a national body being enthusiastically endorsed. However, in view of the government's overriding aim of reducing public expenditure, one feature in particular of the existing arrangements rapidly attracted the attention of the ministerial team. This was the theoretically unlimited commitment of resources for AFE through the open-ended pooling system. Consequently, when the government introduced, in October 1979, its Education (Number 2) Bill, this contained a provision that claims on the AFE Pool would from 1980–81 onwards be limited to a quantum determined by the Secretary of State after consultation with the local authorities, a procedure that was to become known as 'capping the pool'.

Despite some reluctance on the part of ministers to become embroiled at this stage in questions relating to the management of AFE, there was no escaping the fact that, once the aggregate sum allocated to the pool became predetermined (rather than being settled post hoc by the cumulative decisions of individual LEAs), it became imperative for those predetermining it to provide guidelines on how it should be distributed. In January 1980, therefore, ministers in collaboration with the local authorities decided to establish an official group 'to pursue work on unit costs in AFE and to study the possibility of using a range of cost unit indices in the context of regulating local authorities' claims on a limited AFE Pool'. The subsequent operations of this group – the Study Group on the Management of the AFE Pool (GMP for short) – as it laboured to elaborate a more satisfactory methodology than one based primarily on previous expenditure levels, only served to demonstrate the difficulty of the enterprise. On the one hand, the proposal progressively to determine allocations to authorities and institutions by reference to a set of norms based on national averages was to throw into pointed relief the inadequacy of the available database on which such resource allocation decisions had to be made. And, on the other hand, there was the impossibility of devising formulae on which to base financial decisions without the simultaneous introduction of educational judgements – judgements that were outside the Group's remit as well as its competence.

A third and final element in this series of pragmatic devices for the partial management of the sector was the decision to review the system of advanced course approvals for further education at the same time as the pool was 'capped'. In February 1980, a Circular was issued, announcing stringent new criteria for the approval of advanced courses. Henceforth, Regional Staff Inspectors, in determining whether or not to approve new or replacement courses, would have to be satisfied that provision could be made wholly from within existing resources. For a course to be treated as an exception it would have to be demonstrated that it 'would meet vocational need and give students specific employment opportunities'.

In short, during the Conservative government's first year in office, the preferred ministerial approach to the question of AFE management was an incremental, piecemeal one that sought to exploit, in tandem, the potential of the financial instrument now available (the 'capped' pool) and a management tool that had long been available though generally under-exploited, i.e. the advanced course approval system.

At the same time, however, there was another factor ensuring that the subject of PSHE management remained at the forefront of the political agenda. This was the decision of the newly formed House of Commons Education, Science and Arts Select Committee to investigate as its first major topic the funding and organisation of courses in HE. One consequence of this was that it put some pressure on ministers and officials to think strategically about the whole area by reassessing the fullest possible range of options available. Indeed, by the time the committee's report was published in October 1980, evidence was beginning to emerge of a shift within the DES to a more centripetal stance, implying some radical departures from prevailing practice. Partly against a backcloth of generally worsening central–local relations, elements within the Department had begun to question the need to pay overriding regard to LA sensitivities, particularly in view of their manifest inability (or unwillingness) to 'deliver' nationally determined policies at local level. Options involving the removal from LA tutelage of the major providers of PSHE began to be explored in more detail, and it was a paper advocating just such a proposal that was to cause such consternation when its contents were leaked in the *THES* on 6 February 1981.

Whatever the source of the leak and whatever its motivation, there can be little doubt that its effect was catalytic, as it came to affect both the pace and direction of subsequent events. Within six months, the DES had issued (in July 1981) a consultative document, 'Higher education in England outside the universities: policy, funding and management', which served a secondary purpose as government's response to the Select Committee's central

63

recommendation for the establishment of a Committee for Colleges and Polytechnics with substantial LEA representation.

The Document set out two models. Model A (the local authority model) was essentially that developed by the Council of Local Education Authorities in their own recently and hastily published consultative paper, 'The future of higher education in the maintained sector' (CLEA, 1981), and accorded with the Select Committee proposal. According to this model, the local authorities would continue to manage and control the sector, the existing pooling arrangements would continue to operate, and a small, essentially advisory, body would be constituted, representing the various interests involved, to oversee all institutions offering AFE courses. Thus, individual local authorities would retain their involvement in HE but, henceforth, this would be mediated by a national body through its influence on fund allocation, course approvals and LA thinking in general.

On the other hand, Model B (a limited 'centralist' model) had been developed within the DES and was designed to create a new sector of HE directly funded by the Exchequer. This would consist of the polytechnics and some sixty other major institutions providing, between them, approximately 85 per cent of AFE, which would cease thereby to be under LA control. Instead, control of the sector would be vested in a national body, appointed by the Secretary of State, comprising non-institutional as well as institutional members, with a significant weight being attached to industry and commerce.

THE MAIN ISSUES AT STAKE IN THE DEBATE

The publication of the DES consultative document represented one more strand, albeit a major one, in the protracted debate over planning and funding mechanisms for PSHE which had enjoyed spasmodic saliency since the establishment of the Oakes Working Group in 1977. In the course of this debate a number of issues had come to engage the attention of the various groups with a direct interest in PSHE policy. These were: local versus central control of the sector, managerial effectiveness, modes of funding, the scope of the putative national body, the regional dimension, and transbinary co-operation. Since these remain of enduring concern, notwithstanding the advent of a national body in 1982 having within its scope all local authority higher education in England, it is appropriate to review the debate in relation to the six issues in question.

Local versus central control

There was little dissent from the view that any proposed management structure, particularly if it were to inspire confidence and win consent for its actions, should strike a sensitive balance between local accountability, institutional autonomy and central control. What was, however, a matter for dispute was where precisely the balance lay between rigid centralism at one extreme and local authority individualism at the other

In favour of a more central focus, it was argued that LEA control was inappropriate to complex institutions, such as polytechnics, serving predominantly national needs. Indeed, according to the Association of Polytechnic Teachers, given that students were not constrained to attend a 'local' polytechnic or college of HE, 'the national funding and hence the national control of higher education must logically follow' (APT, 1981). Further, it was alleged, the needs of students, the rights of taxpayers and the efficient workings of institutions were of more importance than the monetary, political and prestige-based concerns of LEAs seeking to retain control of HE institutions.

Nor was it self-evident that the requirements of democratic accountability would be best served by a proposal along the lines of Model A for a national body consisting mainly of LA elected membership, especially one on which only a few of the maintaining authorities would actually have members, but whose decisions would have to be accepted by all. It was argued, in the context of major institutions, that accountability to those who paid for and used the system would be more effectively guaranteed through the ballot box at the time of parliamentary elections than through the local authority, seeing that local authority rates accounted *in toto* for only about one-third of the budget of most major institutions and, furthermore, that the local authority in which the institution was situated was unlikely to provide from its own rates more than a modest proportion of the institution's overall budget. It was largely because the pooling arrangements permitted, at best, only tenuous accountability that the Oakes Working Group had recommended, as a concomitant of continued LA involvement, that maintaining authorities should become directly responsible for the costs of a fixed proportion of HE provision under their control, an eventual target figure of 15 per cent being set (DES, 1978, ix and paragraphs 5.25–29, 5.38, and 13.4).

A further argument centred upon the tendency of local authorities, as paymasters and employers, to interpret involvement with institutions as close control over them. To combat this tendency towards tighter control of institutions – evident, for example, in the CLEA consultative paper (CLEA, 1981) – proponents of a more central focus, most notably the Committee of Directors of Polytechnics, emphasized that some form of corporate status (such as the five ILEA-maintained polytechnics already enjoyed) was a desirable precondition for the more effective management and flexible control of major institutions.

Among the reasons given for retaining local authority control was the fact that all public sector institutions fulfilled local and regional as well as national needs and that local–regional priorities and national requirements were most likely to be harmoniously reconciled by a local authority presence, provided that this did not involve local authority intrusion into the detailed management of institutions. Corporate bodies with severed local connections (along the lines suggested in Model B) would, it was alleged, be less sensitive to local and regional requirements.

There were also overwhelming educational and economic reasons for not separating advanced from non-advanced further education (NAFE) – the 'seamless robe' argument so consistently advocated by the main lecturers' union, NATFHE. Similarly, there was the need to maintain the closest possible relationship between part-time (considered to be primarily a local–regional responsibility) and full-time provision.

A third argument related to the need to ensure effective democratic control of AFE institutions at local level, regarded as essential if they were to enhance their responsiveness to the needs of the various sectors of the local community and to employment requirements that, it was averred, are more effectively discerned and met on a local and regional basis. The point was made with particular force in a document produced by the National Union of Students:

> Because of the planning vacuum at national level and the lack of effective local authority involvement, the development of colleges and polytechnics has been largely determined by their senior administrations. We are anxious that institutions should be brought under more democratic control at the local level. This would lead to courses being developed which are of relevance to those who pay for them and those who use them. Higher Education may then be seen to have value to the whole community. (NUS, 1981).

Effective local authority involvement would, moreover, facilitate the development of links between HE and sixth forms and other providers of 16–19 education, and, at the same time, enable HE institutions to participate more fully in a wide variety of local authority services.

Finally, a number of more pragmatic reasons were put forward for continued local authority involvement. For example, Model B entailed the transfer of staff, land, buildings and capital equipment from the LEAs to the institutions themselves, which would become corporate bodies. Such transfers tended inevitably to be complex and costly and likely to occasion considerable upheaval – as the example of the CATs in the mid-1960s had amply demonstrated – despite the fact that, on that occasion, comparatively few institutions had been involved.

Managerial effectiveness
The DES accorded a high degree of prominence to the theme of effectiveness in its consultative document, criticizing both the Oakes and Select Committee prescriptions on this count (DES, 1981). Effectiveness was defined by the Department as the power to take decisions and to secure their implementation and the capacity to plan in a national perspective, coupled with the ability to gain and maintain public confidence. According to the DES, only Model B, with its direct relationship between central body and institution, could guarantee 'delivery'. 'Delivery', moreover, was especially necessary, given the prospect of ever tighter expenditure constraints, if the ensuing contraction was not to be haphazard but co-ordinated from a national perspective.

Such direct links between top and base were considered to be essential to the promotion of institutional dynamism in a system that sought to combine educational excellence with cost-efficiency. An important criterion in judging a system's effectiveness was whether or not it inhibited the response of institutions to new situations and needs, and Model B was to be preferred because it would reduce such response times. Model A, by contrast, implied an additional stratum of control – the local authorities – through whom the authority of any putative national body would have to be mediated. This entailed the risk that the advice proffered on such sensitive matters as course rationalization would not necessarily be heeded, thereby paving the way for the development of major distortions of provision from the national standpoint. Moreover, in response to criticisms about the consequent loss of local control and accountability, it was pointed out that in Scotland and Northern Ireland centralized planning (often involving tight steerage) and funding mechanisms had long been in operation without any evident diminution in responsiveness and with accountability being guaranteed to Parliament through the relevant Secretary of State.

On the other hand, CLEA contended that a central body of the type proposed by Oakes, the Select Committee and Model A was both necessary and sufficient to undertake the planning, co-ordination and rationalization of HE in the maintained sector and to control its finance. It was necessary because only a body that allowed adequate membership to representatives of the responsible providers could be deemed to fulfil the requirements of democratic accountability. And it was sufficient because a body containing LEA representatives was ipso facto capable of carrying the maintaining authorities with it.

Moreover, although direct control might permit decisions to be taken rapidly, these would be vitiated to the extent that they exhibited a procrustean disregard for the views of those involved or the desires of those others outside the system who might wish to influence provision at local level. Short-term powers of 'delivery', derived from the capacity of one stratum of management to dominate, were contrasted with longer-term effectiveness based on a management structure capable of reconciling conflicts between different levels of influence.

Modes of funding
Central to discussion of this theme were the relative merits of direct financing of institutions by means of earmarked grants from central government compared with a continuation of the pooling system, under which the central body would levy funds from LEAs on a formula basis and distribute them to institutions through their respective LEAs.

The Committee of Directors of Polytechnics, the most consistent advocate of direct Exchequer funding, rationalized this preference on a number of counts. First, such a system was economic and consistent with the need to plan HE *nationally* as well as being devoid of the technical complexities that bedevilled the pooling system, described by one commentator as 'an obscure, impenetrable bureaucratic labyrinth' (Howell, 1980, p. 114). Secondly, given the lengthy lead-times characteristic of HE, institutions could only plan their development effectively if they were guaranteed a measure of financial certainty, at least in the medium-term, and the unhy-pothecated nature of monies allocated in the context of the Rate Support Grant militated against this. Thirdly, the importance of institutional freedom, flexibility and, hence, responsiveness was alleged to become all the more apparent in times of constraint, and a system of *direct* central funding was most likely to enhance such freedom. It would, for example, permit savings due to prudent management to accrue to the institution and facilitate the retention by institutions of income derived from such items as fees, research contracts and the hire of facilities. Fourthly, it was argued that, if the purpose of a national body was to make binding decisions, then funds should flow directly to the institutions on an agreed basis in accordance with these, with accountability resting with the national body and the Secretary of State. Finally, criticism was directed at the principle of pooling, mainly on the grounds that it provided little incentive for efficient management, seeing that the ability to commit resources remained largely divorced from the obligation to find them.[4]

On the other hand, it was emphasized that a system of direct central funding would curtail institutional freedom even further, because allocations would be made solely in accordance with the priorities of the government of the day. Moreover, the financial involvement of local authorities was particularly to be valued in the context of a 'capped' pool since, through 'topping up',[5] they possessed the ability to provide independent sources of revenue, thereby helping to protect their institutions from cuts in government spending. And, in addition, there was the interconnected nature of financial and employment responsibilities, so that it was difficult to envisage how local authorities could remain the employers of the staff within the institutions if the latter were no longer to be funded by them.

Concerning the mechanics of funding, it was suggested that institutional freedom within predetermined budgets might best be maximized if institutions were progressively financed on a common unit-cost basis (with appropriate weightings for different subject areas) in relation to agreed programmes. Such a system, however, although apparently apposite in the case of major providers, would be less appropriate to institutions offering only a small proportion of AFE, for whom funding on a course basis was to be preferred. Consequently, if a Model A solution, embracing institutions with widely differing degrees of AFE provision, were to be adopted, it would be necessary to operate a complex mixed system of programme and course funding.

Finally, there was widespread agreement that any national body should concern itself not merely with questions of finance and efficiency but should include within its remit matters of educational standards and institutional ethos. In the words of the CDP, 'The planning and control of Higher Education has too often concentrated on one aspect . . . the financial cost . . . However, the preservation of academic quality appropriate to sub-degree, degree and post-graduate work must be seen as integral to planning and control' (CDP, 1980, paragraph 4.1). In short, the elaboration of sensitive and agreed measures of educational 'value added' was viewed as no less important than moves towards common units of funding.

The appropriate scope for the national body
Discussion of this issue was conducted essentially in terms of the following two proposals: (1) The putative national body would restrict its purview to a newly created sector of HE, separate from the universities, on the one hand, and from other institutions of higher and further education, on the other. (2) All maintained institutions offering AFE courses would fall within its remit in respect of these courses. The first proposal implied a definition of the body's scope in *institutional* terms, whereas the second delimited it by reference to *courses*, irrespective of the institution providing them. While the first proposal afforded the prospect of a reasonably coherent sector of manageable proportions, it entailed the risk of undermining the presumed unity of AFE and NAFE, with potentially deleterious consequences as far as access to AFE was concerned.

Advocates of the establishment of a separate sector (most notably CDP and APT) questioned whether the existence of a large number of advanced courses spread thinly over a broad spectrum of institutions was a sensible use of increasingly scarce resources. Attention was also drawn to the needs of students who found themselves institutionally isolated from their appropriate peer group and without the type of facilities considered to be necessary for their full academic development – a situation which, it was alleged, had arisen because of the way in which, in the 1970s, small pockets of HE had been allowed to develop in numerous institutions. And, finally, with reference to salaries and conditions of service, it was argued that the disparity of treatment between the universities and major providers of PSHE would be perpetuated as long as FE remained linked to HE.

On the other hand, proponents of the second approach emphasized that the creation of such a separate sector would only serve to erect new and arbitrary organizational and institutional barriers, to the detriment of educational opportunity. For example, the possibility of progression incorporated into BTEC courses and the development of post-experience, preparatory and refresher courses threw into stark relief the essential arbitrariness of the AFE/NAFE schism. In particular, AFE provision outside the restricted number of institutions to be covered by the putative body would become precarious, especially if there was to be an end to the pooling machinery. The magnitude of the problem is revealed by the fact that, although approximately 70 per cent of LA institutions had a stake in AFE, only a minority of these were likely to be incorporated into the new body. Furthermore, a high proportion of AFE courses located in institutions that would remain outside the new body were part-time, and any reduction in their number would render access to HE much more difficult for part-time students, who, in 1980, were only marginally less numerous in public sector institutions than those studying full-time. At the same time, uncertainty was expressed concerning the future of NAFE courses remaining in institutions falling within the remit of the proposed new body, particularly as scant attention had been given to the question of who would have responsibility for their funding.

Concern about student access to courses remained an important strand in the debate concerning the scope of the putative body. A Model B type solution received criticism on the grounds that it would damage further the already inadequate opportunities for mature and part-time students. Moreover, PSHE was a crucial provider of trained manpower for industry and commerce: its continued effectiveness in this respect depended largely on its being allowed to improve access by developing new modes of study, involving flexible, distance-learning and modular courses. For similar reasons, the importance of ensuring a balanced geographical spread of HE opportunities – whereby home students might continue to apply for the course of their choice without undue geographical constraint – was also emphasized.

Consideration was also given to the position of the voluntary and direct grant colleges and the need to forge closer links with these, particularly in view of the important role played by them in teacher education. A model B type body would occasion least disruption for these colleges, although their highly valued direct relationship with the DES would be severed.[6] At the same time, there was no organizational reason why a Model A type solution could not ultimately accommodate arrangements for this sector. Indeed, the colleges' needs might be better served through a solution of this type, because it would grant them places on a *representative* body. Initially, however, there were likely to be some problems when a small, relatively coherent group of institutions came to be absorbed into a large and diverse group, with the prospect of tougher competititon for funding.

Finally, mention should be made of one proposal put forward by CNAA in its response to the DES July 1981 consultative document. This sought to incorporate the alleged virtues of each of the two models proposed in the document. According to this third model, the putative national body would embrace the institutional range proposed in Model A, but, to facilitate the management of so large and heterogeneous a sector, institutions would be 'banded' for purposes of planning and funding, according to the amount of advanced work undertaken.

The regional dimension

Although the Oakes report had stressed the importance of co-ordinating AFE provision regionally through newly constituted Regional Advisory Councils,[7] by no means all interest groups were in agreement on the need for a national body with regional sensitivities. The APT, for example, dismissed the whole concept of regional co-ordination in the absence of a concomitant limitation on student mobility, pointing out, for example, that there was little correlation between the regional provision of teacher education and regional teacher supply. And CDP remarked, apropos of the existing arrangements, that a combination of local initiative and the regional approval of courses (by RACs, whose remit, in any case, did not extend to the university sector) remained an unacceptable substitute for national planning.

On the other hand, an adequate regional sub-structure was widely considered to be a sine qua non if proper account was to be taken of local needs by a national body, particularly one dealing with the range of institutions proposed by Model A. Regional bodies would, for example, be crucial elements in the constitution of a sound database, channelling information on courses and student demand to the central body and relating these to NAFE provision in the area. Again, such bodies could aggregate the needs of the disparate LEAs in their area and thereby foster co-ordination between neighbouring authorities. This would be of especial importance in relation to course provision and in affording increased scope for reorganization. They could also provide an effective focus for liaising and co-operating with other organizations with a legitimate interest in HE, such as industry and commerce, the voluntary sector and other public services. And, finally, they offered the prospect of a forum within which the differing interests of constituent LAs and the national body might be reconciled.

Transbinary co-operation

The importance of establishing a body able to command sufficient authority to work closely and collaboratively with the UGC remained a leitmotiv throughout the period in question. The CDP, for example, in its commentary on the Oakes report, had emphasized the need to co-ordinate and plan HE as a whole and had suggested that this might best be achieved through a liaison group of the polytechnics and universities endowed with real powers. In similar vein, the Select Committee recommended that its proposed Committee for Colleges and Polytechnics should establish strong links with the UGC, to permit the overall co-ordination of provision and so optimize the use of resources across the binary line. Thus, the establishment of a public sector body capable of engaging in effective dialogue with the UGC could, it was asserted, play an important part in helping to focus upon problem areas, in stimulating innovation and in arbitrating whenever conflicts of interest arose. At the same time, it was stressed that transbinary co-operation was unlikely to be forthcoming unless the relationship between the two bodies was frank and equal, and that this might best be facilitated by a system of cross-representation.

Another strand to this particular theme concerned the desirability, or indeed the feasibility, of establishing some kind of overarching body with responsibilities for the whole of HE, including the universities, either to supersede the UGC and any body established for PSHE, or, more likely, to coexist with them. NATFHE, for example, alluding to a reference in the leaked memorandum to the need to rationalize the whole of HE, suggested that this objective might be achieved most effectively by amalgamating both sectors under a single body (NATFHE, 1981a, 1981b). And the *THES*, in presenting its 'alternative' memorandum, 'Not the National Body', advocated the establishment of a Postsecondary Education Commission (in addition to a Committee for Polytechnics and Colleges) to deal with the strategic planning, as opposed to detailed management aspects, of the system (*THES*, 6 March 1981).

THE ESTABLISHMENT OF
THE NATIONAL ADVISORY BODY

Although opinions were sharply polarized on which of the alternatives outlined in the DES July 1981 consultative document should be followed – a consequence, in part at least, of the climate of mistrust regarding government's intentions that had prevailed since

73

the publication of the leaked memorandum in the *THES* in February – there was general recognition that government financial pressure was making matters urgent. Without some sort of unified managerial competence for the sector, it was proving impossible to achieve in a planned way a reduction in the costs of provision and, at the same time, to create a shift in the subject balance in order to reflect government priorities more effectively.

In the event, developments were to occur with extreme and, in some respects, unseemly rapidity, given that the closing date for receipt of comments on the consultative document was not until 30 November. A cabinet reshuffle in September resulted in a new ministerial team at the DES led by Sir Keith Joseph, with William Waldegrave assuming responsibility for higher education. Waldegrave, who was less cavalier than his predecessor in his attitude to continued LA involvement in AFE, was determined to act speedily. Consequently, he was ill-disposed to contemplate the sort of time-consuming and contentious legislation that a Model B type solution would have entailed, particularly as this would cause the already strained relations between central and local government to deteriorate even further.

By early October, a paper entitled 'Future management of AFE and distribution of the 1982/83 AFE Pool' had been circulated. It referred to 'resource constraint and the beginning of the decline in the 18 year old age group . . . forcing changes on the system . . . with the clear risk that they will be largely uncoordinated, causing damage to national provision as a result' (paragraph 3). By 20 November, the DES had issued a press notice, 'Arrangements for the management of local authority higher education in England', announcing the proposed establishment of an interim body, to be known as the National Advisory Body for Local Authority Higher Education, and inviting comments by a 4 December deadline. Unlike the UGC, it was to be an advice-proffering, not a decision-making, body. The relationship between it, the government and the local authorities was subsequently to be defined by the Secretary of State in the following terms:

> To Government belongs the responsibility to determine the size of the AFE pool having regard to national considerations and after consultation with the Local Authority Associations, and its allocation between authorities. To the NAB, in offering advice affecting those allocations, falls the responsibility to know the AFE sector and to plan its provision in the light of that knowledge.[8]

74

Thus, the body that came into being on 1 February 1982 was essentially a compromise born of expediency rather than conviction and, hence, accorded only interim status by the Department. As such, it bore a closer resemblance to the Oakes and Select Committee models than to Model B of the July 1981 consultative document or, *a fortiori*, the proposals contained in the leaked memorandum. The relationship between institutions and their maintaining authorities was to continue basically unchanged, and funding would still be effected through the existing pooling arrangements. Moreover, the proposed two-tier structure of a small controlling committee (on which the Local Authority Associations would predominate) and a much larger board (broadly representative of PSHE interests) could be viewed as a neater way of achieving the balance and breadth of representation that Oakes had sought through a single body with a local authority modified veto built into it.

THE NAB IN OPERATION

The circumstances in which the NAB began its work were not particularly propitious. On the one hand, its interim status was likely to make it difficult for it to establish credibility. On the other hand, the prospect of conflict and division was considerable, seeing that its primary task would be to reduce costs in a sector that traditionally had been parsimoniously funded compared with the universities. To its credit, however, it sought from the outset to present itself to the PSHE policy community as a promoter of positive initiatives rather than simply as an instrument for advising the Secretary of State on the distribution of the 'capped' pool. It aimed thereby to provide an effective and credible forum for tackling some of the issues in the protracted and hitherto ill-co-ordinated debate on the size, shape and purpose of PSHE. And, above all, it elected to operate in an open and publicly accountable manner, which contrasted markedly with its counterpart, the UGC. The adoption of such an approach helped NAB rapidly to establish itself as a necessary part of the machinery of central policy-making in the eyes both of the DES and of the various interest-groups involved. Indeed, when its structure, membership and operation were reviewed in 1984, it not only emerged as a permanent body but had its remit extended to include (from 1985) the voluntary and direct grant colleges and capital (in addition to recurrent) expenditure.

Several factors induced the various organized interest-groups influential in PSHE to cohabit with NAB. Foremost among these was the realization that the only alternatives were, at best, a less representative body and, at worst, a continuation of the planning uncertainties of the past. Despite some early misgivings on the part of both NATFHE and the CDP,[9] none of the interest-groups represented on the NAB board has so far felt impelled to withdraw its membership. As a result, the board's credibility, based largely on its claim to representativeness, has been enhanced.

Secondly, NAB was to prove successful in wringing some concessions from central government: or, at least, in minimizing the damage to the system arising from government's determination to effect a 10 per cent reduction in real terms in the AFE quantum over the two-year period 1982–83 to 1984–85. It managed, for example, to obtain an additional £20 million from the DES for the 1984–85 pool, despite the fact that determination of the size of the AFE quantum remained a government responsibility and, hence, outside its terms of reference. And, lastly, it was perceived to be effective in resisting certain DES pressures, particularly those tending towards institutional closures and the further concentration of courses in the major providers, one result of which would have been to curtail access to HE, especially in the case of non-traditional groups.

At the same time, the DES found its proposals broadly acceptable during this interim period. Its establishment coincided with the achievement of considerable 'improvements' in efficiency and lecturer 'productivity' throughout the maintained sector. Between 1980–81 and 1984–85 the numbers of home full-time and sandwich students in the sector rose by nearly 30 per cent while total funding in real terms barely increased. Consequently, overall student–staff ratios (SSRs) tightened significantly from 8.9:1 to something approximating to NAB's own target of 12.0:1 while there was a reduction in the unit of resource (the amount of money allocated per student place) of more than 22 per cent during the same period. Moreover, this policy of admitting the maximum number of qualified applicants without a concomitant increase in resources contrasted markedly with the UGC's decision to restrain student numbers in the light of the cuts announced by government in the March 1981 Expenditure White Paper, with a view to protecting research and teaching standards (HM Treasury, 1981). NAB thus provided government with a convenient alibi at a time when the number of eighteen-year-olds seeking places in HE was at a peak, since many of the students being denied university places by the UGC decision could be absorbed into the public sector.

Another point in NAB's favour, as far as the DES was concerned, was that it sought to effect a switch in the subject balance that harmonized with government's perceptions of the country's needs for qualified manpower. In the 1984–85 planning exercise, for example, a deliberate attempt was made to alter the balance of provision over a two-year period away from arts and social studies towards science, engineering and business and professional studies. In addition, earmarked funds were allocated to selected institutions under the Information Technology and Biotechnology Initiatives as part of government's 'recovery-through-technology' programme.

Thirdly, there is some evidence that the nettle of transbinary collaboration – a prerequisite for a more rationally planned and integrated HE system – was beginning to be grasped. Transbinary groups to plan provision in specific subject areas (e.g. agriculture, architecture, librarianship and information studies) were established. Common themes, such as continuing education, were explored by parallel groups with cross-membership.[10] And, perhaps most significantly, meetings of members of NAB's Chairman's Study Group and members of the UGC were to provide a forum for the exploration of major strategic issues. The culmination of this was the publication, in 1984, of a joint statement to be incorporated in the respective bodies' advice to the Secretary of State on longer-term strategy.

Lastly, there was the commitment of NAB's Technical and Data Group (TDG) further to refine the work on pool allocation formulae initiated by the Study Group on the Management of the AFE pool. This approach emphasized the importance of quantified rational planning techniques, involving scientifically derived criteria, as a basis for decision-taking. This was likely to have two beneficial consequences from the DES viewpoint. On the one hand, it would facilitate the establishment of funding norms for specific activities within PSHE, thereby making institutional disparities less easy to defend. On the other hand, there was the possibility that such ostensibly 'neutral' procedures could be exploited as a means of legitimating essentially political preferences. For example, the TDG's decision to group subjects into fourteen programme areas with different weightings was based upon professional estimates of their relative needs in resource terms, but it also happened to be the case that the most generously weighted were those, such as engineering and science, most favoured by government.

However, the likelihood that NAB will continue to achieve similar levels of acceptance for its proposals during its second triennial planning exercise is open to doubt. The omens to date have scarcely been encouraging, as the following developments indicate.

First, as ever tighter resource constraints have made it increasingly difficult to achieve a satisfactory balance between access and the maintaince of standards, tensions have arisen between NAB's two tiers of board and committee, the one dominated by professional interests determined to see no further diminution in the unit of resource and the other by LA members concerned not to reduce access.

Again, NAB's purely advisory status has been thrust to the fore by the Secretary of State's decision to break with precedent by rejecting certain of its recommendations, most notably on architecture and initial teacher-training provision. In the latter case, the DES has itself reassumed planning responsibility, thereby raising (once again) the possibility that a more centralist body might be imposed on the system, if the Department should continue to find NAB's solutions unpalatable.

There is also the likelihood that NAB's relationships with institutions will be exacerbated by two factors in particular. First, reductions in intakes of the order of 6 to 17 per cent (depending upon the degree of 'protection' accorded to a particular programme area) as envisaged by NAB for 1987–88, would inevitably mean major course and programme closures, particularly in humanities and social studies (subjects which traditionally recruit the highest proportion of non-standard entrants), leading to renewed pressures to concentrate the remaining provision more narrowly.

Secondly, there is the prospect of disruption stemming from proposals to change the methodology by which the AFE pool is distributed. NAB's decision to relinquish the 'sub-quantum' method of distributing the pool, with its differential unit of resource for different categories of institution, derives from a desire to eradicate funding disparities within the sector and so strengthen its case for equity of funding between PSHE and the universities. However, the technical difficulties of devising a uniform funding formula, capable of being applied to all PSHE institutions without at the same time causing widespread upheaval, particularly in the polytechnics (many of which would stand to lose large amounts rapidly), remain immense.

QUALITY CONTROL MECHANISMS

Although the main focus of this chapter has been on control mechanisms in relation to the finance and planning of PSHE, it must be emphasized that the differences between the two sectors of HE are by no means confined to these matters. Equally salient are the very different forms of academic control characteristic of each sector. As was mentioned in the introductory section (pp. 54–5), in public sector institutions responsibility for endorsing the academic quality of courses is generally invested in one or other of a number of recognized external agencies, not, as in the university sector, in the institution providing the course.

The principal degree-awarding body in the public sector, the CNAA, was established in 1964, following a recommendation of the Robbins Report, to replace the National Council for Technological Awards. It was granted a Royal Charter empowering it to award degrees, diplomas and certificates, comparable in standard to university awards, to students successfully completing courses of study organized in non-university institutions of HE in Great Britain. It has become by far the largest degree-conferring body in the country, with approximately 165,000 students (one-third of the total studying for a first degree in the UK) following CNAA-validated undergraduate degree courses.

From its precursor, the NCTA, it inherited a number of features, prominent among which were, first, the concept of the *course* as the key to validation and, secondly, the principle of submitting course proposals to the judgement of academic peers, rather than to that of some remote group of authoritative 'experts'. Thus, from its inception, CNAA operated as an institutionalized system of peer evaluation involving the initial validation of proposed courses and (no less important) regular progress reviews of courses already approved. Although certain of CNAA's practices have evoked critical comment on the grounds that they have been at times unduly cumbersome and bureaucratic, the principle of peer group review has elicited much favourable comment. In particular, it has acted as an important stimulant to curricular creativity:

> The need to defend our proposals forces us to make clear not only the fundamental problems but the coherence of our solutions. And it is out of this greater understanding that most of us can be persuaded to innovate. (Pratt and Burgess, 1974, p. 107).

In its early days the validation procedures adopted by CNAA tended to be highly formalized, with most emphasis on the initial design and balance of courses rather than on delivery and outcomes. Moreover, the validation decision was simply a cut-off decision concerned with the adequacy or otherwise of a specific course and, as such, did not entail an assessment of the course in question compared with similar ones elsewhere.

The prime criterion for assessing adequacy was that the standard of the awards, and hence of the courses leading to the awards, should be comparable to those of the universities, a proposition that begs a number of questions. These include, as Lewis (1982) has pointed out, 'whether the standards in the universities are uniform and, if not, whether it is sufficient for the purposes of approval for a CNAA course to be of the same standard as the worst university course, which in turn implies that such standards can be, and have been, identified and measured' (Lewis, 1982, p. 154). In practice, most board members tended to be guided by some intuitive measure of minimum acceptable standards derived from experience of approving, teaching and examining a range of courses.

By the mid-1970s CNAA had begun to consider ways of modifying its approach to validation. As the interests, especially of the larger and more experienced institutions, shifted from initial validation to the adaptation of existing courses and as the institutions themselves began to develop increasingly rigorous internal procedures for evaluating particular courses before transmission to CNAA, the need to reassess the balance between institutional flexibility and freedom, on the one hand, and accountability to and control by CNAA, on the other, imposed itself with increasing force. A 1975 paper entitled *Partnership in Validation* (CNAA, 1975) advocated a more equal relationship between CNAA and its associated institutions, and this theme was subsequently expanded in a further publication, *Developments in Partnership in Validation* (CNAA, 1979). Under the proposed model, CNAA retained the ultimate right to approve courses leading to its awards, but emphasis was henceforth to be placed on the notion of a joint responsibility for the setting and maintaining of standards.

Among the most striking features of this 'partnership' approach were the procedures applied to the reapproval of courses. The expectation was that well-established courses would no longer have to undergo re-validation every five years but would receive indefinite approval subject to periodic progress reviews, intended to assess the extent to which a particular course was meeting its stated objectives. At the same time, flexibility and experimentation were encouraged, with institutions being invited to propose alternative approaches to validation. The most noteworthy example of this was the 'joint validation' experiment conducted with Newcastle upon Tyne Polytechnic. This involved replacing the final phase of the polytechnic's own internal procedures for course validation and

CNAA's external course reviewvisit by a single merged process, in which courses were reviewed jointly by polytechnic and CNAA members.

Although the emphasis has tended to remain on the individual course as the key to validation, it should not be assumed that course-based validation is the only – or necessarily the most effective – quality control mechanism available to a validating body. Accreditation (either of whole institutions or restricted to certain programme areas) is an alternative that bulked large in the deliberations of the Lindop Committee, which had been set up in April 1984 to review the validation process in PSHE as a whole (DES, 1985b), and was implicit in CNAA's Mode B proposal in December of that year.[11] Under such a system, institutions would be licensed by the validating body to approve their own course proposals and review their existing courses subject only to a periodic review of the institution and its procedures for maintaining and enhancing course standards. The institution, therefore, would have autonomy to design and mount courses in areas granted accreditation without the specific approval of the validating body. At the same time, the standards of the degrees gained by students would remain underwritten by CNAA and the institution would continue to have access to CNAA's network of contacts and expertise.

Such an approach, however, although going some way towards satisfying the demands of the more mature institutions for an appropriate degree of responsibility for exercising quality control over their courses, has its shortcomings from the validating/accrediting body's standpoint. Of paramount concern in this respect is the difficulty of devising procedures that would guarantee an adequate flow of relevant information from the institutions to sustain the peer review principle.

Changes in the nature of the interactions between CNAA and its associated institutions on the lines outlined are likely to have ramifications for CNAA's relationship with NAB. To date, CNAA has experienced considerable difficulties in providing reliable and authoritative information on course quality in a form that is useful to NAB and, at the same time, acceptable to the institutions. Indeed, its first venture into these choppy waters – the decision to rank town planning courses in late 1983 – imposed severe strains on relations with the institutions whose courses it had validated, particularly in the context of the 'partnership' model then being promoted.

In particular, the sorts of developments initiated by CNAA following publication of the report of the Lindop Committee of Enquiry (and subsequently endorsed by government in its response to the report) increased the likelihood that closer links would be forged with NAB, with the possibility of an eventual merger not to be ruled out. Relations between CNAA and individual institutions will inevitably become less intense as detailed course-by-course validation is superseded either by some form of accreditation or by an 'arm's length' validation agreement, under which the institution has the major responsibility for maintaining the standards of its courses. Developments of this type are likely to prompt CNAA to seek closer ties with NAB and, hence, greater involvement in the policy-making process at national level, as compensation for some loss of influence vis-à-vis the institutions. Moreover, peer group review, organized under the aegis of CNAA, is likely to become the prime means of assessing and controlling academic quality instead of, as hitherto, threshold validation of individual courses. Such a shift of perspective would necessitate the monitoring of standards, broadly conceived to include outcomes of teaching and examining as well as course design and structure, across whole subject areas, and probably would lead to the quest for agreed and sensitive indicators of performance that could be applied with a reasonable degree of consistency across courses and institutions. From NAB's particular vantage point, this could considerably enhance the importance of CNAA, given that CNAA's quality advice would be in a form that would make it possible to grade courses in a given subject area against one another according to explicitly defined criteria.

Of course, if a merger of the two bodies were eventually to occur – possibly by linking programme approvals (a NAB function) to institutional accreditation for a particular subject area (a CNAA function) – it would not be without its dangers. In particular, there would be the risk that academic power might be unduly concentrated in a single body, with the possible consequence that a safe orthodoxy would be preferred to academic development and innovation. Such a risk could, however, be minimized if the merged funding/validating body were to be given a strong developmental focus and if its business were to be conducted openly with real opportunities for interaction between institutions and the national body.

CONCLUSION

Among the themes that have figured prominently in this chapter, two at least – forms of control and accountability and relationships between the two sectors – are likely to bulk large on the HE agenda throughout the rest of this decade and beyond.

At the heart of the debate over the first is the need to achieve an appropriate balance between institutional freedom and social accountability. Control over PSHE institutions has traditionally been exercised in a detailed and elaborate manner, with form not infrequently being disproportionate to substance. Such detailed control mechanisms are increasingly resented by institutions that have come to regard themselves as mature and self-critical academic communities. They serve, moreover, to reinforce a widely held perception that PSHE is inferior in status to the autonomous universities. They also do little to enhance the Crosland principle of social accountability, since they inhibit institutions' flexibility and hence their capacity to respond to the changing demands and problems of the communities they are designed to serve.

For some institutions, the preferred option would be to attain university status and the freedom from external controls that, apparently, permeates the university sector. In their view, the binary policy has interrupted the historical pattern of development that brought autonomy in the form of university status to institutions as and when their circumstances and public needs justified it.

For others – probably the majority – there is the feeling that regular interaction with their maintaining authorities and periodic exposure of their courses to external validation are intrinsically worth while. Such pressures, it is argued, act as a stimulus to the sort of institutional dynamism and professional self-questioning that helps to ensure that client needs continue to be met. If, however, external controls over course validation, finance and staffing are to remain broadly acceptable, they will need to be exercised in less inflexible ways than in the past, yet without their effectiveness being in any respect impaired. It was largely the need to find a satisfactory response to this concern that lay behind the (at times) fraught debate on the relative merits of different forms of academic control, following publication of the report of the Lindop Committee. In respect of administrative control, it may lead to renewed pressures from institutions to be accorded corporate status. Alternatively, institutions may seek to negotiate agreements with their maintaining authority whereby responsibilities for management are devolved to the institution in return for its guaranteeing to meet strategic objectives set by the LEA.[12] Or, finally, it may result in further legislation being enacted along the lines of the *Further Education Act 1985*, which sought to place LA institutions on an equal footing with universities and grant-aided colleges in respect of entrepreneurial activities, such as the commercial exploitation of the by-products of their research, the proceeds of which might be used to sustain further developmental initiatives.

Concerning transbinary relationships, the pressures towards further collaboration between the two sectors seem likely to intensify. Developments can be expected in four areas in particular, either as a further series of ad hoc responses to the need to rationalize provision or (less likely) as part of a government-led strategy for HE designed to enhance the positive features of each sector.

The first of these derives from the importance that is being attached to a more flexible and responsive model of HE, based on a wider development of credit transfer, modularized courses and experimental modes of study. This model, which already exists in embryonic form through such initiatives as CNAA's Credit Accumulation and Transfer Scheme (CATS) and the Manchester-based Consortium for Advanced Education and Training (Contact), depends on the establishment of networks of interlinked structures of tertiary awards that transcend both institutional and sectoral barriers.

Secondly, there is increasing recognition of the importance of co-operation on a regional basis, particularly where expensive equipment or specialist facilities are required, coupled with the acknowledgement that the regional machinery necessary for a co-ordinated approach to provision remains distinctly under-developed. Consequently, any reassessment of the relationship between regional and national planning is likely to result in an enhanced role for regional bodies involving the more active engagement of the universities than hitherto.

The prospect of institutional mergers, provided that they are authentically transbinary, is another, and potentially exciting, area for development.[13] Unlike mergers within a common sector, which are unlikely to generate anything other than a more 'rationally' arranged pattern of conventional institutions, transbinary mergers offer the possibility of a fresh beginning; they have the potential to produce a new species of institution transcending the limits established by Crosland's binary policy. They could, in the words of a *THES* leader article, 'harness the academic excellence and the liberalism of the British university tradition to the broader and more practical goals embodied in the polytechnics' (*THES*, 8 November 1985). At the same time, the difficulties of effecting successful mergers of this kind should not be underestimated, given the disparities in funding between the two sectors and their different patterns of academic organization, administration and government.

Finally, the need to co-ordinate the overall finance and planning of HE points to the eventual creation of some authoritative central body, such as has been envisaged for Scotland by the Scottish Tertiary Education Advisory Council in its December 1985 Report.[14] There are various possibilities. A minimalist solution would be to trust that such a body might emerge osmotically through periodic meetings of the UGC and the NAB boards and the establishment of transbinary working groups. Another possibility would be to set up a weak overarching body, which would serve as a forum in which the various public sector bodies (NAB, WAB and STEAC) and the UGC might argue their respective cases. Either of these options might find favour with the DES, because it would enable the Department to play one interest off against another. Under a maximalist solution, on the other hand, a Robbins-type Higher Education Commission would be created with effective powers, formed either from a merger of the UGC, NAB, WAB and STEAC, or as an entirely new body.[15]

NOTES

1   For example, the Robbins projection for 1973–74 of 390,000 full-time students in HE proved to be a considerable underestimate, a figure of 451,000 having already been attained by 1970 when the DES published its Planning Paper No. 2 with substantially revised estimates for the decade ahead.

2   As reported in *THES*, 11 November 1983, 'Robbins IV – Toby Weaver on the inevitability of a binary policy'.

3   For example, Sir Peter Venables, The Vice-Chancellor of the University of Aston at the time, commented that the binary line 'pre-supposes a distinction between the vocational and the fundamental in technological education which belongs to the nineteenth century' (*New Statesman*, 21 January 1966.) See also Lukes, J. R. (1967).

4   This aspect is highlighted in G. Fowler's apothegm: 'Everyone spends what everyone else pays'. See 'Non-university higher education', *New Statesman*, 31 March 1978. The Layfield Committee on Local Government Finance made the following remark: 'The net effect of the system is one whereby some providing authorities are able to precept all others for pooled services', House of Commons (1976), p. 111.

5   That is, contributions made directly by LAs to PSHE institutions within their own boundaries as a supplement to the AFE pool allocations. In some cases these 'topping up' monies have been substantial. According to DES estimates for 1982–83 'topping up' was in the region of £54 million, equivalent to nearly 10 per cent of that year's AFE pool.

6   For an account of this, see 'The acceptable face of DES linkage', *THES*, 27 March 1981.

7   DES (1978), xxv, xxvi and paragraphs 9.12–17, 13.6 and chapter X.

8   Letter to the chairman of the NAB Committee from the Secretary of State for Education and Science, 21 February 1983, reproduced in *NAB Bulletin*, Spring 1983, p. 4. A similar body for Wales, the Wales Advisory Body, was set up in 1983.

9   A motion to force NATFHE to withdraw from participation in NAB was narrowly defeated at its 1983 conference. In mid-1983 the CDP representative on the NAB Board, Dr W. Birch, resigned because he considered that insufficient attention was being accorded to CDP representations. However, it was regarded as a personal resignation, the CDP electing to appoint a successor.

10 Both working groups presented their reports in 1984. See UGC (1984b) and NAB (1984b). Shortly after the publication of these reports, the DES announced its intention to set up a national standing committee on continuing education across the binary line.

11 Consultative Paper on the Development of Council's Relationships with Institutions, CNAA, December 1984.

12 For an example of this, see the report on negotiations between the Royal Borough of Kingston and Kingston Polytechnic, *THES*, 14 February 1986.

13 The one so-called 'merger' to date, that involving the New University of Ulster and Ulster Polytechnic, is in no sense transbinary because the effect has been simply to shift the polytechnic into the university fold. Recent transbinary merger proposals have centred on City University and City of London Polytechnic (see *THES*, 8 November 1985) and Keele University and North Staffordshire Polytechnic (see Staffordshire County Council, 1985).

14 *Future Strategy for Higher Education in Scotland*, Scottish Tertiary Education Advisory Council, 1985, paragraphs 8.13, 8.15–20, 8.29, 8.32 and 9.19.

15 See Shattock, M. (ed.) (1983), especially pp. 205–6. Others remain more sceptical concerning any prospective merger, e.g. G. Williams and T. Blackstone (1983), p. 119, and DES (1985a), paragraph 8.3.

5

The Management of Universities

GEOFFREY LOCKWOOD

BASIC ASSUMPTIONS

It is an exciting and challenging time to work in and write about the management of universities at the institutional level. It is exciting because of the speed of change, and it is challenging because that change provides opportunities, as much as problems.

I start with two basic assumptions, concerned with independence and competition. The first is that universities are independent corporate bodies and not local sub-units of a national system. Each has its legal independence, its history and its local circumstances. They are diverse institutions. In the European context, individual institutions such as Uppsala, Edinburgh and Trinity College Dublin have been shaped by centuries of tradition; they embody the values of university life and work in forms of government and administration that have adapted to the varying demands of society over the years. These institutions need to be cherished: they nurture and transmit the culture. Of course they should continue to adapt to external change, but to insist that they should conform to structures and procedures common to newer institutions would be to put at risk the essence of those older universities; and that essence cannot be re-created or replicated.

Similarly, institutions that have been given roles additional to the normal purposes of higher education need to be allowed to relate their institutional management to these roles. The developmental role (e.g. opening up new geographical regions, correcting national economic/social imbalances) of universities is recognized in the Third World, but it also exists in Europe. In relevant circumstances the governance, financing, etc., of the institution should be adapted to suit the performance of that role. Nevertheless, basic factors of age, scale, primary roles, etc., will result, given the common European tradition, in close affinities across national boundaries. Much as the organizational styles of Uppsala, Edinburgh and

Trinity College Dublin have a degree of commonality based upon history, those of RIT Stockholm, NIT Trondheim and Heriot-Watt have shared features related to their technological bias; those of Limerick, Sussex and Linkoping derive from their common innovatory characteristics, and so on.

Given the variety of pressures towards uniformity, it is important to encourage an atmosphere in which diversity can flourish. One advantage of diversity relates to the enhancement of academic freedom: the increased sense of responsibility that exists when an institution has a degree of choice about the structure of its governance and administration. Another advantage is the degree of choice that diversity presents to the consumer. Yet another is the increased resilience of the system as a whole. Diversity allows limited experimentation with structures and procedures without having to apply them across the whole higher education system. The Universities of Leeds and Manchester, for example, were originally parts of the same Victorian university. They developed and exist in similar urban civic settings a few miles apart in the North of England, they are of a similar size and range of disciplines, they function within a common framework under the British University Grants Committee, their costs are not dissimilar; but in their management they are recognizably different institutions. Their committee structure, the balance of university/faculty/department roles and responsibilities, the organization and style of their administration – all these are markedly different. The existence of those differences based upon history, local circumstance and institutional character need to be seen as a strength of systems of higher education (OECD, 1979).

The term independence has been used rather than autonomy, because it is the legal independence of the body corporate that is the basic factor (Moodie and Eustace, 1974). Autonomy is normally used to refer to the extent of a university's freedom to use public resources in ways in which it thinks best. The extent of that freedom has varied over time, and is likely to decline as the political paymasters specify more closely the results and values they want delivered; but its legal independence provides a university with freedoms, such as the ability to function in markets other than that for University Grants Committee monies. In particular, in the context of this chapter, each university has considerable freedom to determine its managerial style.

The second and related assumption is that universities are in competition with each other. Universities have always competed in the recruitment of staff and students, for research grants and contracts, for private donations, and for public monies. Yet the assumption has to be stated, however obvious it seems, because of the growth since the 1960s of inter-institutional co-operative agencies such as the Committee of Vice-Chancellors and Principals, Universities Central Council on Admissions, Universities Statistical Record, Universities Authorities Panel (see also Chapter 3). These agencies, in conjunction with the increased tendency in Westminster and Whitehall to refer to a planned national system of universities, have obfuscated the root factor of competition between universities.

INTERNAL FACTORS AND EXTERNAL PRESSURES

The two basic factors of independence and competition are reflected in the existence of different patterns and styles of institutional management. Collegiality, or the self-government of an academic community of equal members without other parties (laypersons, administrators, etc.) possessing authority, has been strongly exemplified only in Oxford and Cambridge (the myth of its existence has affected attitudes in other universities, and is an example of the confusion caused by the difference between the beliefs of internal academic members about the nature of university management and the constitutional realities on which that management is based; Keller, 1983). The difference between the large federal University of London and the other civic universities is considerable. The pattern of management of the Scottish universities is different from that of English universities. These differences are evidenced in the various aspects of institutional management, the extent of the involvement of lay members and bodies, the comparative roles of Senate and Council, and the methods of appointment of academic officers.

Therefore it is important at the outset to establish that the forms and styles of management in the British universities vary in more than detail, for reasons that derive from their contemporary situations (location, range of disciplines, extent of research, etc.) as much as from their history. It nevertheless remains possible to generalize about the institutional level of university management (Brooks and Rourke, 1966). Each university is subject to the same range of external pressures; the strength of these pressures varies, but each will experience them to some extent. Demographic trends might affect some universities more than others because of differential mixes of disciplines, degrees of preference among universities and so on, but all universities have to adjust their planning and procedures to some extent in the light of these trends. Each university is also subject to the same internal forces, which derive from the nature of the academic activity of creating and transmitting knowledge (Baldridge, 1971).

Chapter 2 deals with the external factors that impact upon higher education: economic performance, social structural factors, technological change, political stability and public opinion. All of them are conditioned and interpreted by passage through bodies that bring direct pressure to bear, including Parliament, Government, the Department of Education and Science, several other departments of state, the University Grants Committee, the research councils, the Committee of Vice-Chancellors and Principals, trade unions, local authorities, professional bodies, industry and commerce, and colleges and schools. If national economic performance declines, the university has to expect that to affect its future (Ashby, 1974). If technology produces new and economical ways of transmitting knowledge, the university has to recognize that that will change parts of its methods of production. Thus, university management is affected by many key changes on the national scene and (an aspect that is often overlooked) has relationships with a wide range of bodies, most of which reflect these changes by seeking change in the university and its products.

In regard to the internal factors, universities possess characteristics common to other entities, but the combination of those characteristics is unique (Balderston, 1974). This amounts to different forms coexisting in the same body. In some cases they are partial; the form of the firm can be found functioning in fringe units in most universities; the union or the guild form exists in many associations within the university. In other cases, the forms are total, comprehending the whole body; the university is an organization, it is an institution, and it is a community. The university's basic essence is thus multi-formed or pluralistic. In its main purpose it is an organization: it employs labour and capital, which interact through formal processes to generate the products of teaching and research (e.g. graduates, publications). Equally, it functions as a community, both in that relationships among its current members have ends in themselves and in that it provides supports and services for social cohesion (Bailey, 1977). Similarly, it functions as an institution by the intrinsic nature of the values placed permanently (beyond the current community) upon activities such as scholarship. Organizational theorists (e.g. Livingstone, 1974; Corson,

1973) may prefer to use other terms to describe the forms characterized above as 'organization', 'community' and 'institution', but those labels convey effective images of the three forms with their different mixes of structure, power, social base and values (Lockwood and Davies, 1985).

In the university, these forms do not have separate boundaries. Most large industrial or commercial organizations have institutional and community characteristics, but they are distinct, subsidiary, and usually peripheral to the functioning of the organization. In the university, each critical decision, whether it be to employ a new faculty member, erect a new building, change the teaching method of a course, etc., is subject to conditioning by those three forms. It is not a matter of the organizational form governing some areas (e.g. resource allocation), the community form governing further areas (e.g. library policy) and the institutional form determining yet others (e.g. teaching methods). All three intermingle and compete in the milieu within which all activities and decisions take place. The university contains a number of other features that contribute to that milieu and complete the structure of management – complexity of purpose, limited measurability of outputs, diffusion of authority and internal fragmentation are among them (Kerr, 1979). Features of this kind are not merely the result of history and circumstance: they derive from the very nature of the university's activities. Universities are in the knowledge business – a business conducted through individuals and small groups, each possessing a near-monopoly of fields of knowledge, and processed through personal interactions in the activities of teaching and research, which are not capable of being managed from above to the extent necessary for a crude hierarchical structure of management to be effective.

University management at the institutional level is about monitoring, reviewing and evaluating a wide variety of external pressures, about understanding and influencing internal features and processes, and about maintaining a balance between the two in the interests of the long-term future of the university, its basic academic purpose and the needs of its clients and society at large. Institutional management is the skin on the drum: there to provide the barrier and the flexibility to absorb the external pressure, protect the instrument and enable it to perform.

91

ORGANIZATIONAL STRUCTURE

The organizational structure through which management functions is a combination of three frameworks – those of units, committees and officers – which are interlaced rather than integrated, reflecting the complexity of the basic activities, the diffusion of authority and the fragmentation of the academic profession (Fielden and Lockwood, 1974). The elementary particle of academic life is the individual faculty member, but the academic department is the primary unit in the structure. These units vary considerably in size, in the extent to which they have sub-groups, in their possession of facilities and capital, in the definition and permeability of their boundaries (a School of Medicine, with high external recognition and relationships and with a strong monopoly of its subject field, has a firm boundary, whereas in a Department of Social Geography those features are much weaker), and in many other ways. At its root in the base units the structure is thus complex: protected by professional competence, fragmented but not discrete. The units vary in size and importance, but in comparison with many other forms of organization, the structure generally is characterized by a high number of small units. Moreover, the departments share few corporate tasks (they are separate production units), yet they are linked by an interlacing of cross-memberships and common facilities; it is difficult to create cells with exclusive membership in a university (thus an innovator within a unit is usually faced in that group by people who present the constraining views and positions of other units).

In most universities the basic academic units are linked to institutional management through a range of faculties. The extent of the co-ordinating role of the faculties varies considerably across universities: in some the faculties control the key areas of decision-taking affecting the department (for example, resource allocation to the department, the making of academic appointments, the recruitment of students), whereas in others the department has a direct relationship to the university level in those key matters and the faculty is the tier that co-ordinates cross-departmental matters of curricula, examinations and so on. Whichever model applies, the institutional level is involved in the management of, say, twenty-five to seventy-five basic academic units and five to a dozen faculties, none of which are entirely self-contained. When the academic support units (e.g. library, computer centre) and the non-academic units (e.g. catering, health, administration) are added to the list, it can be appreciated that the number of units and intermediary structures is high for what in Britain is usually a relatively small-scale institution.

The second organizational framework is that of committees. It is clear from the constitutional instruments under which most universities exist (normally a Charter and Statutes) that governance is by committee: so, in practice, is management. In the main, the authority of the governing body or bodies is passed down from committee to committee rather than, as in the USA, from the governing body to officers who make use of committees as advisory bodies. This has led to the development of committee systems of considerable scale and complexity, with responsibility dispersed and accountability unclear: indeed, it is normally difficult to determine when a decision has been reached, because the overlap between committees can lead to a decision taken by one being re-opened by another.

The complexity begins at the highest level, where responsibility is in practice divided between a Council (the governing body, with a lay majority) and a Senate (the prime academic agency, and the senior of the bodies consisting entirely of internal members). The constitutional relationship between the two bodies is normally laid down in a Charter: although the Council is the highest authority, it can only act in certain matters subject to reference to the Senate. In practice, the internal characteristics of universities have created a climate in which the relationship is ambiguous and effective power is divided. Again, there is manifest here the complexity, uncertainty and confusion which characterizes the whole of the committee structure.

That structure is divided into the respective sub-structures of Council and Senate (linked at certain points and overlapping at many others), in which an average of fifty or sixty committees are segregated, horizontally and vertically, with authority and responsibility blurred. In the academic field, the tiers in the vertical structure (Departmental Meeting – Faculty Executive – Faculty Board – Senate Executive – Senate) are criss-crossed by the horizontal lines of responsibility of more specialist committees (Library, Planning, Finance, Buildings, etc.).

The operational characteristics of the committee structure (regular rotation of short-term members, intricate timetables confined almost exclusively to thirty weeks of the year, interlaced memberships, the propensity to set up ad hoc bodies, and so on) create further complexities and confusion, as well as having the effect of slowing down and absorbing initiatives for change until a consensus is reached. Business has to go through large 'arenas': it has to get past those with primary interest in it and then those with little interest in it but whose vested resources could be affected by it. Business is conducted by participants, many of whom will not be in office to be accountable for the effects of its implementation or rejection. It is a system of decision-taking that derives directly from the nature of the basic activities of the university, but one that the academic community has extended from its heartland (decisions on curricula, examinations, teaching methods, and so on) to encompass all of the business of the university – an example of the myth of collegiality having proved to be stronger than the primary constitutional instrument of the university.

The third framework is that of the officers. Its features are not dissimilar to those of the committee structure. There is a division at the top of the structure evidenced by the number and nature of statutory officers. There exist certain 'ceremonial' officers, whose powers are usually held in reserve (Visitor, Chancellor). The working statutory officers divide into those with general responsibilities (e.g. Chairman of Council, Vice-Chancellor), and those with specific responsibilities (e.g. Deans of Faculties, Librarian, Treasurer). None of them, as a rule, is solely responsible to one body. The Registrar or Secretary, for example, is normally responsible as head of the Administration, not just to the Vice-Chancellor but also to Court, Council and Senate. Officers are not formed into a clearly defined single hierarchy. The diffusion and ambiguity is enhanced by a lack of specificity and detail in the roles assigned to them. In practice, hierarchies do exist, but they depend largely upon consensus and convention and are less clear than in most other forms of organization. This results in less individual responsibility and initiative and in greater reliance upon informal meetings of groups of officers. The fragmentation of authority and the reliance upon consensus has led to many of the officers being elective and short-term rather than appointed, although not to the extent met within the continental European university.

The officer structure in the British university can thus be characterized by a mixture of lay members and academic staff holding weakly-defined offices, part-time and on short terms, in a complex and ambiguous pattern of responsibilities to other officers and committees. Both lay persons and academics are supported by a 'civil service' of career administrators, of which more later. The pluralistic nature of the university is clearly in evidence here. The phenomenon of extensive part-time senior management is not at all common in other organizations.

DIRECTIONS OF CHANGE

In this chapter so far, two main aspects have been emphasized. First, university management at the institutional level is faced both with a range of external pressures for change, often conflicting and transmitted through a large number of bodies, and with the reality of the loose and multi-formed nature of the university itself, stemming from its basic purposes and activities. The role of management is to keep the institution adaptive to external stimuli while protecting its essential nature. Secondly, the internal organization has been characterized by what is termed 'limited manageability' (Cohen and March, 1974). It is not simply a question of university managers deciding what is necessary and then issuing orders: they have to work through complex internal structures of decision-taking and decision-avoidance, peopled by competent professionals possessing few common corporate interests and tasks.

The remainder of the chapter is concerned with an appraisal of the present situation and a review of how university management might adjust over the next few years. The external issues (see Leverhulme, 1983) include the need to adapt to increasing competition, the requirement to live with external uncertainty, the application of greater selectivity in the allocation of public monies, more direct political 'guidance', 'interference' or 'steering', shifts in the traditional markets (towards science and technology, towards continuing and professional education, towards disadvantaged groups), the need to pay greater attention to serving the needs of enterprises (private and public), the development of integrative relationships in the European Economic Community, a reduction in university influence upon methods of assessment in the secondary schools, the need to build bridges across the binary divide, and many more. There are also growing demands for increased efficiency, value for money, and public accountability, all of which will result in pressures to adhere to common standards, whether they be defined in terms of performance indicators or codes of practice (see, in regard to the latter, the comments in Chapter 3, p. 47, on the CVCP codes of practice). These are only the currently evident problems: lurking around the corner, unless the universities take steps to remove them, are pressures for the external validation of university curricula and awards, the national employment of university staff (in order to achieve rationalization through staff mobility), the closure of some universities, the transformation of the basic core curriculum into distance-learning packs to reduce the labour-intensity of university teaching, and so on.

These pressures imply a need to re-examine the internal milieu and structures mentioned earlier, to determine whether they can enable the university to maintain its essence (academic standards in teaching, scholarship and research) while demonstrating (which involves both achieving and publicizing) its responsiveness to political and market requirements; its flexibility in fulfilling its mission or strategy; its ability to adjust to new technologies and delivery systems (maintaining the educational value of small group teaching while achieving the economies of technologically-based inter-institutional learning packages); its capacity to retain individual innovation in research while benefiting from value for money in the usage of research support facilities. Such a re-examination could well lead to adjustments in the balances between collegiality and leadership, between management and governance, between centralization and decentralization. It could also lead to more open internal planning and evaluation, greater flexibility in personnel policies and a greater willingness to generate resources in activities and fields where it is possible to do so, with the understanding that the 'profits' would be redistributed to safeguard scholarship in those fields that by their nature cannot operate in the marketplace.

In considering how such issues relate to the structure of university management it is important to recall the two basic assumptions, that universities are independent corporate bodies, and that they are in competition with each other and with other institutions of higher education. Whatever their internal complexities, it has to be emphasized that universities are corporate bodies. If this status is once set aside, the pressures not only for nationally centralized allocation of resources and codes of practice but also for the more complete rationalization of university activity will not easily be resisted. Similarly, if the basic assumption of competition is not upheld, the result might well be a system of voluntary co-ordination, through the CVCP and other agencies, which is not much different from that which would be imposed externally.

In the current climate, perhaps the most effective response of the individual university would be to increase the external recognition of its institutional boundary – to establish that it is a corporate entity with historical and local identity, with particular strengths; to increase the internal reality of that institutional boundary (to strengthen the inter-dependence of units, to derive and disperse institutional benefits from the units), to pay more systematic attention to the skills and interests of its members (less emphasis upon the assumption that all faculty members can fulfil every academic and administrative role equally well, and greater emphasis on the selective use of the individual's skills and experience, whether in teaching, research or administration); and to increase the speed of responsiveness to change within the limits set by the guiding philosophy (or mission) of the institution.

These are by no means simple tasks, but they are capable of achievement. It should be possible to create a single, coherent and open structure of government and management; a structure that balances the devolution of decision-taking within an integrated framework, through which the flows of information, analysis, discussion and decisions can be flexibly controlled and maintained by formal processes of communication, planning and evaluation (Lockwood and Davies, 1985).

THE JARRATT COMMITTEE

In essence, this was the approach that the Steering Committee for Efficiency Studies in the Universities (the Jarratt Committee) took in its work in 1984–85. The Committee's Report represents the views of a mixed group of experienced members from lay, academic and administrative backgrounds. The creation, functioning and reporting of the Committee has been fully described in the public arena (*THES*, 28 February 1986).

Because the Jarratt Committee is central to the subject of this chapter, it needs to be considered in some detail. The terms of reference given to the Committee were:

> to promote and co-ordinate, in consultation with the individual institutions which it will select, a series of efficiency studies of the management of the universities concerned and to consider and report to the Committee of Vice-Chancellors and Principals and the University Grants Committee on the results with such comments and recommendations as it considers appropriate; provided that the commissioned studies will not extend to issues of academic judgement nor be concerned with the academic and educational policies, practices or methods of the universities. (CVCP, 1985)

The Committee soon interpreted its remit as being to examine management structures and systems in the universities, particularly with regard to their effectiveness in ensuring that decisions were fully informed, that optimum value was obtained from the use of resources, that clear policy objectives existed, and that accountabilities were explicit and monitored. The Committee did not need convincing about the importance of management structure at the institutional level. It stated unequivocally that, even if universities have a clear strategy, they will not be able to implement it without a management structure that achieves adequate rates of change and the will to change. The Committee saw this as the greatest need for the universities in their preparation for the period to the end of this century. The members of the Committee were fully aware that attitudes affect the functioning of structures as much as the formal or constitutional design and content of those structures. For example, they noted that tenure does not exist in some universities, but that the academic culture was such that the Senates in those universities believed that all academic staff should be treated as if they had tenure, regardless of whether or not this was actually the case. Such attitudinal factors were noted as inhibiting not only change but the very discussion of change. It was partly for that reason that the Committee placed a major emphasis upon the role of institutional planning in bringing attitudes out into the light in the formulation of a strategy. Any university should give corporate consideration to questions of academic performance (for example, in relation to the quality and range of its offerings, and to market conditions) and strategy (where it wants to be in five years' time) – otherwise it will fudge options and drift. Similarly, any university ought to be rigorous and systematic in ensuring the effectiveness of its resource allocation and monitoring procedures – otherwise it is certain to be wasting or under-utilizing its resources, especially the expertise, time and energies of its academic staff, and failing to give the best value for money. The Committee asserted that a well-designed corporate planning process will make explicit the key internal balances between integration and devolution, leadership and partici- pation, Council and Senate, as well as ensuring that the academic, financial, social and physical aspects of decisions are interrelated. A formal planning process should also require the existence of effective management information, monitoring and evaluation systems, and should structure their use. Fundamental to the work and report of the Committee was the first of the assumptions made in this chapter: that 'universities are first and foremost corporate enterprises to which subsidiary units and individual academics are responsible and accountable. Failure to recognise this will weaken the institution and undermine its long-term vitality.' (CVCP, 1985). A key role of institutional planning should be to strengthen the acceptance of reality.

The Committee commissioned detailed studies of six universities, and the terms of reference applied to the general part of each study centred upon analysis of the effectiveness of the organizational structure and decision processes of the university, including the management information systems, and with a special emphasis upon the management and accountability of bodies for the resources allocated to them, including the monitoring of value for money.

The study teams for each university, composed of management consultants and selected members of that university, were asked to recommend changes to the organizational structure and decision processes in order to increase institutional effectiveness and efficiency: to ensure that objectives for policy and administration were clearly set; to specify the assignments of the authority and responsibility for attaining those objectives (and management of resources in doing so); to identify any obstacles in the way of achieving these aims.

Thus, the Jarratt Committee instigated very thorough investigations into the structure and processes of institutional management. Following the studies, and the exchanges of experienced opinion among members of the Committee, the results were summarized in ten brief recommendations, which all universities were requested to consider and to develop plans for achieving within twelve months of the date of the Committee's report (the latter stipulation signifying the Committee's view of the ability of universities to procrastinate). The recommendations can be paraphrased as follows:

(a) The governing bodies (Councils) should assert their responsibilities, notably in respect of strategic plans being drawn together into one corporate process linking academic, financial and physical aspects. This recommendation reflected the view that Councils, composed to balance external and internal viewpoints, had in the expansion period since 1961 allowed internal bodies to dominate decision-taking (or non-decision-taking).

(b) Senates should continue to play their esssential role in co-ordinating and endorsing detailed academic work, and to serve as the main forum for generating an academic view and giving advice on broad issues to Council – a recommendation that concentrates upon the constitutional role of the Senate and, by exclusion, rejects the attitude that the Senate is the 'internal Parliament' of a university, responsible for all aspects of decision-taking.

(c) Each university should develop a rolling academic and institutional plan, which should be reviewed regularly and against

99

which resources should be allocated. This recommendation underlined the Committee's belief in the necessity for corporate planning, especially in conditions of uncertainty. The Committee wished to dispel the view, commonly held by senior university officers as well as other members in the universities, that universities could not plan unless Government gave them clear long-term guidelines and assurances. If universities are independent corporate bodies they should act as such. Independence, or autonomy, is not simply a legal fact embodied in a Charter locked in a strongroom: it is a freedom that has to be exercised to survive.

(d) The Vice-Chancellor should be recognized not only as academic leader but also as the chief executive of the university. This again was no more than a confirmation of the constitutional reality in most universities, but the fact that it was felt necessary to assert it is significant. The reaction has been illuminating and has served to underline the need for the recommendation. Rather than being recognized as a confirmation of both the constitutional and traditional state, it has been seen as one of the attempts of the Jarratt Committee to introduce the concepts of industrial and commercial management into the universities: a concern illustrated by the debate in one university on whether the first letters in the term 'chief executive' should be in upper or lower case in the advertisement for a new Vice-Chancellor.

(e) Each university should establish a planning and resources committee of strictly limited size reporting to Council and Senate, with the Vice-Chancellor as chairman and with both academic and lay members. In fact, most universities already possessed a body with those essential features, but the Committee was anxious to stress this method of overcoming the division between the sub-structures of the Council and the Senate, and to provide a small non-representative body through which the leadership could function openly rather than operating through a 'kitchen Cabinet'.

(f) There should be budget delegation to appropriate centres, held responsible to the planning and resources committee for what they have achieved against their budgets. The key words in this recommendation are 'held responsible'. Budgetary devolution is a common practice in many universities but, with a few exceptions, although units are accountable their resources are not necessarily adjusted according to their performance.

(g) Reliable and consistent performance indicators need to be developed, and a greater awareness of costs and more full cost charging: a recommendation simple to state but more difficult to implement, especially given the genuine problems of measurability in a university. However, the Committee wished to emphasize that performance indicators were a necessity for both external and internal assessment. The subsequent reaction in the universities is again interesting, in that concentration has been placed upon the accuracy of indicators. It is a virtue of universities to search for perfection in an imperfect world, but it seems not altogether consistent for academics to repudiate indicators of their own performance unless they are perfect, while they readily accept and use crude indicators in other aspects of life (no one pretends that the scoring of goals in soccer is an accurate reflection of the quality of play, but goals are none the less regarded as a proper criterion for evaluation).

(h) Heads of Departments should be appointed by Councils, on the recommendation of the Vice-Chancellor after appropriate consultation, with clear duties and responsibility for the performance of their departments and their use of resources. This might well turn out to be the most contentious of the proposals in many universities, given the rise of the practice of electing such officers since the late 1960s. However, as with all the Committee's recommendations, it is for each university to consider in the light of its local circumstances, provided that it preserves the essence of the proposal: the designation of one person in each budgetary centre who is personally accountable to the Council for its use of resources.

(i) Arrangements should be introduced for staff development, appraisal and accountability: a proposal to which everyone pays lip-service but which will have to await basic changes in attitude, and to some extent structure (except among administrative staff, where it has been adopted for many years).

(j) Staff time should be saved by having fewer committee meetings, involving fewer people, and more delegation of authority to officers – especially for non-academic matters. This proposal combines two motivations: first, a wish to shift more decision-taking, especially in non-academic affairs, from committees to officers; secondly, in a time of economy, to concentrate the primary resources of the University (the time and expertise of its academic staff) upon its primary functions (teaching and research).

These short crisp recommendations cover most aspects of governance, management, leadership, planning, resource allocation, accountability and staff development in a university. It is important to recognize that, given the variety that (as has been noted earlier) exists in university management (and for good reasons), the Committee did not attempt to lay down blueprints. Apart from the reference to a need for a planning and resource committee, its recommendations were about directions of change in university management and did not stipulate model lines of procedure.

The Report of the Jarratt Committee summarized most of the external pressures upon university management at the institutional level, and indicated desirable directions of managerial development. It was, however, only one of many such stimuli. As noted in Chapter 3, the University Grants Committee in 1985 had clearly expressed its intention to change in two main respects the basis on which it would allocate public funds to the universities from 1986–89. First, historical differences in the unit costs of teaching across the universities would be eradicated by the imposition of a fixed funding formula for teaching. Secondly, monies for teaching and research would be assessed separately. Research funding would be allocated on a more selective basis that would take into account both previous research performance and the judgement of peers about future potential in each main subject group in each university. In terms of the immediate effects upon the academic priorities and financial management of the universities and upon their attitudinal responses to external pressures, the changes in the UGC's procedures and criteria have proved more significant than the report of the Jarratt Committee.

A further consideration is that of the overseas student market. The Government's policy since 1979 of funding home and EEC students but of expecting the universities to provide for overseas students on a self-financing basis forced the universities, for the first time in the history of many of them, into a market economy. The effect has been dramatic. It has taught university management the techniques of marketing (e.g. how to mount sales missions, the value of investment in people who can recruit, the importance not only of promotional literature but also of avoiding damaging publicity) and has underlined the need to differentiate in the distribution of internal rewards in accordance with market success. None of these results were intended by a Government policy directed simply at reducing public expenditure, and the results have not been fully understood by the universities – but that is often how effective change occurs.

Whether it be Jarratt, the UGC, or the overseas markets, the effects have been the same. The managerial systems at the institutional level are becoming more explicit, more capable of internal differentiation, able to generate an increased speed of response to outside stimuli, more internal evaluation and better external projection of the university's values.

CONCLUSIONS

The future must surely lie in building upon those directions of change. For all the reasons given earlier in this chapter, it would be wrong and damaging to be radical in seeking innovation in the management of universities at the institutional level. That management has evolved over centuries, and is well suited to the production processes of the university. It is possible to construct radical models (just as it is for the stock exchange or the building societies), but increased efficiency and effectiveness can best be achieved through continuing evolution, which ensures that the basic functions of the institution are modified rather than disrupted.

It is perhaps useful at this point to underline four aspects of university management that will continue to be key determinants in the ability to adjust to the challenges of the next decade or so.

Leadership
First and foremost among these aspects of management is leadership. The lay leaders (e.g. Chancellor, Chairman of the Council) have important roles to perform: the internal appreciation of the value to the university of those roles needs to be maintained. They are not to be seen as external forces interfering in the life of the institution or the work of the collegium – they are full members of the corporate body, whose interest in any aspect of the life and work of the university should be welcomed, and who should be employed in the task of balancing external and internal realities.

However, the dominant leadership role is that of the Vice-Chancellor (Baldridge *et al.*, 1978). It did not need the Jarratt Committee to inform universities that the Vice-Chancellor is their chief academic and administrative officer (though that might have been a useful reminder to some Vice-Chancellors): the more important question is what the role should be of such a chief officer in a university. The answer is that it is to provide leadership. The styles of this provision can vary according to the individual and the institution (Mortimer and McConnell, 1978), but it is not sufficient simply to chair meetings or make one's views known. Leadership involves a deep, and manipulative, involvement in the internal politics of the institution, requires a close acquaintance with key external influences and supporters, and should stem from a clear belief in a strategy for the future of the university. In a university, leadership is about consensus-building – because by the nature of its activities the institution cannot be authoritarian – but that is different from consensus-seeking; 'building' implies educating internal members about the external realities, structuring internal forces in a positive direction, and industriously creating support for the strategies that will best help ensure institutional growth. Leadership also involves the dynamic projection of the values and potential of the university to its various external publics and markets (local, regional, national and international; specialized and generalized).

No constitutional changes are required in most universities to allow the Vice-Chancellor to assert leadership in strategic planning, in the appointment of staff, in the selection policies for student recruitment, in the budgetary process and in most other main decision areas. The Vice-Chancellor, however, needs to have a predominant voice in the selection of key officers (e.g. Pro-Vice-Chancellors, Deans) so that he or she can build up a senior management team or cabinet. In that regard, the Jarratt Committee's recommendation that the Heads of Departments should be appointed on the nomination of the Vice-Chancellor is both one of its most crucial and one of its most controversial suggestions: in making that recommendation, Jarratt placed its emphasis firmly on the need for leadership.

If universities are to return strong leadership (which used to be the tradition outside Oxford and Cambridge), it is equally important that their leaders should be selected carefully, trained appropriately and held accountable. It is likely, therefore, that Vice-Chancellors will increasingly be appointed for fixed terms of office rather than until the normal retirement age, and will be expected to submit themselves to regular performance appraisals by representatives of their Councils.

Strategic planning
The second important direction of development is that of strategic planning; that is, the process of creating a guiding philosophy for the university and of translating it into a rolling plan. The days when individual universities could both see and promote themselves under a generalist or collective image of all universities are on the wane. It is becoming a matter of each university having to deter-

mine and promote what is distinctive and valuable in its teaching, research and public service. Because inter-institutional competition is likely to increase rather than diminish, the individual university's strategic planning will need to be based upon either its distinctiveness or its relevance to particular markets or opportunities. For example, there is likely to be a shift of emphasis towards the local or regional area where the university can prove its economic and cultural value and where it can meet the developing market for part-time and in-service courses: hence the growing interest in science parks, continuing professional education and so on. Some universities have claimed that they cannot undertake strategic planning in the environment of uncertainty engendered by governmental policies. To describe their attitudes as disingenuous is not to defend such policies. Planning is not a discipline that requires conditions of certainty or predictability: on the contrary, it is a process essential for survival in conditions of environmental uncertainty. It is a matter of determining what the institution wants that is also of value to the wider society, and of seeking ways of financing the appropriate activities. As in any sphere of competition, the institution will be as much dependent upon the knowledge, judgement and ability of its management as upon the performance of its staff.

Flexibility of the institution
The third direction of development is towards increasing the flexibility of the institution: a simple statement to make but a difficult state to achieve. In essence, it means the creation of a margin of readily redistributable resources and the generation of an attitude in favour of regular structural change. It requires a significant number of academic staff not to be on full tenure and a willingness to accept frequent change in the governance and management structures within the provisions of the Charter and Statutes. There is no one way to achieve these conditions: in general, however, they will best be generated by a managerial philosophy of devolution within an integrated framework. The more the individual units are held responsible and accountable for what they do, the more they are likely to exercise responsibility. It is a matter of liberating their enterprise and initiative within a framework of quality controls and institutional assessments of the futures of each unit.

Professional administration
The fourth major issue concerns the professional administration of each university. Even though, during the past quarter of a century, the British universities have developed a high quality internal civil

service (far higher in quality than in most public enterprises, such as the National Health Service or Local Government), that service needs to be accountable for its performance. The function of the administration is to help ensure the future of the institution that it serves. There is no satisfaction in knowing that when the institution flounders its committee minutes are immaculate and its financial accounts superbly maintained: the administrators' task is to avoid the floundering. That objective needs to be made more prominent in administrators' job descriptions; they have a responsibility for the future of the university and not just for keeping their aspect of the administration in good order.

In the United Kingdom universities are independent corporate bodies whose futures remain largely in their own hands; those futures are significantly dependent upon the internal attitudes to the managerial system in the individual institution and the efficient functioning of that system, and upon a recognition that the stability of academic performance is dependent upon structural flexibility. The guiding philosophy of each institution, directed at basic and distinctive aims, can only be fulfilled by taking advantage of political and economic (including market) opportunities through that structural flexibility. The external environmental conditions and pressures will change – that is the only constant. It is the task of management at the institutional level to ensure that the university is capable of reacting to such changes in ways which continue to serve its basic aims.

6

The Management of Polytechnics and Colleges

STEPHEN JONES AND GEORGE KILOH

INTRODUCTION

The development of public sector higher education in England and Wales is the history of an attempt to create a sector that could establish parity with the universities but would operate under social control. It was a decision that had profound implications for the internal governance and processes of management of the new institutions. The essence of the university's style and status seemed to lie in its freedom from any external control except that of the academic community, which by its nature transcended institutional boundaries. The system devised to manage the universities, there-fore, could not be adopted without change to meet the needs of the new public sector institutions. A solution was sought in an amalgam of the structures and ethos of the university model with those of the local authority model, which it was thought would allow a measure of political control while retaining academic control over academic matters. The derivation of the powers of the constituent elements of governance of PSHE institutions, the tension existing between them, and the effects of recent developments on the relationship between these elements form the central theme of this chapter.

When Anthony Crosland came to develop the public sector of higher education in 1965–66 (see Chapter 4) there was already an established means of controlling colleges of further education. It was a means that he and his successors, with one short-lived exception, continued to find acceptable in principle, however much they might judge aspects of its practice inimical to their concept of higher education. Crosland spoke of the need for the sector to be 'directly responsive to social needs', and he linked this otherwise ambiguous concept with the desirability of local government 'keeping a reasonable stake' in higher education (Crosland, 1965).

At the time when Crosland was speaking there was no substantial model of institutional self-management other than that evidenced by the universities. Like later Secretaries of State, no doubt he despaired of the possibility of bending independent university-like institutions to the national will, and there was no tested alternative to dependent status. It took almost twenty years to make any significant change in relation to the first obstacle. However, an example of successful public sector autonomy was much nearer, and its beginnings should have been evident to Crosland while he was still at the Department of Education and Science in 1965.

THE INHERITANCE

The traditional methods of local authority control of colleges have been described in terms that would surprise those accustomed to university operations (Robinson, 1968; Goldman, 1973). Up to the late 1960s and in some cases beyond, the standard pattern was to reserve to the authority and its officers all decisions affecting the college and its internal workings except, in practice, the day-to-day organization of teaching. Governing bodies were uncommon before Ministry of Education initiative in 1959 and became a statutory requirement only in 1968. In those early days the principal was not necessarily a member of the governing body where it existed, or even in attendance at its meetings. The governors were serviced from county hall, not from the college. In effect, all power resided at county hall.

Direct management had a number of aspects. First, the local authority remained unambiguously in control of employment. Whether posts were filled, at what level and in which areas, was a matter for county hall. Trade unions negotiated with the authority, not the college; staff conditions of service and salaries, both collectively and individually, were outside college powers. Approval of study leave and any associated expenditure was also for the authority. Staff budgets were frequently controlled by the authority's general establishment committee rather than by the education committee.

Secondly, the authority controlled all equipment and space. The college had no control over leases or over alterations to buildings. Decoration and maintenance was authorized by the authority, again frequently on the decision of a committee other than the education committee. Equipment was provided directly by the authority, down to pencils and pads of paper.

Thirdly, even where the principal (and later the governors) had power to spend, they were limited not only in total sum but also by strict rules of virement. When the Weaver Committee looked at this area in 1965 it noted that the DES itself, in the large number of colleges it funded directly, recognized only five broad heads of expenditure, within each of which the governors could exercise virement. For maintained colleges the Committee settled on fifteen such heads (DES 1966b, appendices A and B).

Lastly, the academic programme was itself under authority control. No course could be offered without the authority's prior approval; it could be discontinued at the authority's direction. From 1947 a system of Regional Advisory Councils arose to ensure that neighbouring authorities did not offer excessive advanced course provision. It was recognized that for these courses at least the colleges had more than a purely local role, but the RACs were creatures of local government, not of the colleges.

Historically there was a further reason for the close association of colleges and local authorities. Though voluntary agencies, such as the churches, have always played a significant role in the provision of teacher education, and indeed provided most of it until after the Second World War, the great expansion of places after 1945 was driven largely by the desire of local authorities to provide for themselves as employers of teachers. There was a very close relationship between authorities and teacher training colleges, which was supported by generosity from central government on a scale that is still obvious. Though very few colleges still exist devoted solely to teacher education, any college of higher education or polytechnic that has among its antecedents a residential college of education will know the kind of provision made for prospective teachers and will compare it sadly with the poverty of the technical education sector. Many authorities kept a toe-hold in higher education through teacher training, and the abandonment of monotechnic colleges of education has not necessarily been accompanied by an appreciation of the rather different character of the sector as it is now constituted.

In administering colleges of any kind the local authorities had little or no regard for any university paradigm, even where courses were offered for the internal degrees of the University of London. For many years, and in the great majority of colleges, such a paradigm would have been irrelevant. The colleges were not only growing within a system whose main activities would always be in the schools, but university-level work was with few exceptions a small and recently acquired part of their provision. The number of degree-level students outside universities and the colleges of advanced technology was insignificant up to the early sixties; the degree of BEd followed on the Robbins Report of 1963. There are even now complaints that local authority members, and sometimes officers, fail to recognize that major colleges operate very largely, and sometimes exclusively, at university level, that higher education is intrinsically more expensive than secondary, or that it may need different patterns of control.

A NEW MODEL OF GOVERNANCE

It was the Robbins Committee that first drew attention authoritatively to the shortcomings for higher education of the traditional methods of local authority management. It recommended that 'finance should be given to governing bodies under the broadest possible categories of expenditure. Detailed earmarking and control on items of expenditure by an outside body are unnecessary and wasteful not only of time but of money. Economy is more readily achieved through prudent management and careful buying by those responsible than by a rigidly detailed allocation of funds for particular purposes' (Committee on Higher Education, 1963, paragraph 680). The Robbins Report has been described as 'the high-water mark of the autonomous tradition in England' (Locke, Pratt and Burgess, 1985, p. 135). As paragraph 40 of the Robbins Report has it, 'In the past our universities have tended to set the tone and the pace for other institutions and it is probable that in the future they will have a similar role to play'.

Thus the Report says of the CATs for which it recommended university status: 'We consider that the present powers and status of the colleges are not commensurate with the work they are now doing. They lack many of the attributes of university self-government; they have not full power to award their own qualifications, and in particular cannot award degrees . . . ' Similarly, it says of the teacher training colleges for which it recommended federation with university schools of education: 'The training colleges . . . feel themselves to be only doubtfully recognised as part of the system of higher education and yet to have attained standards of work and a characteristic ethos that justify their claim to an appropriate place in it' (Committee on Higher Education, 1963, paragraphs 390, 308).

Robbins had a plan for teacher training but effectively none for technical education. In 1965 Crosland rejected the one and supplied the other, and one of his first actions was to commission the study

110

chaired by Weaver on the government of colleges of education, whose report was to form the foundation of the model of governance developed for PSHE more generally.

The Weaver Report began by noting the Robbins Committee's view that the relationship between the universities and the training colleges should be further extended through the development of the institutes of education. However, the government had concluded that the administrative and financial aspects were separable from the academic, and that there should be no fundamental change to the maintained or voluntary status of the colleges. None the less, arrangements for the internal government of colleges would be reviewed in the light of the Robbins Committee's recommendations on that subject. These recommendations had in fact been sparse, being more or less confined to repeating what had already been said, in the context of universities, about the relationship between lay and academic elements on governing bodies and the desirable integration of teaching staff into academic counsels, and that these should apply also to the colleges of education. Weaver shared Robbins's conviction that 'academic freedom is a necessary condition of the highest efficiency and of the proper progress of academic institutions', and sought to transfer this notion into the maintained sector of higher education as represented by the colleges of education. Robbins had accepted that the executive governing body of the university should control its finance and influence its general policy, but had added that that body had no business to interfere in internal academic organization, and had extended this view to the colleges of education. Similarly, Weaver recommended that 'the governing body should be responsible for the general running of the college and . . . for the broad pattern of courses' and that 'the academic board should . . . be responsible for the academic work of the college' (DES, 1966b, paragraphs 24, 25).

Thus a university-derived view contributed to the model for PSHE government. None the less, the Crosland approach was to retain local control. Later actions by the DES showed that it was aware of the managerial problems implicit in such a policy, but it had no alternative once it had rejected any notion of quasi-university independence for public sector colleges. Evidently it recognized that colleges were unlikely to reach their full potential if kept in close local authority control, but there was little or no relevant experience of any middle way between full local authority control of the traditional kind and the independence enjoyed by universities. One had to be established by agreement between the DES and the local authorities, achieved only by a process in which DES prompting fell at times little short of direction. There was considerable resistance to the Weaver proposals, which envisaged powers being exercised on behalf of, but not by, the local authorities, but they were commended in the DES *Notes for Guidance* (for the establishment of polytechnics) in 1967. The 1968 Education (No. 2) Act made the legal adjustments thought necessary to allow a college to exercise delegated functions although not a subcommittee of the local authority concerned. In 1970 the *Notes for Guidance* were adapted to serve for all FE establishments. Even then, however, the designation of some polytechnics was being delayed by argument about the proper balance of powers, and argument was to continue to disturb college/authority relationships.

One of the Robbins recommendations accepted by the government was the creation of the Council for National Academic Awards (see Chapter 4). Significantly enough, however, CNAA was born of an attempt to continue a non-university tradition. Its predecessor, the National Council for Technological Awards, had been established by the Ministry of Education in 1955. It provided a model for the CNAA to follow, and allowed it to develop procedures that, although serving the purpose of ensuring the university standard of its awards, owed nothing, overtly at least, to university practice. All the same, these procedures came to be infused with university-derived characteristics.

By 1973, the end of the transitional period initiated by Robbins, each college had a measure of internal self-government while its local authority retained control over its general educational character, its main budgets, course approval and the conditions of service for staff. There was a governing body on which authority representatives were usually in a minority and which always included a substantial lay element. There was an academic board with a balance of ex officio, elected and student members. There was a director with duties perhaps only loosely expressed, and a range of committees closely resembling, *mutatis mutandis*, those to be found in universities. In some way there was a parallel with the decolonization process, when internal self-government was the first major step towards independence. The analogy was clearly understood and sometimes feared. To some local authorities even the current amount of independence, let alone any more, was a clear infringement of their rights and statutory duty to manage. To many colleges a fuller independence became an objective.

THE SEARCH FOR AUTONOMY

The binary system was described by Sir Edward Boyle as 'inherently unstable' (Kogan, 1971, p. 128). Polytechnics continue to press for corporate status. At their fringe there are those who would like to include the word 'university' in their titles, although remaining in the public sector, and at least one that would prefer straight transfer to the University Grants Committee. In 1980 the Select Committee on Education and the Arts supported the call for corporate status and for an access of freedom at the administrative level (House of Commons, 1980). The local authority associations, however, have resisted what they regard as yet further encroachments on their rights and on occasion have sought a return to traditional practice. Much of the same tension is evident between the institutions and their main academic validator, the CNAA, which until the 1980s made limited concessions to the growing maturity of the major institutions (see Chapter 4), despite the intimacy of a relationship in which – unlike the administrative course approval system – those charged with approving courses come face to face with those proposing them. Tension may be growing around the relationship with the other main national validator, the Business and Technician Education Council, whose practices demonstrate less regard for institutional autonomy than those of CNAA ever did.

But what does autonomy mean? In a traditional university it means the freedom to determine its own objectives, its own standards and its own management within the context of a Royal Charter. By this test the modern university falls short of its ideal, but all PSHE falls shorter still. A college lacks the essential characteristic of autonomy: the freedom to identify a market and to reach it. The local authority determines the general character of the college. PSHE courses are subject to administrative approval by the local authority and the regional advisory council, the National Advisory Body and DES; DES retains specific control over matters relating to teacher education. Courses given administrative approval are then subject to academic validation, usually by a national validating body. Staff devise these courses and, after validation, teach them, but they do so under licence. Students are assessed by the staff concerned, but the award of a diploma or degree is subject to the approval of the validating body.

Nevertheless, the formal legal position of English public sector institutions is varied. They divide into those funded via local authorities and those funded centrally by DES, albeit both are now co-ordinated by NAB. But even in the first category the five

113

polytechnics in inner London have corporate status as companies limited by guarantee (as does, for example, the university-sector London School of Economics). Among the centrally-funded 'voluntary' colleges there is a great variety; some are not corporate bodies, being legally parts of their providing bodies. This chapter does not attempt to deal substantively with Scotland or Wales, but it may be noted that in Scotland the central institutions are corporate bodies funded and controlled directly by the Scottish Education Department. The norm in England (and Wales), however, is for a college to be 'maintained', that is, owned and operated by a local authority under arrangements approved by the DES, but this shorthand approach must not obscure the variety that continues to exist, particularly among former colleges of education. It may be that in some circumstances a maintained college can have a legal personality, but such a view has not yet come to a test.

On any test applied at institutional level, therefore, the public sector college is likely to be considerably less 'free' than a university, even less free, for example, than a college of London University. This may not be true of the individual, and collective tolerance of what appears to be intolerable may owe much to the comparative freedom of staff to behave in the ways traditionally associated with the academic. Lecturers may tend to use particular teaching methods or to adapt their behaviour in other ways to satisfy the expected preferences of the validators, but for the most part they are free to adopt whatever approach they find appropriate. These are characteristics of universities also, and external validation may therefore be tolerated as equally as is the need to convince a Senate committee. In both types of institution there will be pressure to conform, and some resistance to innovation.

Institutionally, there is status to be gained by distancing oneself from the validator, thus making oneself more like the self-reliant university, but it is by no means clear that academic staff are as convinced as institutional leaders that this object is in fact desirable. There are two reasons for this. The process of seeking and gaining academic approval is generally a positive one, despite occasional frustration. It creates a strong feeling of community while the process is in train and, since most courses are approved, the course team and the department experience a feeling of satisfaction and public recognition. Above all, however, external validation can powerfully endorse the academics' own views within the institution and, if necessary, against it.

The situation is even clearer at departmental than at course level. Departments in universities and colleges look outwards to the wider academic and professional communities. The college department will have additional links, which may sometimes be helpful to it, with validating bodies and Her Majesty's Inspectorate. A department is subject to a range of pressures in relation to its balance and type of work, and this range can itself protect it from succumbing to any one influence. By developing a wide variety of work a department can respond more flexibly to new pressures and, therefore, in effect can largely determine its own line of development. An astute head of department can always find powerful external allies to support a particular approach, which the institution will find it difficult to challenge. It is extremely difficult for any institutional pressure to be brought to bear upon a department that has a strong and supportive relationship with the major external bodies upon which the college itself depends.

The position of the staff, then, is not greatly affected by the lack of institutional autonomy; the position of the department may in fact be enhanced by it. The demand for autonomy – linked often to the argument that current controls are needlessly expensive – comes from more senior management, who can be bypassed by current structures. It is they who most insistently advance the claim for greater status through autonomy, one outcome of which would be the institution's ability to present courses in response to local need without having to seek the range of approvals now required.

This claim can draw for support on practical experience elsewhere. In August 1964, less than a year after Robbins, a major report was issued on non-university higher education in Australia. Its recommendations were for a new sector, later to be called 'advanced education', whose activities were precisely defined and appear to be what Crosland had in mind for the polytechnics, albeit more clearly expressed than anything from any English equivalent (Commonwealth of Australia, 1964).

From the transitional period of 1965–72 the colleges of advanced education emerged as autonomous bodies with limited powers, including the authority to award their own degrees under certain conditions. The rationale for autonomy was twofold. First, it was felt that a college 'would need freedom to shape courses to suit both local and national needs, and it should not be unduly hampered by existing patterns of curricula and syllabuses' (Commonwealth of Australia, 1966, paragraph 5.1.3). Secondly, autonomy would enhance rather than diminish local responsiveness. 'One of our main concerns was to give people in the area the feeling that the college belonged to them and was not controlled from Sydney' (Government of New South Wales, 1968).

The relevant point here is not that the context of the Australian public sector was the same as that of the United Kingdom – it differed in some important respects, particularly in the lack of local education authorities below state level – but that autonomy was seen as desirable, immediately feasible and entirely compatible with the requirements of the funding bodies, requirements very similar to those of the UK. One investigating committee was 'unanimously of the opinion that the College should be established as a strong and independent corporate body with a status similar to that enjoyed by universities in Australia and the United Kingdom' (Commonwealth of Australia, 1966, paragraph 5.1.1).

Such thoughts were unthinkable in England, whose governments were struggling and still struggle with what are essentially adaptations of the traditional management model, interpreted in as many different ways as there are local authorities. Some authorities give considerable latitude; some seek to bind still closer. Greater independence is resisted for reasons that have never been formally and comprehensively stated. To the National Association of Teachers in Further and Higher Education, the major teachers' trade union, always a strong proponent of a unitary further education sector under local authority management, it is distasteful because it is 'the first step on the road to ... freedom from local authority control' (Bocock, 1980). Such an attitude begs the original question, quite apart from the fact that some voluntary colleges and the inner London polytechnics have forms of corporate status yet remain firmly within the public sector. The solid reason for adhering to local government appears to be that particularly at a time of contraction the superior resources of a local authority are seen as a protection against institutional caprice or even bankruptcy.

NATFHE is not alone in seeing the granting of corporate status as the first step on the route taken by the CATs, which abandoned sub-degree work: local authorities saw the institutions they had founded for sound local purposes being given autonomy and adopting different aims. The development of further and higher education in Manchester has been cited as an outstanding example of successive local and municipal initiatives being subverted by aspiration for higher status (Pratt and Burgess, 1974, pp. 25–6), but most large cities show the same evidence. Many observers see considerable virtue in the close association of all kinds of tertiary course, whether advanced or non-advanced, perhaps partly as a reaction against the elitism implicit in the creaming off of advanced work into university-style institutions, but also because it is claimed that the simultaneous presence of varied courses in the same college leads

116

to easier transfer of students as they find their own levels. This argument leads less obviously to the belief that all types of course should coexist within the same municipal management structure. How far these claims are based merely on ideology can be disputed. It has also been claimed that the large sums that local authorities receive from the government to run PSHE are of considerable assistance to them in maintaining cash flow at difficult times.

CNAA's relationship with institutions contrasts sharply with that of the local authorities (see Chapter 4). CNAA lays down principles and guidelines for courses leading to its various awards, but its role is then to respond to proposals. The chief variable revealed by recent developments is the extent to which free rein is given to this institutional initiative. It is commonly agreed that, in the years since its establishment, the CNAA has been conspicuously successful in establishing the academic credibility of awards offered in developing institutions of PSHE, both in polytechnics and colleges. It has done so in large measure by translating into its processes the characteristics of the universities. If higher education in the public sector was to be taken seriously, the university-derived notion of academic autonomy had somehow to be carried over, and it at least demanded that only the institutions could propose detailed academic programmes. Because research is an essential accompaniment to teaching in the universities, the CNAA has always laid emphasis on the requirement that teachers in PSHE should undertake research. Above all, perhaps, and as elaborated in Chapter 4, the CNAA has embraced the notion of peer assessment, drawn from the self-regulation of the academic community embodied in both university and UGC attitudes and procedures.

Although autonomy in the sense of possessing the initiative rests with PSHE institutions as with universities, the difference lies chiefly in the extent of overt accountability. Universities' accountability (apart from the requirements for particular courses recognized by professional bodies) lies as much in their reputation through the career performance of their graduates as in their relationship to, for example, the UGC. It is in this sense an indirect accountability. In the interests of establishing comparability with university awards and thus the credibility of PSHE awards, CNAA's early procedures demanded an overt and detailed accountability to peers before a course was offered. One way of describing developments in CNAA procedures from, say, the mid-1970s to the present is as a progressive withdrawal of the overt accountability of institutions to CNAA – although too slow a withdrawal for many institutions – towards a joint and indirect accountability of the kind that characterizes the universities.

If the existence of the CNAA draws the institution towards the traditional university model of peer review, where authority lies with the individual teacher and with the teachers as a collective rather than with some higher individuals, the emergence of the NAB has had the effect of strengthening the central authority of the director and his immediate staff and of emphasizing their influence upon academic decisions.

The behaviour of colleges' internal governmental machinery is thus decisively affected by the freedom of action permitted to them by individual local authorities (behind whom stands the NAB) and the validating bodies. Much formal power is retained outside the institution, and it can be argued that the functions of a university council are in a college exercised largely by the local authority and those of a senate by the CNAA. Conversely, although a director may be seen as a substitute vice-chancellor, for historic and practical reasons his office is one of greater formal executive authority.

RELATIONSHIPS WITHIN THE INSTITUTIONS

The relationships between the governors, the director and the academic board inevitably differ in practice from one institution to another. In principle they were laid down by the 1978 Oakes Working Group (see Chapter 4) in that part of its report that dealt with intra-institutional government. It stipulated that the nature and aims of each college were to remain under the control of elected authorities. This is a direct and physical control. Although a university can in principle introduce a course in, say, Serbo-Croat even if the UGC objects – provided that the money can be found – a maintained college cannot.

Oakes drew a clear and potentially rigid distinction between resource and academic matters, and construed the latter narrowly: 'We wish to emphasise that the governing body is ultimately responsible to the LEA for all expenditure on the running of its institution . . . In exercising this responsibility it will, no doubt, as a matter of practice, delegate authority to the principal, who may in turn wish to delegate authority for expenditure in particular areas to his deputies, heads of faculty or department or other subordinate officers, but it should be clearly understood that in exercising such authority they do so on behalf of the governing body. The academic board, on the other hand, or its sub-committees may well make recommendations which have expenditure implications but it has to be understood that the authority for deciding on them must remain vested in those who are responsible for the management of the institution, and this principle must not be eroded' (DES, 1978, paragraph 8.20).

According to this view an academic board and its substructure have no authoritative role in staffing, the allocation of space or the allocation of money for academic purposes. These things are for the director or the governors. How far they in their turn have any real power depends upon their relationship, formal and actual, with their local authorities.

GOVERNORS

If the director and the academic board are, in their different ways, vital to the good running of a college, so are the governors. Their role is, however, muted. Just as so much of the power of university councils has passed to central government (conditions of service, capital expenditure, some aspects of planning), so have college governors a diminished role.

The business of governing bodies and the attitudes of their members have not been fully analysed. One survey, not in the UK but in Australia, where circumstances are comparable, showed that governing councils knew little about their institutions and approached their tasks with widely differing, indeed contradictory, perceptions (McCaig, 1973). It is likely that much the same would be found of polytechnic and college governors. Their role is mixed. By the articles of government the governors are meant to approve all estimates and all expenditure, and to be responsible for the college generally; it is, however, very difficult for any governor to challenge the estimates presented to him or her because the amount of data will not usually permit the construction of approaches alternative to those suggested by the director or the local authority. The membership of governing bodies is designed to allow an expression of views by those connected with the professional or industrial concerns relevant to the college, but course proposals rarely come to them in any form. They are restricted, in effect, to querying the details of financial data and to making statements of broad principle. They also play a role in the appointment of senior staff and in student and staff discipline and appeals, where the lay membership is regarded as detached and impartial and able to overrule the director if the facts of the case demand it.

Nevertheless, the governors are publicly thought to have a significant role beyond this. 'A Court of Governors ... bears the responsibility for the institution when necessary but more normally oversees and supports, particularly in any wider context, its polytechnic's development. This is a sensitive and important role which requires above all that the Court be satisfied that the powers delegated to and through the director are adequately exercised' (ILEA, 1985, p. 16). The relationships of governors, local authority and institutional head are a continuing subject of national debate. The position of governors will, however, remain equivocal as long as they must attempt to play their independent roles according to agendas determined by the director and the local authority, and on the basis of information supplied from those sources.

Governors none the less can act as a protection against what some would see as arbitrary power; thus, in 1980–81, the governors of Huddersfield Polytechnic, an appreciable number of whom had been appointed by the maintaining authority, stood for the institution and against the authority when a crisis over alleged mismanagement developed from what appeared to be very trivial beginnings. Governors are therefore a buffer: between director and students, director and staff, academic board and local authority, director and authority, and sometimes director and academic board. With the CNAA, they are the only real safeguard against lapse into the *ancien régime* of direct local authority control. The sensitive local authority may therefore need to propitiate the governors in the same way that the college needs to propitiate the authority. One observer has written that in practice the role of the governors of a public sector college might not be very different from that of a university council if they enjoyed the confidence and support of the authority; but he thought that such occasions must be rare (Matterson, 1981, p. 71).

CENTRAL INSTITUTIONAL MANAGEMENT

It is clear from Oakes that the position of a polytechnic or college director cannot formally be the same as that of a vice-chancellor. The bare description of the role may hardly differ: conventionally a director is the 'Chief Officer ... and ... responsible under the general direction of the [governors] for furthering the objectives of the Polytechnic, including the organisation, management and discipline of the Polytechnic' (City of London Polytechnic, 1970). But in fact it is as difficult to define the role of the director as it is that of the vice-chancellor. So much depends upon the particular context in which the individual holds the post and so much more upon the character of the individual.

Vice-chancellors have written at length on the peculiarities of their position. One remarked that 'If a British vice-chancellor has an original idea it would be the height of ineptitude to publish it to his faculty and fatal to issue a directive about it . . . Naked enterprise from the administration, which in industry creates confidence, in a British university creates suspicion not to say alarm' (Ashby, 1970, p. 7). Another, of a rather later generation, wrote 'If a vice-chancellor is doing his job properly, he must take decisions without going through the full democratic process; but they should always be those decisions which, given adequate time, would have been taken by the majority in a democratic vote' (Perry, 1976, p. 215). A third confirmed that 'For academic management the optimum structure lies nearer the democratic end of the range' (Aitken 1966, p. 74). How far these views will survive the 1980s in the universities must be a matter for conjecture, but they probably still represent the majority view of those directly affected.

If the essence of university management lies in the need to secure the consent of the academic community for desirable change, the role of the vice-chancellor, in so far as domestic behaviour is concerned, must be that of a chairperson. The task is to identify ways forward and to obtain majorities for them in committee. The college director does not need this degree of formal consent except where the matter in hand has sole and unarguably academic relevance. He or she sits, moreover, in a less precisely defined relationship to the governing body: the appointment is recommended by the governors but is subject to the local authority's veto; it is an appointment to the authority's staff. The director is responsible formally to the governors, but the authority will regard him or her as personally responsible for the college. At least one authoritative commentator regards the director as the 'chief executive of the LEA within the college' (Waitt, 1980, p. 146). Like the vice-chancellor, the director presides over the main organ of academic government, but unlike the vice-chancellor the director has a substantial measure of executive authority comparable with the prerogative of the monarch in Tudor or early Stuart England. One observer has remarked that school government follows the model of a renaissance princedom, and that its politics have been that of the court (Baron, 1975, p. 83). The same remarks would fit the college tradition. The extent to which a director can exert his ostensible powers is limited in practice. Some directors would doubtless think it extremely limited.

The way in which the director exercises power rests heavily on the further education tradition in which the colleges and their directors are steeped – a tradition which in somewhat ungainly fashion has adapted itself to a situation in which the colleges are large, complicated and self-confident. One characteristic of college government is the survival of the tenured assistant director. Unlike the university norm, in which pro vice-chancellors rise from the ranks of senior academics and, their tours of duty done, sink back again, the public sector has preferred to appoint permanent assistants. This is a clear inheritance from further education. A small college had only a principal and a secretary to conduct its internal administration. As it grew it attracted a vice-principal and perhaps more secretaries. When polytechnics were established conventional thinking had it that their size indicated several more vice-principals, and in general these were appointed. As mergers took place the principals and vice-principals of other colleges were co-opted to the bigger college's service, and it is said that one polytechnic had twelve such people on its staff before rationalization became inevitable. The high tide of the assistant director appears to have begun to recede, and given the costs involved it is likely that recession will continue.

The survival of the tenured assistant director is evidence of the FE practice of individual rather than collective decision-making at all levels. Traditionally, the director relied heavily upon assistant directors rather than on committees, and where committees existed they were often chaired by the assistants, with a resulting confusion between the kinds of decision that were properly for the executive and those properly for the committee. Even where there is a genuine attempt to find common consent, internal committees will often be seen in the light of experience as devices to ensure the compliance of staff in whatever course of action is desired for them. This historic position appears to be under attack as academics find them places for expression of fears in the face of likely contraction, and as they continue to be encouraged in the university-derived perception of their role and position.

This has had an impact on the position of the administration. Before the early 1970s it is unlikely that a university observer would have been able to see much of an administration at all in PSHE, but things have had to change. The former view – that administration belonged to county hall – is now much modified in that substantial professional administrations are appointed to all polytechnics and many colleges. They are, however, the poor brethren. They stand in an anomalous position to the assistant directors, who are almost invariably appointed from among the teachers and whose heights they can scarcely hope to reach. Although paid on substantially lower salary scales than their university counterparts, they conduct an administrative process considerably more complex and much more prone to unpredictable and unwelcome outside intervention. Oakes recognized their difficulty, but no action has followed. Their importance in academic processes, among them the sensitive area of the academic board, cannot be overestimated.

THE ACADEMIC BOARD

The restricted role of the academic board has already been described. It is difficult to identify any action that it might take that does not require the later approval of the governors, the director, the local authority or a validating body: the appointment of internal examiners may be the only one. Yet board members would probably adopt a very traditional view of the academic's role within an institution of higher education, and they do not chafe unduly at the constrained role allotted to them. It is a necessary implication of the college's position within the public sector that the main, indeed almost the only, expression allowed to the board is through the approval of courses, but even here the board has much less power than a university senate. Though it can initiate course approval it cannot complete it; the external mechanism is lengthy and uncertain in outcome. Oakes accepted the limitations on the academic board by which it was restricted, subject to the general guidance of the governing body, to the planning, co-ordination, development and oversight of all the academic work of the college, including the admission and examination of students. Different colleges interpret this remit with varying degrees of imagination, but in the context of external control of resources, course approval and validation it must be seen as short commons indeed.

It is likely that most academic boards fail to exercise the kind of responsibility that one would expect, both for academic work and for advising the director on resources. They have little real power except to say No; they have little effective experience of governing. The concept of collective decision-making has made only limited inroads into the ancient principle of individual accountability. Some of the classic polytechnic crises are due partly to a lack of understanding about how collective decision-making must proceed: an unfamiliarity with what committees and individuals must do together if the institutions are to prosper, and on the one hand an unwillingness to compromise or alternately to use authority, and on the other an unwillingness to question or to inform.

The board might not only be unfamiliar with the practice of collective decision-making; it may also lack the power to challenge departments who have direct access to external academic decision-makers. Early practices in highly departmentalized and specialized institutions may have encouraged this access, and when resources for expansion arrived in the 1960s and 1970s the academic board had no real part in allocating them and no desire to do so. As resources have shrunk and academic developments have become circumscribed, the poverty of the role of the academic board has become more apparent. Its role as adjudicator of demands for additional funds is largely in abeyance when most funds are swallowed up in historic budgets needed to preserve existing work. It has failed to develop adequate planning mechanisms for the institution as a whole or to evolve into a collective academic leadership.

THE IMPACT OF NAB

One of the features of NAB's funding methodology (see Chapter 4) is the differential weighting of subject areas. The fact that this favours some departments and prejudices others makes such factors more divisive than cohesive. It is liable further to exacerbate the weakness of the academic board's influence, since the board's representational character tends to a requirement for consensus, and its inability to achieve this produces stalemate. In this context it would require a whole institution to feel under threat for a board to play a positive and influential role.

Directors are now involved in discussion on behalf of their institutions not only with their local authorities but also with NAB officers. They must respond to NAB enquiries and surveys; they must interpret the institution to NAB and NAB to the institution. On the decisions of the Secretary of State, advised by NAB, hang the future of the institution's courses and departments and possibly the future of the institution itself. Renewed pressure from non-NAB bodies, such as the Audit Commission, helps to create a situation in which the director is in a real position to translate the pressure on him or her into pressure on his or her colleagues.

Thus, in 1983, one polytechnic had no choice but finally to accept the rationalization of nautical education, recommended by NAB and endorsed by ministers, which meant the closure of two departments. The director, having secured the consent of the local authority, notified the academic board which, by a majority, gave its support. It is highly unlikely that so sharply focused a proposal to reduce staff would have been accepted by the board had the director not been constrained by a NAB-induced decision.

More generally, and less dramatically, the target student–staff ratios (SSRs) that are an essential part of NAB's funding methodology provide institutional management with a mechanism for change sufficiently powerful to overcome the doubts felt by staff about their validity and academic consequences. Since academic debate is rarely conducted without reference to resources, and since SSRs determine resources, SSRs are coming to be crucial factors in institutional planning. Moreover, even if of shaky validity in places, they are observable and verifiable. It is often stressed by NAB that a view it has taken of, for example, the balance between subject areas nationally is not meant to condition that balance in each and every institution: institutions are indeed free to depart significantly from the national balance should their circumstances justify it. However, there is no doubt that a department whose courses are of a kind looked on favourably in national planning feels a good deal more comfortable within an institution than a department not so favoured. Similarly, a department whose SSR matches or is higher than the level underlying NAB funding feels secure within the institution in a way that a department in the opposite position does not.

These are not yet overriding considerations, nor do they signify a change in kind from what has long applied. Yardstick SSRs, against which the position of a particular department was judged favourably or unfavourably, predate NAB by a long way; similarly, favoured and unfavoured subject areas are not a new concept. NAB has, however, sharpened these perceptions. The central management of an institution, desirous of shifting resources between departments, can make use of what NAB allocations imply by way of institutional priorities. This applies particularly where some departments feel that another subject area is being unfairly subsidized by receiving more than its NAB-determined due to run its courses, while they see their own NAB-determined due being diverted away from them. Only a powerful policy and a persuasive head of department can secure the maintenance within an institution of an imbalance, compared with NAB funding, in favour of any particular subject area.

Although NAB does not take detailed notice of institutional finances, its decisions determine what these funds will be. As national support for higher education comes under strain, the importance of the institutional relationship with NAB becomes the greater. NAB shows signs of having had a significant impact on the relationship between some institutions and their maintaining authorities. Where an institution is wholly or almost wholly funded on NAB advice the individual local authority's influence upon finances is likely to diminish. The authority may cease to have a direct financial stake in the institution and become rather the route by which NAB-determined resources reach it. This must reduce the local authority's ability, notwithstanding its continuing role in governance, to influence the institution in the provision it makes.

DECISION-MAKING IN A PERIOD OF CONTRACTION

The institution must live not only with the need to adjust to difficult decisions about contraction: it must also live with two conflicting cultures. It must behave both as an academic community and as a corporation able to implement hard decisions about the way it will contract. It is here that the Oakes principle is strained if not broken. In the sort of discussion in which colleges and funding authorities are now likely to be engaged, there can be no clear distinction between academic and resource matters, even if one could previously have been detected. The ability of directors to perform their duties effectively depends upon the degree of co-operation they receive not only from the local authority but also from their staff. Thus directors are in general most careful to make sure that they carry the academic staff with them in their decisions, though formally they cannot shelter behind an unwillingness by the staff to be carried. That a senate does not consent to a particular proposal may be an absolute defence for a vice-chancellor facing outside pressure, but it is a defence open to a college director only where the issue is one relating solely to academic matters, and even there the position is not entirely clear. It may be that a director who makes an open use of statutory powers loses the ability to influence colleagues, through the effects of the inevitable confrontation. A director who wishes to guide an institution into different paths had better do it with caution. To this extent, director and college operate more closely to the university pattern than might be thought.

Directors are not obliged to consult their colleagues, and some do not make an obvious practice of doing so. Directors may well be supported by their local authority in taking unilateral action, and in most cases they will have cleared the way by previous consultation with the authority's officers; but that is not the end of the story.

Despite its apparent distance from matters relating to college management, the CNAA can be a powerful force for the traditional view that management is about obtaining consent from those affected by one's decisions. Thus it is not uncommon for CNAA institutional reviews to comment privately on the style or capacity of the director and, having regard to his or her impact on the institution and its standards, it is entirely proper for them to do so. Less commonly, the comments are published. In extreme circumstances a college that could not show that it was a nascent if not an established academic community, rather than a set of teachers dominated by an autocrat, would lose CNAA validation. At least two major institutions have had to face this possibility, and in one of them the director made fairly prompt arrangements for early retirement. At the other side of the circle, private comments are again made where a director is thought seriously deficient but not autocratic. Comments of this kind are made public only after considerable heart-searching and, in at least one case, after taking legal advice.

The role of director has rarely been one in which initiatives can be taken, unless there is money to oil the wheels of consent – and in recent years there has been little enough of that. More recent developments require that directors take the initiative if contraction is to be implemented without disaster or if, better still, it is to be avoided altogether. They are, however, not the only points of contact with the local authority. In fact authorities continue practices that appear to subvert the formal mechanisms set up for decision-making. Such practices vary according to the habits of the authority and the acquiescence of college staff, but at their worst they can compromise the internal authority of the director, the governors and the academic board. The intimacy of the college/local authority relationship is not limited to financial matters: where the authority has subject advisers, they are frequent contacts, and their support is almost always necessary for a course proposal to achieve approval. The quality of advice from all these varied sources is itself varied. One jaundiced director commented that, of the various public bodies with which he had to deal, 'Few . . . seemed to contain people who might be supposed to understand the approximately university-level education that I thought I was supposed to be concerned with'. They were 'grey-faced men in dismal offices shuffling innumerable forms and totting up endless columns of figures' and he was 'appalled at the mediocrity I have encountered throughout the system' (Miller, 1980). This view is extreme, but it is not unrepresentative; it underlines the truth that, whatever the

127

brakes on the process that DES may think it has provided, colleges will be exposed to the differing wills and habits of individual local authorities, who vary in their quality and behaviour, allowing freedom or imposing control, encouraging or discouraging, as they think proper.

The Oakes analysis of where power lies is therefore a statement of theory rather than of reality. It cannot be realistic, given the inseparability of the academic and resource sides of the college. It gives considerable power to the governors (which in practice means the director), power which can be exercised only in the context of the need to propitiate the household gods: the local authority, the validating bodies, the staff, to name only three groups. To some extent, Oakes recognized the impracticality of the principles he emphasized, suggesting that there was merit in involving governors in some internal committees – and much the same point was made in respect of the universities by the Jarratt Committee (CVCP, 1985). Indeed, some universities do this already. Paradoxically this kind of joint endeavour may be the only means by which the separation of powers can be made to work.

The resource constraint of recent years has tended to underline within institutions the incapacity of the academic board to achieve academic consensus, the separate rather than the common character-istics of academic departments, the enhanced influence of the administration and the executive power of institutional manage-ment. Had the constraint allowed some secure knowledge of the scale of budget reductions sufficiently far ahead, it is probable that most institutions' processes could have coped with it. As it is, the period from 1980–81 has been characterized by a series of notifi-cations to local authorities and institutions, shortly before the event and subject to change thereafter, of substantial budgetary shifts, usually downwards, and all this from a base which in 1980–81 represented a far from lavish provision. Institutional responses have had to take, in various forms, the character of crisis management even where there was no real crisis.

In conditions of crisis management a process of participative decision-making, internalization of institutional goals by academic staff and the pursuit of desirable change through consensus are conspicuous by their absence. Centralism rather than devolution is in evidence. This is no surprise, given the character of the director's or principal's role already described, and given that the director and the administration control an informational network on students and staff, which is suddenly of real importance. Centralist ten-dencies are further encouraged by short time-scales that preclude or at least inhibit participation, by the absolute need to secure desirable change quickly, and by the fact that staff are understandably reluctant to co-operate in a process that could bring about their colleagues' departure, and possibly their own too. But initiative in academic matters continues to rest with the departments, who may in turn draw yet greater strength from the expected delegation of powers by the CNAA. Delegation may also give the academic board greater moment, but its strengthening is likely to be formal rather than actual.

CONCLUSION

There seem now to be first signs that the greater institutional autonomy evidenced by a direct relationship with NAB, and foreshadowed in the possibilities held out by CNAA, has led to reconsideration of the historic tie between college and local authority. Polytechnics and colleges can still be seen as the ground upon which national, regional and local considerations in higher education are searching for a *modus vivendi*. The Conservative government of 1983 produced circumstances in which a radical review of the role and functions of local government might have to be undertaken: in 1987, the position of PSHE remained for resolution.

This chapter has sought to show how the constituent parts of PSHE institutions' governance derive from a conscious attempt by government to bring about some fusion of university and further education models, and how they exhibit the tension between the influences brought to bear by CNAA and NAB. Comparing government attention to questions of institutional status with that given to matters of academic substance, Pratt and Burgess convincingly argued that 'Paying teachers equally for work of equal value, providing comparable resources for institutions different but equal, rewarding the system of vocational education in its own right would go a long way to make the question of status irrelevant' (Pratt and Burgess, 1974, p. 177).

PSHE looks to be as far as ever from rendering questions of status irrelevant. Public expenditure policy seems set to ensure a continuing disparity in resource levels between the two sectors of higher education, and the government's Green Paper of 1985 appeared to argue that there was an essential rightness about this state of affairs. The system of control means, too, that PSHE departments and institutions lack any long-term security, being open, apparently continuously, to national scrutiny by bodies with the direct power to close them – bodies that have not hesitated to do just that in the recent past.

What, then, is the future of PSHE, facing as it does a declining resource level and a declining quantum of 18-year-olds, most of whom will continue to regard the universities as first-choice institutions?

The principal safeguard for the future must lie in a positive promotion of those features of PSHE that are distinctive within higher education as a whole. If major colleges and polytechnics simply became indistinguishable from universities the return on any investment of resources would risk being insignificant in development terms.

National policy should be directed at rewarding these distinctive features at their true value and thus imparting greater status and impetus to them. Their distinctiveness derives mainly from the institutions' place as a conscious part of a wider network of educational provision. Institutions should come progressively to see justification for their existence not in offering university-style higher education to a greater number of students than the universities themselves could accommodate, but in making explicit the links between their form of higher education and the forms of post-fourteen education and experience that have not traditionally led to study at that level. They are able to make available a wide variety of courses and programmes for older students and those without conventional entry qualifications. The obvious vehicle for such developments, demonstrably effective in the UK as overseas, is the unit-based scheme in which credits are accumulated and which facilitates the movement of students between general and specialist programmes and between institutions.

Institutional management structures reflect the existing patterns of power within the college as well as the need to service relationships with outside bodies, and they may be inadequate to the purpose of effecting major change of the kind that will be called for. Attitudes and techniques need to be developed that will allow change to be managed in conditions of contraction through consent or at least by an agreed process. The present process is too frequently one of management having to take initiatives, often at inadequate notice and therefore with inadequate consultation, thereby provoking resentment and alienation among staff, who feel uninvolved, impotent and at risk. The strong executive centre of the further education tradition, which is the tool by which rapid decisions can be made, already and increasingly has to accommodate a range of internal and external pressures; it will need consciously to be adjusted to acknowledge the indissolubility of academic and resource issues and to involve the institution at large in the decision process. Equally, academic departments should be prepared to identify themselves with the institution more than in the past, and participation in decision-making is a precondition for such a development. There needs to be a growing recognition that the strength of PSHE lies as much in its readiness to establish and exploit relationships between different aspects of its provision as in the excellence of individual departments. A priority task for institutional managers is to create conditions in which the academic board is obliged to come to terms with the full range of its academic and associated resource responsibilities and is thereby encouraged to transcend the limitations of Oakes's theoretical model.

Institutional agreements with CNAA, made in the wake of the government's response to the Lindop report (DES, 1985b), have served to reinforce the recognition that responsibility for quality in higher education is located within the college and to encourage the further development of institutions with the capacity to make decisions for themselves. Institutions' perceptions of the extent to which their destiny lies in their own hands would also be enhanced by a reduction in the range of external administrative controls over their activities. This applies to the college's relationship both to the local authority and to the regional and national agencies that control it. Policy objectives could now be secured in the main through the process of resource allocation, allowing a separate administrative course approval process to be dropped.

Were these developments to take place, transbinary experiments would be easier to contemplate; nor would such experiments necessarily compromise the distinctiveness of what PSHE would bring to the new institutions. 'Distinctions [between institutions] based on adventitious grounds, whether historic or social, are wholly alien to the spirit that should inform higher education' (Committee on Higher Education, 1963, paragraph 35). There are features of the way universities are managed that could desirably be carried further into the public sector: in particular, freedom of action within an overall budget and a fuller recognition in structure and process of the interrelatedness of academic and resource questions, so that decision-making within the PSHE college would require responsible participation by a greater number of staff than is now usual. There is, in the medium term, no logical objection to the creation of institutions that would 'combine the status and excellence associated with universities with the range of opportunity, responsiveness and innovation associated with the polytechnics: a prospect of extending the range of that elusive concept "Quality" and doing so in the context of responding to the growing and well grounded demand for social accountability in higher education' (Staffordshire County Council, 1985). Such institutions will not, however, arrive without some considered changes to the procedures by which many now operate.

NOTE

The authors acknowledge with thanks the assistance of Kate Van Haeften.

7

Staffing and Academic Structure

TONY BECHER

ORGANIZATIONS AND INDIVIDUALS

This chapter marks a change in focus. Discussions about the politics of higher education, about the management of the system as a whole, and about the management and control of its constituent institutions, have necessarily to concentrate on structures rather than on the people who work within them. But once attention is shifted to the level of the subject departments and other basic units of academia, it becomes essential to take into account human as well as organizational factors (Becher and Kogan, 1980). The individual becomes as much the centre of attention as the corporate enterprise.

The discussion that follows is based in large part on a study of the ways in which groups of academics in a variety of different fields organize their lives and shape their careers, how they interact with one another, and what their professional values are. This exploration of the cultures of academic disciplines (Becher, 1981) has involved in-depth interviews of some 200 individuals in ten subject areas – ranging from pure to applied and from quantitative to non-quantitative – covering fourteen institutions.

The main purposes of the chapter are twofold. The first part, focusing on the individual academic, sets out to explore the processes of recruitment and subsequent employment of academic staff; to underline the variety between disciplines of forms of professional contact and communication; to examine the importance of research reputation as a driving force; to identify the extent of career choice. In the second part, the emphasis shifts to the relationships between individuals and institutions. An important element in the argument is that what academic staff are motivated to do and what patterns their careers take reflect and are reflected in the form of organization in which they find themselves. Not only institutional features but

133

those concerning the particular type of basic unit have to be considered in attempting to understand this interplay between structure and staffing (basic units in British higher education are in general small enough – occasionally as few as six or seven people, and rarely more than about forty – to allow for a direct understanding of how the values and aspirations of their members are related to their collective policies and practices). The chapter concludes with a brief discussion of the uneasy balance between individual and institutional autonomy on the one hand and public accountability on the other.

THE POPULATION OF HIGHER EDUCATION

This chapter is about one particular group of people – members of academic staff – who inhabit the world of higher education. Some mention ought to be made, however, for the sake of completeness, of three other categories, each significant in its own way, though not directly relevant to the present discussion.

The largest of the three (whose importance is indirectly acknowledged in the discussions in the following two chapters, concerning respectively the curriculum and teaching, and learning and assessment) is the student body. The undergraduates comprise a nomadic and transient group, who only inhabit the academic scene for three years (except in Scotland, where the norm is four years); the postgraduates, much smaller in number, will often stay somewhat longer. Almost by definition, students are not expected to take an active part in the professional affairs of the basic units to which they are attached (though they may justifiably comment on matters of teaching provision or – at the institutional level – on questions affecting collective welfare). One might say that students are the beneficiaries or clients of the higher education system, not its providers: and hence that, as suggested in Chapter 1, their participation is (rightly or wrongly) limited in rather the way that pupils' participation is in the school system or patients' is in the National Health Service.

A second group comprises those who administer the system, as against those who operate within it. In the university sector, the past two or three decades have seen a move away from the earlier tradition of appointing senior academics to key administrative posts. At one time, registrars and bursars were commonly chosen from within the ranks of academics, or occasionally from retired servicemen or civil servants. In the post-war period, however, a career line of professional university administrators has developed (see chapter 5), which has almost entirely replaced the gentleman-amateurs of previous generations. A few full-time or near full-time leadership positions – vice-chancellors and pro vice-chancellors – remain, and are generally (but not invariably) filled by academics. The public sector has taken a somewhat comparable route. Its lower-level clerical and administrative posts have generally been filled by the relevant local authority out of its own cadre of employees; there is also an emergent category of more senior career administrators; the highest managerial posts have continued to be recruited from among those who were originally members of teaching staff. The central concern of this group of inhabitants of higher education is, in any event, with the organizational and policy issues discussed in Chapters 4 and 5, rather than with predominantly academic matters – although the two cannot be neatly separated. As far as the development of particular areas of teaching and research is concerned, the battle for approval and for resources has to be fought at the institutional level or above – but, after that, the detailed working out of academic strategy is almost invariably left to those with expert knowledge within the relevant basic unit.

Finally, there is a large body of ancillary employees in all higher education institutions – technicians, secretaries, clerks, porters, telephonists, catering staff, maintenance and ground staff and the like – whose importance is only clearly recognized in the relatively rare context of a strike. Nearly all such people are local inhabitants; many of them have long periods of service. Although this group provides an essential underpinning for the system as a whole, its members would not expect, and would not be expected in terms of relevant expertise, to contribute actively to the policy of the institution or of its basic units, except in relation to staff welfare and conditions of service.

While it is right to acknowledge the importance within each institution of higher education of these three categories – students, professional administrators and ancillary staff – the particular parts they play are not directly related to the present theme. We shall accordingly focus attention on those holding academic appointments within the system. A distinction needs to be made at the outset between mainstream academic staff and those recruited to research posts. The mainstream academics comprise the permanent establishment of their institutions, usually taking part in its internal governance (through officerships and membership of its committee structures) as well as having recognized teaching commitments.

They are also expected (but not contractually obliged) to do research. Those recruited to research posts are in a relatively marginal position, having no role in institutional affairs and at most a minor involvement in teaching. They are normally employed for defined research activities on fixed-term contracts of between one and five years, and in many cases work under the supervision of a senior member of the permanent staff. A number of the younger research fellows and research assistants may in due course be appointed to teaching posts, but the translation is by no means automatic. The main concern in what follows will be with mainstream academics.

ACADEMIC IDENTITIES

The traditional department based on a single subject (history, physics, engineering and the like) remains the most common form of basic unit.[1] For its students – those who applied for, and were admitted to, the available places – it often provides a source of social as well as intellectual activity. One might say that such departments more or less define and justify the existence of their undergraduates. But the same point can be made even more strongly in relation to their teaching staff: the department forms a long-term base for academic and collegial relationships, and creates a professional identity for its members.

The pattern of recruitment for academic staff changes with the subject-matter. There are nowadays two basic routes into a lectureship – the doctoral and the professional. Nearly all 'pure', as opposed to 'applied', subjects will appoint new staff on the basis of their intellectual or academic credentials: a doctorate in the subject concerned has tended to become a minimum requirement, although in some of the more competitive disciplines (especially on the science side) one or more spells of postdoctoral research may be called for as well. In some vocational fields, in contrast, new appointments are made at least partly on the basis of competence as a practitioner: the appropriate doctoral qualification is expected to be acquired after the member of staff is in post. This approach is a matter of deliberate choice in some fields – teacher education or nursing, for example (Barnett *et al.*, 1987). In most branches of engineering, however, it results from the fact that starting salaries for graduates are so high that virtually nobody stays on to do a research degree – most recruits come from those in the middle ranks of industry who see more promise in an academic career.

The profile of staff qualifications varies over time as well as over subject discipline. Understandably enough, in the period of rapid expansion of British higher education from the mid-1960s to the early 1970s, it was relatively easy in most subjects to get a job in either the university or the public sector. In some new and expanding subjects even the incumbents of chairs did not always have strong qualifications in the field (a number of sociology professors, for example, migrated across from social administration or social anthropology). More than a decade later, the quality of many of these appointments contrasts sharply with those of current applicants. This is because the cutback in academic jobs has left the profession with little mobility. There is a large cluster of people in their forties and fifties, few of whom can expect either to be promoted in their own institutions or to move elsewhere. There are only occasional vacancies, and these are usually the subject of intense competition among the ablest of the current generation of young scholars, many of whom will never get an academic post.

Academics are, almost invariably, recruited to a basic unit and not to an institution as such (though their formal terms of appointment relate to the second rather than to the first). They correspondingly see themselves primarily as members of that unit. But they also have a wider sense of identity, to their parent discipline (or, more rarely, interdisciplinary field), as voiced in the assertion: 'I'm a historian'; 'I'm a physicist'; 'I'm an engineer'. The attachment to one's academic specialism is more than mere sentimentality. The 'invisible college', as the national or international network of academics dedicated to a particular subject area of enquiry has sometimes been called, offers a wider social and intellectual arena than one's own basic unit, a source of useful ideas and congenial contacts, and a means of acquiring a reputation in research (Crane, 1972).

Again, the nature and functions of the invisible college vary from one field to another. In English literature and history, to cite two library-based subjects, most of the communication takes place through books and journals, or through written correspondence with colleagues elsewhere. The pace of interchange is relatively slow – for example, publication delays of two years for journal articles are not uncommon. Conferences are not as frequent, their function tends to be social as much as intellectual, and most academics would be likely to attend one a year at most. By way of contrast, in some areas of experimental subjects such as chemistry and physics the interaction is intense. People make contact by phone rather than by letter: an important discovery can be briefly announced in print within a few weks, and a journal article is expected to appear within six months. Conferences, symposia and mutual visits are commonplace: active researchers will reckon to go to perhaps five or six conferences annually, two of them at least run on an international basis.

Academics in British higher education operate within a framework of shared assumptions, comparable conditions of service, and standardized salary scales.[2] None the less, there are marked differences between the ways of life that characterize different academic fields – many of them arising from the particular intellectual tasks that those fields embody. It is important to be aware of such differences, because there is a common tendency, when discussing higher education, to assume a fairly simple and uniform pattern of academic activity, independent of the type of institution or basic unit or subject field. As we shall see later, nothing could be further from the truth.

One of the reasons why academics may devote a fair amount of intellectual energy to their involvement in invisible colleges derives from the specialized nature of academic enquiry. Research reputations, in an increasingly competitive academic world, typically derive from achieving a high degree of expertise in a closely-defined field – in the barbed words of the cliché, from 'knowing more and more about less and less'. For a surprisingly large number of people in a variety of subject areas, the world total of fellow-academics whom they know to share a close common interest will tend to lie between half a dozen and twenty.[3] The chance that even one of these will be found in the same basic unit is minimal, particularly as a typical unit will be concerned to recruit a group of staff who can cover the whole spectrum of undergraduate teaching in its field and, therefore, will aim to achieve a wide spread of specialisms. Only the larger units can normally afford to take on more than one academic with a given specialism. Accordingly, where the subject-matter calls for or may benefit from collaborative research, this is often carried out between a number of institutions rather than within a single one.

SCHOLARLY REPUTATION

'The advancement of learning' has increasingly become a central concern of higher education (Rothblatt, 1976). Academic reputations are made, on the national or international scene at least, in terms of research excellence – usually manifested through specialist publications. It is for this reason that the highest goal for the more ambitious members of the academic community is prowess in research. In those fields of enquiry that depend on high-cost apparatus (particle physics is a prime example), the necessary experimental facilities may have to be provided on a co-operative basis between several institutions or even between several countries, and will often involve large research teams. Reputations are less easy to establish in such contexts than they are in smaller, less expensive research programmes (for example, in theoretical chemistry or ecology).

In many branches of experimental science, those putting up research proposals have to argue the case for the necessary funding. The pattern of research awards is itself a rough indicator of academic capability. The research councils, foundations and other grant-giving agencies – operating as they do mainly on the basis of peer review (on which more shortly) – are expected to be reasonably good judges of the timeliness of the topic and the promise of the researcher or researchers concerned. Some of the more applied fields of science and social science (geology, for example, or business studies) provide opportunities for consultancy as well as for research – that is, work calling on particular expertise, commissioned and paid for by an outside agency. This tends to be less highly regarded (because it is less clearly directed towards intellectual progress), but it is nevertheless an activity that counts towards one's professional reputation.

But there are many fields of enquiry where outside funding is the exception rather than the rule. Research in anthropology or the social aspects of law may involve travel expenses, and sometimes the costs of research assistants and secretarial staff, but the sums involved are very small compared with the costs of 'big science' (Price, 1963). Many researchers in the humanities need access to a good library, and not much else. Philosophy and pure mathematics can be done with no more elaborate equipment than a pencil and paper. So while some groups of academics are geared to maximizing their grant earnings as a route to reputation, this criterion is more or less irrelevant for others.

There are other contrasts in the working values of different disciplinary communities (such as their attitudes towards the issue of vocational relevance): but they share an overriding common concern with reputations in research. Publication is only the means to achieving scholarly recognition, not an end in itself. The often-quoted injunction, 'Publish or perish', is misleading in much the same sense as the complaint that one's research output is assessed by how much it weighs, or at least how many titles there are. Both underplay the extent to which judgements of quality are made by one's colleagues in the same field.

This body of close colleagues, or professional peer group (a concept not far removed from that of the invisible college mentioned earlier), performs a number of key evaluative functions (Zuckerman and Merton, 1971). It not only forms the basis of the grant-awarding process in the case of many funding bodies (proposals are commonly sent out to two or more independent referees with appropriate expertise), but is also used in assessing articles submitted for journal publication and eligibility for membership of learned societies. Members of the peer group will also be invited to act as external examiners for degree awards, to participate in the process of appointment to senior posts, and to offer comments on candidates for internal promotion within an institution. The peer group principle can again be seen to operate, in somewhat modified form, in the work of the specialist subcommittees of the UGC (see Chapter 3) and the subject panels of the CNAA (see Chapter 4).

This principle of mutual judgement by specialists of one another's work seems well-founded, in the sense that only those with a mastery of the particular field are capable of making an informed appraisal within it. Peer review, one might argue, helps to maintain overall standards as well as to reward individual excellence. But there are some countervailing dangers too. The peer group's protection of established procedures can have an inhibiting effect on desirable changes; the prevailing orthodoxy, as represented in a few influential figures, can systematically penalize those who fail to subscribe to the party line. Fortunately, few academic groups are completely insulated from external judgement, whether this is exercised by colleagues in neighbouring fields or by those completely outside the arena in question. Nor, in the environment of the 1980s, are they altogether unaffected by broader social and political concerns (see Chapter 2).

To summarize the argument so far, scholarly reputation can be seen as the prime value in academic life. It is manifested, in some fields, by the extent of grant funding; in others, it rests mainly on published output. But neither criterion should be seen as merely quantitative, since both are functions of the qualitative judgements inherent in the process of peer review.

A consequence of the emphasis on reputation is the academic's concern to guard his or her intellectual property. Powerful taboos exist against plagiarism. Taking and using other people's ideas without acknowledging them is regarded as no better than theft of a more material kind: it may lead to the ruin not only of one's reputation but of one's whole career. The legitimate inverse of this is the process of paying a tax on intellectual borrowing, in the form of the citation of relevant sources (Cronin, 1985). Although there are many possible reasons for citing another author's work (again, the reasons differ to some considerable extent from one subject to the next), behind them all lies a concern to give formal acknowledgement of previous contributions to the field – even when one happens strongly to disagree with them. Being cited is itself of relevance in reputation-building, and the currency accorded to it has been enhanced by the development in some disciplines of 'citation indexes', listing where and when the works of particular authors have earned a published reference by somebody else.

The concern for recognition among one's professional colleagues can – for those who are strongly caught up in it – exercise a powerful motivating force. So too can the related involvement with an intellectual issue or problem. Academic life, for those who subscribe actively to its dominant values, can at times become obsessional, demanding a high commitment of time and energy. People will often work for long hours, cutting down on outside interests and even on family commitments. When questioned about why they do this, they typically comment on their high level of job satisfaction and their sense of close personal identification with what they are doing.

THE EXERCISE OF CHOICE

Academics, by the nature of their work, are largely self-motivated. Not all of them choose, or indeed enjoy the opportunity, to involve themselves closely in the contest for public recognition, but all of them have a high degree of autonomy in their work. True, they have certain specific obligations related to their roles as teachers, but even these are to some extent consequent on their own choices or open to negotiation. The life-style of academics has aptly been compared with that of one-man businesses (Halsey and Trow, 1971). Within the overriding constraint of professional survival, each academic has in effect to operate as an independent entity, seeking as best he or she can to capitalize on both skills and opportunities.

The range of choice in shaping one's academic career is in fact quite substantial (Becher, 1987). In terms of research, the initial selection of a specialist field is usually made at the doctoral stage. In the nature of most disciplines, there is a range not only of subject-matter but of modes of working. For example, within the biological sciences, microbiology is a more gregarious and competitive field than taxonomy; among specialisms in psychology, experimental studies of behaviour are more quantitative and less philosophical in emphasis than psychiatry or humanistic psychology. There is thus a good opportunity to match one's topic to one's temperament and style of approach.

No decision, moreover, need be seen irrevocable. Although an academic may opt to remain within a particular specialism throughout his or her working life, it is surprisingly common to make at least one significant change at some intervening point between recruitment and retirement. (It is less common, but far from unknown, for people to change disciplines – from physics to engineering, say, or from archaeology to history.) Shifts of specialism are easier to make in some fields than in others. In certain areas of mathematics, entering a new specialism may entail two or three years' introductory study; in history and English literature, change can be relatively painless, even if it involves a move – to take an actual example – from Renaissance drama to modern poetry. But though people can and do re-define their interests in mid-career, there is a price to pay in terms of professional visibility. A reputation in one field does not normally carry over into another, so the business of making a name for oneself may have to begin all over again.

According to legend, mathematicians do their best work before reaching their late twenties. (Older mathematicians generally deny this, but acknowledge that mathematical research makes particularly strenuous intellectual demands, because one has to be able to concentrate intensely enough to see the whole solution to a problem in one's head.) There are other subjects in which 'burn-out' is a recognized phenomenon (though it is not generally acknowledged in the humanities and social sciences).[4] It may be a matter of having specialized in a particular research technique that becomes outdated; or having focused on a topic that has now gone out of fashion. Not all those whose work is affected in such ways are willing, or able, to reshape their careers as active researchers: but there is usually a fair range of choice open to those who want to opt out of further competition.

Some science subjects, in particular, leave room for elder statesmen to adopt a generally philosophical and reflective role, reviewing trends within the subject and producing general overviews of the research activities of others. It is a fairly typical move, in many disciplines, to take on a sizeable administrative commitment, either in one's own basic unit or at the institutional level (an added option is to seek office in a learned society or in one's professional association). But the most common choice of all is to concentrate on undergraduate teaching at the expense of doing research and supervizing the research of doctoral students.

Although, in terms of the prevailing values, teaching enjoys less prestige than research, many academics besides those whose research careers have burned out are committed primarily to teaching.[5] Some lack the facilities, or find it hard to set aside the necessary time, to be active researchers; others consciously back out of the rat race, and settle for a role as 'locals' within their own institutions rather than as 'cosmopolitans' inhabiting the wider academic scene (Gouldner, 1957). Those who none the less maintain a strong disciplinary loyalty concentrate on the pursuit of scholarship. They keep in touch with current developments in their subject, and aim to achieve an expert command of the corpus of relevant knowledge. Although they do not themselves contribute to the advancement of their chosen fields, they often have a more extensive mastery of their subject area than those whose main energies are devoted to research. Scholars of this kind can play an important, if localized, role in knowledge transmission (a role that can be widened by producing student texts and other teaching material).

It is sometimes argued that, in higher education, teaching must necessarily be underpinned by research. Whether or not one accepts this argument, it does not follow – and indeed is manifestly not the case – that all good teachers are necessarily good researchers, or all good researchers necessarily good teachers. As Martin Trow has argued, there is in most basic units an informal but usually quite effective division of academic labour:

> Thus, the formal characteristics (and the quality) of departments and their members are preserved, while a considerable variability in individual talent, preference and disposition allows people actually to distribute their time and energy very differently among the various functions of the department: graduate and undergraduate teaching, research . . ., administration, consulting, and 'public service'. (Trow, 1976, p. 22).

He concludes that this division of labour allows any given basic unit 'to perform in actuality a wider range of functions than would be possible if its members were more homogeneous in orientation and personal preference'. It would seem to follow that the wide scope enjoyed in the academic profession for the exercise of personal choice is of benefit not only to the individuals concerned but also to the organization in which they work.

INSTITUTIONAL INFLUENCES

So far, this review of staffing and academic structure in higher education has been based on the perspective of the individual, and has explored questions of identity, value and choice. A proper understanding of what it is like to work in a university, polytechnic or college depends on a recognition that reputations are gained, and motivation is powerfully stimulated, by contributing to the advancement of knowledge in one's field. This is itself made possible by the reasonably free exercise of intellectual choice and initiative – there are few fields in which personal enterprise in research is for good reason subject to political or managerial control. It is also important to recognize the diversity of academic life-styles, not only between different areas of enquiry but also within them: a diversity that stems at least in part from the types of intellectual task that are defined by particular specialisms.

But any such argument has to be complemented by one that offers a different emphasis. As was remarked in the opening section of this chapter, individuals both influence and are influenced by their institutional settings. Their choices, though wider than those in most occupations, are constrained in quite significant ways by their environments. Indeed, a critic of the account in the preceding sections might object that its portrayal of academic activities is idealistic and unreal: that only a small minority of staff in higher education make any noticeable research contribution to their subject fields in the course of their whole careers, and that the opportunities for making such a contribution are effectively confined to those in a few elite institutions.

My response would be twofold. There is indeed a covert, but quite clearly articulated, 'pecking order' or hierarchy of perceived merit, which lies beneath the polite fiction of the egalitarian 1960s and 1970s, that all institutions of higher education are equivalent (and what is more, offer first degrees whose values are also equivalent, according to a notional gold standard defined by the universities' external examiner system and the Council for National Academic Awards). The place of an institution within the covert hierarchy admittedly affects the degree to which an individual within that institution is likely to achieve visibility as a researcher. But, even so, I would argue that the aspirations and values of academics in non-elite institutions are clearly influenced by the collective view that research is important and that the quest for professional reputation is a prime good.

The influence of institutional environment on research motivation has both an external and an internal aspect. In terms of outside expectations, the relevant peer group is likely to be affected, in its judgement of merit, by its awareness of the rating of the institution and of the relevant basic unit in the hierarchy. A researcher from a relatively low-status institution thus has an inherently lower chance of professional recognition than a colleague from a high-status one, even when their two contributions may be of comparable merit. The acceptance of this fact is unlikely to prove encouraging to the individual in question. In terms of inside expectations, if the climate of both the institution and the basic unit is one in which research is not actively promoted, and most colleagues are not engaged in it, there is likely to be a disincentive to stepping out of line – a disincentive perhaps reinforced by the individual's feeling that in any case he or she has not 'made the grade' by achieving a post in a more prestigious institution.

Like most accounts based on human expectations, this one is open to qualification. It is by no means the case that all well-regarded research comes from Oxbridge or the more prestigious constituent colleges of London University. It is true that, in the more competitive areas of pure science, a well-established and well-equipped research laboratory is a considerable asset, and that as a result, what has been called the Matthew effect (recorded in St Matthew's Gospel) tends to operate: 'to those that have shall be given, and from those that have not shall be taken away even that which they have' (Merton, 1973). The result is that much research in 'big science' is indeed clustered in relatively few institutions. But such clustering is less evident in other areas – particularly those, such as some branches of engineering, where money for equipment and research expenses may come from industrial sources, or those in which no significant costs are involved.

In terms of general funding, universities have traditionally had an element in their UGC grant attributable to research costs, including staff time. This means that the teaching commitments of university teachers tend to be lighter than those of their counterparts in polytechnics and colleges, and their arrangements for study leave more generous. The polytechnics, deriving mainly from an ancestry in technical and further education, have for the most part retained the notion of heavy teaching timetables for their students and relatively heavy teaching loads for their staff.[6] This is compounded by the fact that their financial allocation per student is substantially less than that for the universities, and that no explicit allowance is made in their funding arrangements for research. Almost inevitably, the emphasis on teaching, the transmission of knowledge, is stronger than that on its advancement. Moreover, the need to keep costs down has led to a managerial concern with ensuring that teaching groups remain at an economically viable size. One strategy that has been found effective is to produce modular courses (see Chapter 8), involving students from a variety of subject backgrounds taught by multidisciplinary course teams. The weakening of their identity with their original discipline, to which this arrangement gives rise, is likely to put the staff involved at a further research disadvantage in relation to those who remain firmly within traditional single-subject departments.

The arrangements in most colleges of higher education are rather different, although the outcomes are usually much the same. In the main, the colleges have derived from institutions originally concerned with teacher education. Their predominantly vocational traditions and programmes have led to a strong emphasis on practice (and perhaps a somewhat less enthusiastic commitment to theory and research). The requirements made of their staff accordingly tend to include sizeable periods of practical supervision of students working in a vocational setting. The time they have available for personal study is as limited as that of their counterparts in the polytechnics: their institutional budgets are equally unfavourable to research activity.

Despite these organizational and financial disincentives, however, those who work in public sector institutions cannot by any means be said to have abandoned an involvement in research. If, almost inevitably, they accord research a lower priority than do teachers in universities, that is not because they regard it as being of lesser importance in the catalogue of academic virtues. Many of them will have carried out doctoral research before or during their appointments to tenured posts. To that extent they will have been imbued with the sense of intellectual commitment and achievement that is fostered by working successfully for a higher degree. Over and above this, however, the emphasis placed by the CNAA (see Chapter 6) on the need for degree teaching to be accompanied by research offers an organizational incentive to supplement the motivation of individual staff members.

The picture, then, is considerably more complex than the one that might have been expected in 1965, when the then Secretary of State, Anthony Crosland, announced the setting up of a public sector of higher education separate from the universities, with the strong implication that the former would turn away from research activity. Not every academic nor yet every basic unit within the university world has a nationally or internationally visible research reputation, any more than every academic or basic unit within the public sector lacks one. If the institutional will is there, the scope exists to divert resources in polytechnics and colleges into research activities, and there are indeed a number of cases in which this has been done. A map of research excellence, assuming it were possible and meaningful to draw one,[7] would show a patchy distribution, complicated by considerable variations in the peer group ratings of prestige in different subject areas. This patchiness is in large part a result of the career histories of key individuals.

CONGLOMERATES AND CONFEDERATIONS

Basic units, as they were defined in the first chapter (see p. 6 above), are comparatively small collections of individual members of academic staff, clustered round some particular activity or programme. As has been subsequently remarked, the individuals concerned have a high degree of autonomy in relation to people in most other occupations. Although, typically, they will spend most of their time on undergraduate teaching and assessment, many will also have a research commitment that is only partially and indirectly related to their teaching and may be largely independent of the research done by their immediate colleagues. In respect of their research – which enjoys higher prestige, if not necessarily higher priority, than their teaching – individuals act in an essentially entrepreneurial role, being ultimately accountable to the wider peer group in their specialist field rather than to their basic unit or their employing institution. The closest analogy here is perhaps with medical consultants, who are responsible as a group of colleagues for covering between them the needs of their patients, but who work independently and autonomously in maintaining and extending their specialist skills.

The lack of close correspondence between teaching and research will sometimes call for flexibility in the planning of courses. Most people are appointed to academic posts on the basis of their potential teaching contributions as well as on their performance or promise as researchers. From time to time a choice has to be made between one candidate with appropriate teaching experience but virtually no track record in research and another with the opposite characteristics. The answer will differ with the circumstances, but will generally favour the second candidate, bearing in mind the prestige factor mentioned above. It then becomes necessary either to persuade the new appointee to develop a new area of teaching expertise, possibly quite far removed from his or her own specialism, or to reallocate the teaching duties among the rest of the unit's staff, or to modify the curriculum in order to capitalize on the new appointee's particular specialism.

Because higher education is concerned not only (as all other parts of the education service are) with passing on existing knowledge, but also with generating new knowledge that may, in the long run, affect what is taught in the rest of the system, it has to contend with a unique form of structural complexity (Clark, 1983b). As has already been noted, departments and other basic units are fairly loose conglomerations of their constituent staff members, in that academics enjoy – by virtue of their specialist knowledge and their free-standing external reference groups – a relatively high level of independence from the organizations within which they work.

However, this independence is qualified in one particular sense. If a member of staff wins national or international distinction within his or her field, that automatically adds to the academic prestige of the parent unit. One might indeed go on to suggest that the academic prestige of any given basic unit is made up of two components, the first and most significant being the sum of the professional reputations of its individual members, and the second the reflected prestige of the institution to which it belongs. This leads to a further complication, because (as we noted in the previous section) the individual academic's standing is at least to some extent derived from that of his or her basic unit. To put the point another way, a department or other unit stands to gain, both as a collectivity and as a set of individuals, from the professional success of any one of its members; by the same token, an individual stands to gain from belonging to a basic unit that has good academic standing.

From the same set of arguments, a case can be made for the claim that institutions are little more than loose confederations of their constituent basic units. The interdependence of research reputations between institution and units is closely parallel to that between units and academic staff. The institution has no reputation for research excellence that can be separated from the sum total of the reputations of the units (and via them from those of individual staff members). It has, moreover, only limited academic authority over the content of the undergraduate and taught postgraduate courses put on by its constituent units, since they are able to argue from a base of specialist knowledge that the rest of the institution does not possess (standards are in general safeguarded here by the peer group operating in one of its many guises, rather than directly by the managerial hierarchy).

This somewhat anarchistic view of academic institutions – reflecting one school of thought that characterized the management of universities as 'organized anarchy' (Cohen and March, 1974) – has to be set against the more comprehensive accounts in Chapters 4 and 5 of how universities, polytechnics and colleges are managed. Even so, the need to recognize the looseness of structure, and to appreciate the reasons behind it, will perhaps become evident in the next, concluding section of the argument.

ADAPTABILITY AND AUTONOMY

The increasingly uneasy relationship between the academic world on the one hand and the politicians and civil servants on the other has been charted in some detail in Chapter 2. The desire of Westminster and Whitehall to control the higher education system more rigorously is related, of course, to financial considerations. Two terms of office of a strongly monetarist government, committed none the less to relatively generous expenditure on law and order and defence, has led to an inexorable tightening of resources for education in general and for the universities, colleges and polytechnics in particular. But the impression has also been given that more than purely economic issues lie behind the policies that have evolved in the current decade. It is as if there were also an urge to curtail the freedom that academics appear to enjoy – a freedom that can readily be interpreted as irresponsible self-indulgence. This impression has been reinforced by the discussions about the abolition of a tenure, a notion that has a clear functional value in the system but that of late has been portrayed as an unwarranted privilege.

It will be apparent, from what has already been said in earlier sections about the nature of specialist knowledge, that it is not easy for those outside the specialism itself to assess the demands and the claims of academic research and development programmes. One obvious management strategy is to call for a clear statement of objectives, whose eventual realization can be independently assessed (Jedamus *et al.*, 1980). Accountability of this kind has been fashionable for a decade and more, carrying with it the implication of rewarding achievement and penalizing failure: a comfortable way in which those in positions of power can prove themselves capable of exercising it.

Management by objectives calls in its turn for a rational (which is to say neatly hierarchical) structure of decision-making. Such a structure (although with all the limitations noted in Chapter 6) has formed the basis of management within the public sector; it is now, as Chapter 5 has indicated, part of the new mythology of the university sector as well. Like most 'top down' reforms (i.e. those imposed by outside agencies with little reference to internal views and values) it fails to take account of an important feature of higher education: the inherent unpredictability of its environment.

In appropriate managerial jargon, the inputs to higher education institutions can only to a limited extent be foreseen, let alone controlled. Governments have come and gone, each with a firm insistence that (useful) science and technology places should be increased and (useless) arts and social studies places reduced in response to national need: but (as was noted in Chapter 2) the prospective students themselves have obdurately refused to fall in with this pattern. Statisticians have predicted dire consequences of the demographic trough of 18-year-olds created by the fall in the birth rate in the early 1970s, but the age participation rate (the percentage of each relevant age group opting to apply for higher education) follows no standard pattern. Mature students (those aged 25 and over) now occupy one in eight of the available full-time places in higher education, a figure which would have seemed inconceivable at the time of the Robbins Report two decades ago. A myriad of factors affect recruitment, not least the state of the nation's schools and the availability of teachers in various subjects.

If inputs are not easily subject to managerial manipulation, no more are outputs. The employability of graduates changes in ways that have consistently undermined the credibility of rational manpower planning. Sometimes – as occurred with the embarrassing surplus of chemical engineers in the early 1970s – forecasts are upset by rapid shifts in industrial demand. In other cases, even sectors that are subject to close national control, such as the education and training of teachers, appear to lurch from one planning crisis to another (acute shortages are discerned in one curriculum subject and then another, and priorities shift from secondary provision to primary and back again).

It seems often to be overlooked by the advocates of a strong central hand on the reins that fairly powerful controls already exist within the system against waste and against unwise policy decisions. Every basic unit is (and, apart from the few years of apparently limitless expansion, always has been) acutely aware of its student recruitment pattern, since a consistent failure to enrol enough students will quite quickly be penalized by a withdrawal of resources by the parent institution. Similarly, a poor graduate employment record will lose credibility not only with the rest of the institution but, in the long run, with potential applicants as well. Internal sanctions of this kind, though informal and largely implicit, arguably have more force than formal sanctions imposed from outside, which occasion collective resentment more noticeably than willing compliance.

When it comes to research, there are – as we have seen – even more powerful forces within higher education to reward achievement and penalize the lack of it. But, quite apart from this, the generation of new knowledge and new know-how is almost by definition unamenable to central control or predictive planning. No medical research unit, except one that knows itself to be on the verge of a breakthrough, could honestly undertake to find a cure for a hitherto incurable disease within (say) a five-year timespan; similarly, no group working on the economic and large-scale extraction of fresh water from the sea could accurately forecast how soon it would achieve its goal. The uncertainty is, if anything, greater in some areas of pure research. Particularly high career risks attach to work on topics that are unfashionable or in opposition to current orthodoxy. Einstein's exploration of relativity is a classic case in point: had his intellectual gamble failed to come off, he would have wasted several years and remained a little-known, eccentric figure. It is one of the useful purposes of academic tenure to allow scope for maverick, and occasionally important, work outside the main stream. Research orthodoxies can exercise a strong influence on what is and is not allowable; tenure provides some curb on the extent to which they can eliminate the dissenters within a given field.

The established system of management within higher education, which permits a relatively loose connection between institutional structures and academic processes, may seem from an external standpoint ramshackle and ineffective. In practice, it allows for extensive and rapid adaptability to new circumstance. Two unpredictable factors were mentioned earlier: changes in input demand and variations in output requirements. The possibility of what Lindblom (see Braybrooke and Lindblom, 1963) has called 'disjointed incrementalism' – a pragmatic, responsive and short-term strategy directly opposed to rational long-term planning – has enabled higher education to cope with, for example, the steep decline in student numbers in classics (where the compensating shifts of staff have been mainly into teaching and research in

151

European civilization and linguistics) and – to take a contrasting case on the output side – with the extraordinarily rapid growth in employers' demands for graduate accountants, which has led to the setting up of new departments in more than forty institutions in the last decade.

As Chapters 8 and 9 indicate, the innovations within the system have by no means been confined to centrally imposed structural reforms or to institutionally determined changes in the pattern of basic units. There have been numerous, and not always small-scale, modifications in curricular patterns, course rationales, the content and structure of degree programmes, and methods of teaching and assessment. Innovations of this kind are not easily visible from the outside, in the way that large organizational changes are – so it is easy in political terms to criticize the system as a whole for its conservatism, protection of its own interests, and lack of responsiveness to national needs. If academics respond angrily to such criticisms, it is because they have an insider's view of what is going on, and because they work in a professional environment in which change and development, not stability, is the normal expectation.

The temptation for politicians and administrators to argue for a more tightly rational and more readily controllable higher education system is perhaps natural enough. But the imposition of rigid links between national government and academic policy is not in practice either productive or efficient, especially if the activities of universities, polytechnics and colleges become subject to political ideology. The proposed closure of social work departments in the mid-1980s, at a time when the demands on social work practice were becoming particularly acute, offers a good case in point. As the experience of the major U68 reforms of Swedish higher education has shown, the responsiveness of the system is reduced rather than increased as a consequence of strong external requirements for accountability. Moreover, the instrumental values implicit in central control are likely to overplay the aspects of higher education concerned with directly vocational courses at the expense of those whose main value lies in promoting more generally reflective, analytical and critical skills.

All this is not to suggest that academics should be any less answerable for their activities than doctors, civil servants, or those who work in other professions. There may well be issues that – as in other largely self-regulating occupations – call for the judicious exercise of external pressure. For example, some academic institutions when viewed from a wider national perspective may be considered not to have distributed their resources wisely; the student admissions policies in others might appear to be unduly weighted in favour of some groups and against others; the academic world as a whole could be held to be insufficiently responsive to the needs of contemporary society in general and to those of industry in particular; and so on. It is the nature of the intervention against such examples of professional self-interest that is likely to prove crucial. The foregoing argument has suggested that the superimposition of a centralized structure of managerial control and external account-ability on the strong existing process of internal accountability could do serious damage to the enterprise as a whole. As a number of centralized systems of higher education clearly demonstrate, once reputation ceases to be a prime value, yielding its place to conform-ity with external regulation, the fires of professional enthusiasm slowly die out, leaving not much behind except a grey, featureless residue.

NOTES

I am much indebted to Eric Hewton, Sheldon Rothblatt, Geoffrey Squires and Martin Trow for their perceptive and helpful comments on an earlier draft of this chapter.

1 Other types include those devoted purely to research, which are not here considered as a separate category. It is an interesting taxonomic question whether colleges on the Oxbridge model should be classified as basic units; however, their functions and composition are very different from those of subject departments, and much of the sub-sequent discussion would not be applicable to them.
2 The lack of variation in financial opportunities serves to reinforce the emphasis on academic prestige. If one cannot expect significant changes in income over a professional lifetime, reputation becomes an even stronger driving force for career advancement.
3 The small 'inner circle' of research colleagues related to one's current, highly specific interests forms a marked contrast to the much larger (usually 100–200) 'outer circle' of those contacts working in the same broad field. One's longer-term career potential depends on maintain-ing a reputation with the outer as well as the inner group.
4 Although the legend of early success and rapid decline is powerful and strongly-entrenched, the empirical evidence does not support it. Lehman's classic researches into *Age and Achievement*, 1953, show a fairly consistent peaking of intellectual productivity in the late thirties (in some subject areas even later). Harriet Zuckerman, in her com-prehensive study of Nobel prizewinners, 1977, concludes (p. 168) that

'Among Nobel laureates at least, science is not exclusively a young person's game; evidently it is a game the middle-aged can play as well'.

5 There is something of a paradox here. A mainstream academic appointment is essentially an appointment as a teacher, even though research capability carries considerable weight in selection and pro- motion. An appointment to a (non-teaching) research post, on the other hand, is less prestigious, and is usually on a temporary basis. Yet it remains true that in professional terms, research counts for more than teaching.

6 There is in this respect a difference between subject areas as well as between institutions. Generally speaking, vocationally oriented pro- grammes such as engineering, pharmacy and veterinary science make heavy demands on their students (of the order of 20–25 teaching hours per week); pure science courses tend to be roughly comparable; but the norm for arts and social sciences is much lower (around 10–15 hours): see Squires, 1986, p. 37.

7 The attempt was made by the UGC in its 1986 grant allocation exercise (see Chapter 3), but the general view – also attributed to the Chairman of the Committee – was that there was a significant error of judgement in relation to at least one department in each university.

8

The Curriculum

GEOFFREY SQUIRES

PATTERNS OF THE
UNDERGRADUATE CURRICULUM

The curriculum is what is taught, and the study of the curriculum is concerned with what is taught and what ought to be taught. Since the purpose of education is typically defined, at least overtly, in terms of teaching something, the curriculum lies at the heart of the educational enterprise. It is, as one writer put it rather more prosaically, the stuff of education.

Within the broad field of curriculum studies there are several sub-divisions. Curriculum theory asks questions about the nature and justification of curricula. Curriculum development is concerned with how curricula change, in a planned or unplanned way. Curriculum evaluation investigates the effects of curricula, both intended and unintended. Each of these aspects of the curriculum is of interest and importance, but each presents it own difficulties, and indeed the study of the curriculum is a rather complex and some-times messy business in two ways: first, it overlaps with the study of teaching and learning on the 'one hand, and that of educational organization and management on the other; secondly, it necessarily draws on not one but a range of academic disciplines, notably philosophy, psychology and sociology.

A good, general view of the field can be gained from the introductory book by Taylor and Richards (1985) or from the much wider-ranging annotated bibliography produced by Richards (1984). Both of these however, refer mainly to the schools, and this is typical of the writing on the subject. There is relatively little on the curriculum in higher education, and nothing in the UK that corresponds to the survey of the American scene by Levine (1978).

In this chapter I would like first to give a brief description of the pattern or patterns of curricula in British higher education, and then to discuss some of the issues that arise from those patterns. It is very difficult, of course, to generalize about the patterns of curricula, and I shall concentrate on the broad features, ignoring some of the subtler institutional and disciplinary variations. Likewise, the issues will simply be raised, rather than discussed in depth. I hope, nevertheless, to give some sense of what it is that students are taught during their three or four years in a university, polytechnic or college, and also of the questions that preoccupy those who plan and teach such courses. First of all, however, something must be said about the term 'curriculum' and its use (or rather lack of use) in higher education.

American usage is much tidier, in this case, than British. The American undergraduate follows a degree programme, which is made up of courses, each of which typically earns a credit, based on the number of hours taught. In Britain, the word course is used both of the total programme, and the parts that make it up. The word subject may be used both of the entire field of study (e.g. physics) or of one particular part of it (quantum mechanics). Whereas the term 'curriculum' is widely used in the USA to describe the total programme of any one student, it is not common in British institutions, where the word 'syllabus' is often preferred.

One must be careful about inferring too much from the use of words. It is true that the study of the curriculum has moved well beyond the traditional notion of the syllabus in several ways. It has focused attention on aims and objectives, for example, where the conventional syllabus simply lists content; it asks what the curriculum does, as well as what it is. Secondly, it unpacks concepts like 'coverage' and 'level' much more carefully than is usually the case. Coverage at O-level obviously means something different from coverage at degree level, but what exactly is the nature of the difference? Why are higher level courses higher? In what way do they get more difficult? And the study of the curriculum is very much concerned with what may be called the curriculum-in-practice, rather than the curriculum-on-paper, i.e. the syllabus. This raises interesting questions about the ethos or experience or milieu of learning, about the roles of lecturers and students, about the effect of the format of learning (timetables, physical environment, etc.) on the content of courses, and indeed everything that has come to be referred to by that useful, if rather distended concept, the 'hidden curriculum'. Curriculum studies has come a long way, both in terms of methodology and conceptual sophistication, since its beginnings in the US school system a century ago, without perhaps achieving much theoretical coherence. But does the fact that lecturers typically do not use the word, or its associated terms, mean that they are unaware of all these phenomena?

The immediate answer must be no. The very process of planning courses and teaching and assessing them makes such issues and facets inescapable, and the fact that they are often articulated in a commonsense or vernacular way, rather than in educational jargon, does not mean that the analysis of them is necessarily less penetrating or precise. Nevertheless, it is a striking fact that the curriculum is one of the least studied aspects of higher education. The Robbins Report (Committee on Higher Education, 1963) managed to say remarkably little about it, and the more recent Green Paper (DES, 1985a) even less. It was one of the weakest areas of the Leverhulme study carried out in the early 1980s. No detailed description of the British undergraduate curriculum exists, beyond the Careers Research and Advisory Centre degree course guides prepared for applicants (CRAC, 1985). The general references given in Powell's bibliography (Powell, 1966, 1971) are mainly north American. There is, of course, continual discussion of the curriculum in particular subjects, which sometimes shows up in professional journals, and there are some accounts of the curriculum in particular institutions where there is an unusual pattern. But, in general, a great deal of descriptive and analytic work remains to be done (Squires, 1987) and what is said in the remainder of this chapter will reflect that fact.

The pattern of studies in higher education in the UK depends on two things: where one studies and what one studies. The first of these is easier to describe. There are national, sectoral and institutional variations. The Scottish (and especially the Scottish University) pattern differs from that in England and Wales in being broader. First-year Scottish students may well study four or five subjects rather than the maximum of two or three followed by their English counterparts, and will typically be admitted to a faculty rather than a department. Specialization in Scotland comes in the third and fourth years of the degree (in England three years is the norm) and a much higher proportion of students take general, ordinary or pass degrees (more than 40 per cent, as compared with about 11 per cent in England and Wales, excluding the Open University.) The greater breadth of the Scottish first degree reflects different traditions (Davie, 1961), a different pattern of secondary school examinations and a somewhat earlier age of entry to higher education.

The national patterns are complicated and overlaid to some extent by differences between the university and public sectors. Degree programmes in the latter are in general broader than those in the former, reflecting one of the CNAA's principles that 'The student must be encouraged to appreciate the nature of attitudes, modes of thought, practices and disciplines other than those of his or her main studies. He or she must learn to perceive his or her main studies in a broader perspective' (CNAA, 1986, p. 23). The Council's guidelines on particular subjects may have more influence than general principles such as these, but there is no comparable statement in the university sector, nor could there be, given the curricular autonomy of each institution. The CNAA's espousal of breadth as a general principle may reflect the liberal studies tradition in further education, the 'progressive' ethos of the 1960s, or the fact that many departments in public sector institutions are applied multidisciplinary ones anyway.

Within the university and public sectors, there are of course institutional variations in the curriculum, although nothing like the variety that are found in the United States. At Cambridge University the curriculum is divided into Part I (usually lasting two years) and Part II; a minority take advantage of this to switch subjects at the end of Part I, usually but not always to cognate fields. Given the general influence of Oxbridge on the system, it is not surprising that this pattern has been copied elsewhere. At Sussex University, all students do a two-term preliminary course before choosing their main field of study in one of a number of schools rather than departments. At Keele, there is a very broad foundation year (previously compulsory, now optional) as part of a four-year degree course. At the Open University, students take foundation courses followed by largely optional 'credits', and unit-credit or modular curricula are found elsewhere, particularly in the public sector (Oxford and City Polytechnics especially). The public sector institutions, and a few universities, have 'sandwich courses', which alternate periods of study with periods of related work experience. There are innumerable institutional variations in the pattern of assessment and examinations, and in the regulations governing 'ancillary' or 'contextual' courses. All in all, however, there is perhaps less variation in the system than might be expected in one that consists of about 150 institutions. This may reflect the fact that, although institutions are relatively autonomous as regards what they teach and how they teach it, the system is in other respects a fairly standardized one, with common admissions procedures, common grant regulations, (largely) common funding, common staff salary scales, and various mechanisms (such as mutual external examining, and inter-library co-operation) that tend to reinforce the norm. In fact, the main factor determining the pattern of studies is what one studies, rather than where.

The pattern of *what* is studied is more difficult to describe and classify than differences of location, but a rough division can be made between three kinds of courses. First, there are *professional* courses. These comprise the traditional, recognized professions such as medicine, law and engineering, and the newer aspiring or quasi-professions of which there are many: social work, town planning, management, public administration, pharmacy, accountancy, teaching, nursing, and so on. It is difficult to define what is or is not a profession (see Jackson, 1970, for one example) and the term is increasingly vaguely used. As regards higher education, the crucial thing is not the list of supposed attributes, but rather a direct and substantial manpower relationship. Where a consistently high proportion of graduates in a particular subject go into a particular kind of occupation, we can speak of a professional connection with, as economists put it, little elasticity of substitution and the typical tensions between 'theory' and 'practice', of which more later. In recent years, professional education has been growing in both numbers and importance in higher education (see Goodlad, 1984), although there are those who would argue that, despite all the rhetoric about the liberal tradition, it has always been the main business of higher education, whether in producing medieval clerics, Tudor bureaucrats, Victorian civil servants or teachers in public schools (Bell, 1971). However, we have not yet reached the point where more than a fifth of all graduates are in business studies, as is now the case in the United States, although there is considerable policy pressure on higher education to produce graduates who will, it is hoped, contribute to the renaissance of the British economy.

Where no consistent connection between the course of study and the graduate labour market exists, it is much more difficult to define the nature and purpose of the undergraduate curriculum. However, in many courses, the absence of external pressures and requirements contrasts with the presence of internal pressures and norms, and it is in this sense that we may speak of *academic* courses. Although only a small percentage of graduates from such courses go on to postgraduate research – usually less than 10 per cent, although the figure varies from subject to subject and from institution to institution – such courses prepare for and seem to be heavily influenced by the demands of graduate study. They tend to be specialized in terms of content, to emphasize the 'process' or methodology of the discipline, and to socialize the student into the ethos or culture of the discipline/department. The single honours curriculum in, say, history, sociology, physics or mathematics is the prime example of the academic first degree; honours courses involving two subjects are a diluted form of the same thing, although arguably a better preparation for some careers, including teaching. But the high status of the specialized honours degree is maintained not only by its evident association with postgraduate research and eventually the academic profession itself, but also by oblique or indirect arguments that it 'trains the mind' and 'teaches one to think', and is thus useful in just about any human activity that does not require codified, specialized knowledge. The 'trained mind' argument thus allows many more students to study for specialized degrees than the job market would apparently warrant; a fact that conveniently accommodates the internal priorities of the academic profession. It is an argument that cuts less ice in some other countries.

Apart from professional and academic curricula, there are others that can only be classified residually or negatively, although a case can be made for calling some of them *general* in a purposeful way. Thus degrees that involve three or more subjects – classics is a traditional example; PPE (politics, philosophy and economics), environmental sciences and European studies are newer ones – can be justified in terms of giving students a broader base of content than they would otherwise have, and also some sense of the relativity of methodologies and disciplinary perspectives. However, there is no real tradition of general education at degree level in the UK (except residually in Scotland) as there is still in the United States, and consequently courses that are neither clearly professional nor clearly academic tend to be regarded as dubious or inferior, except (as with classics) where they tap older traditions and hierarchies. For the same reason, modular schemes that allow the student to select and combine elements of various subjects are rather suspect in the academic world. In a few courses, particularly ones that allow the student to do much of his work in the form of independent projects, the rationale may be less in terms of general education than in terms of individual development. This kind of rationale has been pursued further in the United States than in the UK (see Chickering, 1981), although it may grow in importance here if the proportion of mature students in the system (much higher in the public sector than in the universities) continues to increase.

There are thus two clear curriculum patterns at the undergraduate stage (professional and academic), and the remaining courses can be broadly described as general or developmental. Of course, these headings are not clear-cut: a degree in chemistry, for example, may be seen as being both academic and professional; a degree in law can only be classified in terms of the use the student makes of it: to enter the legal profession, business, or something quite unrelated. (The use of the 'trained mind' argument tends to reflect the extent of the over-supply of graduates for the relevant profession, and we hear more these days about the general value of a law degree than we used to.) Likewise, where some European studies degrees were initially justified in quasi-professional terms, the relative lack of growth of such opportunities and the widespread disillusion with the European ideal has led to more generalized arguments in recent years.

What issues and problems do such patterns throw up? There is not room in one short chapter to analyse these properly; indeed, some of them raise profound questions about the nature of knowledge and the purpose of higher education. However, something needs to be said, and the comments that follow will be grouped under six headings: intradisciplinarity; interdisciplinarity; breadth and depth; theory and practice; the structure of courses; content and process. The chapter will then conclude with some general points about curricular policies and priorities.

INTRADISCIPLINARITY

The term intradisciplinarity is not widely used, but it is being employed here to refer to the internal structure or style of disciplines or fields of study. The basic building-block of the higher education curriculum is the discipline, a word usually preferred to 'subject' because of its greater resonance. Such disciplines are typically embodied in departments, and they thus have a material as well as a mental existence: as well as having theories, concepts, content and methodologies, they have chairs, rooms, journals and conferences. In fact, these material facts tend to obscure some interesting epistemological questions; for it is often assumed that because there is a building or corridor called 'Department of X', inhabited by lecturers in X, that X must therefore be a unitary, cohesive and even indivisible entity with its own distinctive and defining logic, structure, approach and view of the world. In other words, the form or format influences the perception of the content, and the rather difficult abstraction that is the discipline of X is conveniently made concrete. Of course, the lecturers in X will, from the inside, have a much more complex view, and may indeed stress the lack of unity/coherence/commonality in the discipline and its department; but they can do this only within limits or they will begin to undermine their epistemological, institutional and professional existence.

The internal structure and style of disciplines is a very complex matter. To judge from the general remarks made about each field or discipline in the CRAC degree course guides, there is a good deal of variation. Some disciplines have a settled and substantial core, others do not; some have clearly defined sequences, which vary little from one degree course to another; with others, it depends very much on where you study. Historically, too, questions arise. Is mathematics less of a 'whole' than it used to be? Are the biological sciences more of a 'whole' than they used to be? How has geography changed in the last twenty years? Is environmental sciences a discipline? If so, how long has it been so, and how does it now relate to, for example, geography? What exactly is the relationship between engineering science and the various types of engineering? And are the traditional demarcations between each type (civil, mechanical, electronic, etc.) being cross-cut by newer developments, e.g. in information and control systems, or in materials?

An equally interesting question relates to unities of style and ethos, rather than theory and method. Some disciplines – for example, psychology or modern languages – can be approached from a number of different angles or aspects. If this is so, wherein does their unity or identity lie, if anywhere? It may be that disciplines that do not have an obvious epistemological unity nevertheless have a pervasive and unifying style, ethos or culture (Becher, 1984), which can only be assimilated by 'living' it for a period of time. Such styles or cultures are subtle and elusive, but they allow one member of the discipline to recognize and relate to another, through shared references, tensions, jokes and even silences. For example, there may be peculiar concerns in being a sociologist, peculiar certainties in being a chemist, which sociologists and chemists understand but others can only guess at.

The typical single honours degree involves the study of one discipline in depth, though students typically choose one or two ancillary courses, usually in cognate subjects, and usually in the first or second year of a three-year degree. A combined honours degree course involves the study of two, usually cognate subjects such as two modern languages, mathematics and physics, economics and politics. This pattern is sometimes called 'joint honours', but the title is misleading because there is usually no attempt to teach the two subjects in relation to each other. Such courses can be described as 'multidisciplinary'; whereas the term interdisciplinary is reserved for courses which in some way integrate two or more disciplines

(OECD, 1972; Squires *et al.*, 1975). It is necessary to say 'in some way' because, as the preceding comments suggest, we cannot logically discuss the relationship between two disciplines until we have first analysed the nature of each one: the nature of the relationship depends partly on the nature of each party to it.

INTERDISCIPLINARITY

There was a good deal of interest in and writing on interdisciplinarity in the 1970s, and a wide range of courses that crossed the conventional disciplinary boundaries was developed: area studies in the arts and social sciences (e.g. European, American studies); period studies (e.g. medieval studies, the Enlightenment, modern studies); problem-oriented studies (urban development, developing country studies, environmental studies); and others, such as cognitive sciences and systems sciences, which seemed to promise not simply the integration of existing disciplines but the birth of new ones. It should be remembered that some existing courses were also interdisciplinary in nature without necessarily being labelled as such. For example, the study of medicine, particularly at the pre-clinical stage, draws on several basic sciences, although the extent to which they are integrated with one another at that stage depends on the design of the course: there is less integration in the conventional pattern than where the teaching is organized around bodily systems (cardio-vascular, nervous, etc.). Likewise, engineering has always drawn on several subjects, such as physics, mathematics and materials science, and education is typically regarded as being based on several foundation disciplines (philosophy, sociology, history, psychology, etc.). Rather like the character in one of Molière's plays who discovered that he had been speaking prose all his life, academics in these fields were sometimes a little surprised to find that they had been teaching interdisciplinary courses all along. The essential point is that labels such as these are to some extent relative to existing practice, and the term interdisciplinary meant most when it signalled a change from existing single or joint honours patterns.

Since that time, the enthusiasm seems to have waned somewhat, partly because the general academic climate is more cautious, not to say embattled, and partly because the practical difficulties of running such courses have become more obvious. Disciplines are bodies of people as well as bodies of knowledge, and interdisciplinary courses tend to fall foul of existing institutional and professional structures. Where the impetus for such developments is research-led, they have high status, but may be thought appropriate only at postgraduate level; where there is no strong drive from research, they are often stigmatized as lacking in rigour, wishy-washy, superficial, and so forth. Most new academic developments have received a similar welcome in their time: witness the struggles to introduce science and professional subjects in the early nineteenth century, the initial doubts about whether history and English were fit subjects, the continuing skirmishes over some of the social sciences. There is perhaps greater recognition now that the map of knowledge, like the map of Europe, is not as it was a hundred, even fifty years ago, and may change again; but the current climate in relation to new, interdisciplinary developments is still cool.

BREADTH AND DEPTH

The arguments against interdisciplinary or merely broad courses (involving, say, three or more un-integrated subjects) are to some extent the arguments for the specialized, single honours degree. These latter arguments are of several kinds (Squires *et al.*, 1976). First, there is the claim that such studies are good 'for their own sake'. This may well be true, but intrinsic arguments of this kind tend to apply to education (if not training) in general, and do not point to one kind of curriculum rather than another. Then it is sometimes argued that students tend to choose specialized degrees, although this rather ignores the fact that such choices are strictly limited by what is on offer: even if a student wanted to study (say) a tripartite degree, he could not do so in most institutions. Thirdly, it is said that it takes three years to study a subject properly, and anything less is inadequate, if not downright dangerous; but it is suspicious that it takes exactly three years (and why three and not two or four?) to reach degree level in nearly every subject. Could it be that 'standards' are a function of time available, rather than the reverse?

It is yet another argument, however, that is most debatable. The specialized study of one subject for three years is justified on the grounds that, even if only a small proportion of graduates in that subject find employment (including research or teaching) directly related to it, it nevertheless functions as a general-purpose education that fits the remainder for a wide variety of jobs, not to mention life itself. And this belief is held not only by many academics but by many employers, who do not specify the subject or content of a degree in about one-third of all jobs for graduates. There are various explanations.

One is that employers in this case are simply screening for general ability, which is indicated by the class and source of the degree rather than the subject. Another is that the employers are interested in the general intellectual capacities and social attitudes that a higher education is assumed to develop or inculcate. On the supply side, the assumption is that what is learnt – and, even more, how it is learnt – in some way transfers to situations and problems that are quite different from those experienced in the course of study. This assumption is difficult to prove or disprove (What has enabled you to do the job you now do?) although the recent 'cognitive revolution' in psychology tends to view transfer as a function of the person rather than the situation (as was the behavioural view) and hence to believe that it can be developed in the form of high-level or general-purpose 'strategies' or 'programmes' or 'protocols'. However, it is arguable that the 'trained mind' argument has been pushed too far in this country, partly for social and ideological reasons rather than for educational or psychological ones. It has allowed the continued dominance of a non-technocratic elite, which in an increasingly technological age is a dubious benefit; it has reinforced the peculiarly English tradition of the amateur as against the professional; it has exalted the values of analysis and reflection above those of application and action. Such issues, of course, raise much wider issues about the place and effect of higher education in the culture and, in particular, in the economic culture of this country, which will be taken up again at the end of this chapter; but the point to be made here is that 'depth-transfer' assumptions are a cornerstone of the current curriculum in higher education, particularly in non-professional courses.

This fact helps to explain why repeated calls for greater breadth from Robbins onwards have had so little effect. It is, of course, partly a reflection of the overall structure of education in England and Wales. In the United States, a relatively general education in the high schools is followed by a four-year first degree and (in many important professional fields) a two-year Masters. Here, crucially, the Masters often takes twelve months, and the normal degree takes three years. There is thus a strong downward pressure from the very top of the educational system to specialize, and this affects not only the undergraduate curriculum but also the secondary schools, leading to subject selection (and therefore omission) from the age of twelve or thirteen onwards. Since each part of the system interacts with the others, it is difficult to change one in isolation: hence the continuing and usually frustrated attempts to reform O- and A-levels. In the current economic circumstances, the four-year first degree that some have argued for is out of the question; but the length of the Masters degree could be extended at much less cost to the public purse. This might make more breadth possible at every level beneath.

However, it would not automatically lead to greater breadth at first degree and A-level because the norms of specialization are well-established and, as we have seen above, bolstered by a range of arguments, from the sound to the dubious. Besides, the current system is good at doing some things – for example, at producing an annual crop of excellent young researchers and mandarins – with low drop-out rates in (by international standards) a very short time. But such a specialized and compressed pattern of higher education has negative consequences for the rest of the educational system in curricular terms, leading to premature specialization and weakness in science and mathematics, and making it very difficult to devise a secondary school curriculum that meets the general needs of the school population. Paradoxically, the 'efficiency' of higher education entails 'costs' in the rest of the system, and it may be these, rather than any internal pressures, that will in the end bring about changes in the higher education curriculum.

THEORY AND PRACTICE

So far, we have looked mainly at the academic and general courses in higher education. What of professional, or quasi-professional courses? Some of the issues associated with such courses are long-standing and familiar; others are relatively new. The relationship between theory and practice has been a bone of contention for several millenia, and seems likely to continue to be so; indeed it is perhaps the defining characteristic of a professional course. As such it is not something that can be 'solved', although the extent of the 'gap', 'mismatch', 'dialogue' or 'relation' can vary enormously; in institutional and professional terms, the theory–practice issue translates into issues of control, negotiation, accreditation and so on. The close relationship between higher education and the professions has been noted by many writers on both subjects, and there are about 100 professional bodies that have a direct interest in higher education curicula in the UK. In many cases, the curriculum is constrained by the need to qualify students for exemptions from some professional examinations, and the gradual elimination of the alternative, non-graduate route to professional membership in many occupations means that the relationship between the professional body and higher education becomes even more important. Although tensions between academic and professional norms and needs do exist, and conflicts arise from time to time, on the whole the relationship is quite harmonious. This is partly due to the fact that there is a good deal of overlapping membership of relevant committees, and also perhaps points to the deeper consensus about the role of the professions in society; an issue I shall return to at the end of this chapter.

Following Lobkowicz (1967) one might hazard the suggestion that the theory–practice issue is better seen in terms of types of context rather than types of knowledge. This leads away from attempts to define or relate theory and practice in epistemological terms towards an emphasis on the contexts in which theorists and practitioners work. After all, all theorists practice, and all practitioners have theories, even if they are rather low-level or implicit ones; rather than getting into finely graded distinctions between practical theories and theorized practice, we might make more headway by looking at, for example, the time-frames within which people operate, their relationships with their colleagues and institutions, and the criteria used in judging their performance. The academic who works alone for five years on a problem and comes up with a 'no significant difference' conclusion may be applauded by his or her peers; by contrast, the practitioner, working to a strict remit, may have to come up with a decision, even with inadequate evidence, within a few months or weeks. If they change places, it is the context rather than the content of their work that is likely to strike them as different.

The theory–practice issue is a venerable one, and is complicated by related dichotomies, such as abstract/concrete, contemplative/active, and even mental/manual. But some of the issues that confront professional courses are newer. There is more emphasis on 'people' skills, teamwork and management skills in some professions now than there used to be, reflecting the changing social and economic circumstances of professional work. Above all, the rapidity of technological and sometimes other changes have led some courses to aim for a broader and more durable foundation, and/or an increased emphasis on continuing professional development, sometimes accompanied by 're-licensing' requirements. Such changes seem likely to blur the general boundary between higher and continuing education and, if they lead to a more general recognition that one cannot hope to pack everything into a first degree, they could alter the balance of undergraduate studies as well.

THE STRUCTURE OF COURSES

Alongside affecting the content of first degrees, a greater emphasis on continuing education could influence their structure as well. Currently, such structures are best seen as a spectrum. At one end, there is the degree course which is totally prescribed, with no options apart from perhaps some choice of ancillaries, or dissertation/project topic. Such courses are rare and reflect staff shortages as much as curricular logic. Much more common is the course with a substantial core in the first two years, and some options in the third. This pattern is very common in science and technology, and in professional courses that have to meet professional body requirements in order to qualify for exemptions from professional examinations. Further along the spectrum is the course with a small core, or cores, mainly in the first year, followed by a wide choice of options; this pattern exists in many arts and social science courses that are not constrained by professional requirements. Finally, at the far end of the spectrum is the modular course. Here, the curriculum is built up of relatively self-contained units or modules, each of which earns its own credit or credits, which are aggregated to form a degree. In modular schemes, the course units are usually though not always standardized in terms of size or length, and the student typically has a much greater choice of combinations than in the conventional linear structure, although there are usually some restrictions for both educational and practical reasons, such as timetabling. Modular schemes also allow intermediate qualifications (e.g. certificates, diplomas) to be earned en route to a full degree, and this is believed to motivate part-time students who may otherwise face a long haul over five or more years.

The majority of courses in higher education lie in the middle of spectrum, with something between one-third and two-thirds of the total work prescribed. There was considerable interest in modular schemes in the 1970s (Billing, 1974; Mansell *et al.*, 1976), but this made only a moderate impact on the public sector and comparatively little on the universities. There is now some revived interest in modular-credit schemes, particularly in relation to part-time and continuing education, but it is not easy as yet to gauge how much impact this will have (Squires, 1986). Apart from anything else, the pattern of academic terms, especially in the universities, makes it difficult to assess first- and second-term modules on completion, and to timetable full third-term modules. This is because, with the present pattern, the first two terms are almost entirely devoted to teaching, and in the third term often half the time is devoted to examinations, leaving only half the term, or less, for teaching. For a modular system to work smoothly, there would have to be equal teaching time in all three terms (say 9 or 10 weeks) with an increasing amount of revision/examination/marking time at the end of each term (1, 2, 3 weeks) to allow for the existence of two- and three-term modules as well as one-term ones. The alternative of the two-semester year has never really caught on, and is found only in a few polytechnics, while the newer American quarter system – which involves a four-term year – has not been seriously mooted. Such changes would entail a major restructuring of the current academic year, of a kind which is taking place in non-advanced further education and has even been suggested for the schools, but has not so far been seriously placed on the agenda for higher education.

Even if such structural obstacles to modularity were removed, however, there would remain many academic objections. Modularity cuts across the 'holistic' paradigm of higher education (Squires, 1979), which views it as an indivisible, total experience, deeply embedded in its socio–institutional setting. The fact that, after more than fifteen years of discussion and experience, modular schemes remain relatively rare in higher education suggests that they will never spread widely, in their original conception. What may spread more rapidly, particularly in part-time and continuing education, is a modified 'tariff' system, such as has been set up recently by a consortium of polytechnics in the south-east with the backing of the CNAA. Unlike a modular system, a tariff system does not attempt to standardize all courses to the same size or length, or to make most of them optional. However, it does provide a currency of course credits, which makes it easier for students to transfer from one course, institution or mode of attendance to another, or to interrupt their studies or even terminate them with an intermediate qualification. The currency is based on a convenient number of credits (e.g. 60 or 120) for an academic year's work: convenient because the varying size of courses means that the number has to be subdivisible in various ways. Agreement on levels and marking scales is also necessary. This kind of system does not maximize flexibility and student choice in the way that a modular system does, but it is much easier to map on to the existing structures and norms of higher education, and might therefore become more common (see also the concluding section of Chapter 4). Any curriculum structure in higher education has to accept the fact that, with the current three-year degree, between one-third and two-thirds of almost any course is likely to remain non-optional, for either academic or professional reasons, or both.

CONTENT AND PROCESS

The above comments have been about the structure of the curriculum, but something must also be said about the curriculum process, although this shades into the subject of the next chapter on teaching and learning. The curriculum was defined at the outset as what is taught, but it is not only content or subject-matter that is taught; to be more precise, content and subject-matter are never disembodied, contextless, learnt in a vacuum: they are always taught by particular people, in particular ways, at particular times and places. The curriculum-on-paper is only a script: the real curriculum is acted out and lived through. Thus, in a sense, we can say that the lecturer is also a kind of content, and so are the methods he or she uses, the department he or she works in and, last but not least, the assessment that is made. The point can be established simply by asking: What do we remember of school? Of college? Of university? Often, when much of the course content seems to have disappeared without memory trace, we recall the way the lecturer fidgeted over his notes, the buzz in the departmental common-room, the tension of the examination hall. And beyond these perhaps trivial recollections, some more significant things may have become embedded in our consciousness: the idea that knowledge is divided into precincts, that there is always doubt, that the most intense learning takes place between individuals, that achievements have to be certified and sealed with approval.

The very diversity of the curriculum process makes it difficult to say anything general about it, but two points can be hazarded. First, higher education in the UK is more personal than it is in most countries, contrasting with the organized impersonality of some large US institutions and the disorganized impersonality of many continental ones (Squires, 1980). That personal emphasis, embodied in good staff–student ratios, tutoring systems, and the general ambience of departments, makes the curriculum less rigid than it appears on paper; indeed, at the extreme, the curriculum becomes merely a vehicle for relationship and community. This seems to me a valuable inheritance (appreciated more perhaps by foreigners than natives) and it would be a pity if it were eroded by worsening staff–student ratios, increasing bureaucracy, and the dominance of the visible over the invisible.

Secondly, the image, and to some extent, the reality of higher education as being slow to respond and change may be due to the fact that the informal aspect – what Martin Trow once called the 'private life' – finds ways of complementing, modifying and bypassing the formal structures and mechanisms. One would not want to press this argument too far, but it is a caution to those who look, or see, only the official or overt curriculum. Education is inherently a rather imprecise and unpredictable business, and therefore it needs systems that can cope with uncertainty. The informal or personal side of higher education allows it to educate despite, through, and for uncertainty.

POLICIES AND PRIORITIES

I have given a short account of the patterns of curricula in higher education, and discussed very briefly some of the issues and problems that arise from those patterns. Finally, something should be said about current and future policies. I shall concentrate on two topics, out of the many that could be addressed. The first is the relationship between higher education and the economy, and the second is the way in which curricula have become professionalized.

It is common ground among all the main political parties that the UK has been in relative economic decline for many decades, and that the higher education system should help to reverse this trend. There is thus a 'switch' towards science and technology, and an increased emphasis on vocational and professional subjects, both in initial and continuing higher education. This has led to some (and may lead to more) cuts in apparently less 'relevant' arts and social science subjects. A similar emphasis and trend exists in many OECD countries. How well-founded is this policy?

Higher education relates to the economy in two direct ways and one indirect way. Directly, it supplies the economy with research and with high-level manpower. Research is one of the themes of the previous chapter; all that will be said here is that few have doubted the excellence of basic research in the UK during recent decades, as measured, for example, by the number of Nobel Prize winners or the number of patents taken out. The problem, it seems, lies mainly in the take-up, development, application and marketing of the basic research.

The situation with manpower is more complex. There is little obvious evidence that shortages of high-level manpower have held the economy back in the last twenty years (Lindley, 1981), apart from the pockets of shortages that exist even in centrally planned economies. Nor does the percentage or the distribution of graduates in the labour force differ much in the UK and in Germany (Hollenstein, 1982) despite differences in initial enrolments;

171

however, both the United States and Japan have much higher percentages. (The major difference between the UK and its industrial competitors lies in the percentage of those with low or middle-level vocational qualifications, where the UK scores very poorly.)

It can be argued that the UK does not produce enough graduates in technology or business/management. But it seems to be the indirect relationship between higher education and the economy that is the important one, and this is an elusive matter of culture in general and economic culture in particular (Wiener, 1981). Some writers have accused the higher education system (mainly the universities and especially Oxbridge) of transmitting and reinforcing anti-commercial and anti-industrial attitudes that ill serve a trading, manufacturing nation. Not only have relatively few graduates gone into the traditional sectors of industry and commerce (see Hollenstein, 1982); even those who have carry with them attitudes that are more suited to professional or administrative contexts. The making of money or things has therefore been regarded as rather below the salt.

Arguments based on 'attitudes', 'culture' and 'ethos' are notoriously difficult to verify or falsify. Nevertheless, some economists admit them to be important factors in production, in terms of the 'intensity of labour' and the incompleteness of labour contracts (which do not and cannot specify attitudes to the job). And at a macro level, it is very difficult to explain how countries with education and training systems as dissimilar as Germany, the United States and Japan manage to achieve similar economic success. In the general debate about education and the economy, I suspect that too much emphasis has been placed on manpower and skills, and too little on attitudes and culture. If a firm or a country takes training seriously and does it well, it will of course be a contributory cause of economic success; but it may also be a consequence of an underlying attitude to work and production, a sign of a certain kind of economic culture. Indeed, what come through strongly in reports such as *Competence and Competition* (NEDC, 1984) are the consensual foundations for economic success (different in each case) in Germany, Japan and the United States. In that light, the actual structure of the education and training system, and the detail of manpower policy and trends, are of secondary importance.

This suggests that the problem in the UK is not that higher education has failed to supply the requisite manpower for the economy, but that there is a general 'dissensus' about the economy and its social and political aspects in the country, a dissensus that higher education reflects and perhaps exacerbates. The conflict is partly about the ownership and control of the means of production, and can therefore be expressed in conventional ideological terms. But there are other elements as well, more difficult to put one's finger on: among them a nostalgic-utopian dream of the pastoral, not only pre/post-industrial, but pre/post-economic, in the sense that the production imperative no longer holds sway. The anti-industrial ethos identified by Wiener and others draws on ancient and powerful traditions, of which Blake's *Jerusalem* is perhaps the alternative anthem.

In the short term, there would seem to be little choice in the matter. The UK economy is increasingly part of an international economy, with major movements of capital, goods and services, and even labour, across national boundaries. None of the main political parties now contemplates a serious reversal of this trend; thus, the economic and social fortunes of the country depend squarely on its economic, and in particular its trading, performance. The social, political and cultural consequences of economic failure could be dire. Therefore it is reasonable to expect higher education to play its part in turning the economy around, and this is likely to mean that employment and economic criteria in curriculum planning will loom large for the foreseeable future. However, working out the curricular implications of 'economic relevance' is a tricky business. In part it implies an increase in obviously vocational courses, such as business studies, information science or biotechnology, especially where there is clear evidence of actual or potential manpower shortages. However, the relationship between graduate output and labour market intake is quite elastic (graduates do not always do jobs directly related to their studies) and, besides, the labour market to some extent adapts itself to what the higher education system produces (and in this way may 'collude' with it to the national disadvantage). It is arguable that economic relevance is more likely to be attained not by increasing the number of vocationally specialized graduates (what happens to them if the employment situation changes?) but by giving graduates a broader base of studies, which would equip them better in a general way to perform a wide range of jobs. This might mean, for example, ensuring that all graduates have a range of useful competencies (in mathematics, computing, oral and written communication, interpersonal skills, etc.) in addition to their main subject or subjects. It might also mean giving more students the opportunity to work in industry and commerce for short periods (tasters rather than sandwich courses) so that they get a better understanding of those environments; staff would benefit from a similar scheme.

In fact, all these kinds of developments are already taking place in the kind of patchy, pragmatic and generally unsung way that is typical of the system's capacity to adapt and innovate without the need for central decree. The contribution of higher education to the improvement of the country's economic performance is thus most likely to be enhanced by a mixture of changes: some more emphasis on vocational degrees per se; the addition of skills and competencies to the main expertise the graduate can offer; a shift of attitudes and climate, brought about in part by closer links between higher education and industry and commerce. Over and above these, there is a special case for upgrading engineering and technology, which for many decades have had unusually low status in the UK (vis-à-vis science as much as the arts) compared with other countries; but, as the repeated attempts to remedy this have shown, the problem has deep social and cultural roots.

One must not underestimate the historical and existing links between higher education and industry (see Sanderson, 1972) or the capacity of the system quietly to adapt, through changes in student choice, course content and teaching, research emphasis and related activities. And the immediate need to contribute to economic salvation should not obscure the long-term perspective. The 'dissensus' about industrialization and the market economy is a real and valid one: there are serious arguments on both sides. It would be unrealistic to expect higher education to resolve such issues on its own; it exists as much in the national culture (and its tensions) as apart from it. But there is perhaps a long-term cultural role for higher education in helping to articulate what may become increasingly tacit and assumed in a culture that is not forced to explain itself to itself: one that is in many ways a subtle and oblique culture that values the understated and the allusive. Countries, like companies and individuals, which become unable to make explicit and thereby assess what they are about and what they are doing, find it difficult to make more than minor adjustments to their ways; they cannot change radically, because they can no longer map that change. If there is a broad cultural justification for higher education, it may lie in the general effect of higher-level studies in forcing students to explicate, analyse and reflect on what they are doing. There is nothing new in that claim, but, whereas it often takes an institutional form (the university as 'critic' of society), it seems to me more realistic and less grandiose to see it in terms of the impact of individual graduates on the accepted, taken-for-granted and often tacit norms and practices that exist in all organizations – universities, polytechnics and colleges included.

The final point is concerned not with knowledge, but with knowledge about knowledge. From the description at the beginning of this chapter, it will be clear that many higher education curricula are professional curricula, in that they prepare for and lead directly on to work in identifiable professions or quasi-professions. That much is obvious. But it can be argued that most academic courses are also professional, in that they implicitly prepare students for a career in research or lecturing or, *faute de mieux*, schoolteaching. Indeed the single honours degree has all the hallmarks of the traditional apprenticeship: the close relationship between master and apprentice, the clear demarcation of craft boundaries, the emphasis on learning by imitation, the socialization into the craft ethic (even the jokes), the stages of initiation and progression, the final Masterpiece. Of course, as was said above, the process of the curriculum may vary a great deal in practice, and some courses that on paper look like an apprenticeship for an academic or similar career may in fact be a quite different kind of experience: the curriculum may only be the vehicle. But, if most higher education courses are in fact professional courses, leading to the external or internal professions, where does this leave the concepts of liberal or general education?

Liberal education, as a concept, has become virtually unusable. Not only has it become detached from its original philosophical base in metaphysical realism, which allowed it to mean a liberation from error and illusion (Hirst, 1974) but it has been variously interpreted: as the education of a particular kind of person (the free man or gentleman); education to become that kind of person; an education in particular subjects (classics, the liberal arts); an education through particular subjects (virtually anything except vocational/professional ones); an educational process involving true dialogue, discussion, etc.; an education that aims variously at enlightenment, autonomy, tolerance, good taste, an informed citizenry, and so forth (for a historical account, see Rothblatt, 1976). All these ideas are important and defensible, but to crowd them all under one umbrella concept invites confusion.

Yet there is a strong tradition, expressed not only by English writers, but by others as diverse as Veblen, Ortega and Jaspers, that higher education should go beyond professional education, that it should in some way be concerned with basic questions of truth, reality, knowledge and understanding. Some interpreters give these ideas a more social gloss than others, but in all cases they are concerned with something more than professional expertise and

175

values. The common stereotype of the university, as being in but not quite of this world, and a place where the great questions are debated late into the night, bears witness, however naively, to that tradition.

To some extent, the American commitment to general education stems from this kind of view; the dual problem is that general education keeps expanding (there is more and more to know) and higher education requires some specialization and depth; besides, general education in US universities and colleges is by no means an unqualified success. The periodic calls in this country for greater breadth (see not only the Robbins report, but Robbins, 1980) also stem in part from this tradition, but higher education in the UK is even more compressed and specialized than in the United States – three rather than four years for a first degree, one rather than two for a Master's – so there is simply not the time (so the argument goes) for depth and breadth.

Without structural changes, that is likely to remain the situation. I would argue that all students should ideally have substantial contact with three disciplines, to the point where they can experience the 'absoluteness' of each perspective or disciplinary culture and yet the 'relativity' of each in relation to the others. I would also like to see a common course concerned with knowledge about knowledge, with the philosophical, historical and social aspects of both organized knowledge and professional expertise; a course that would lead the student to reflect on the disciplines he or she is studying, and give him or her some feel for the nature of others. It seems to me that an emphasis on knowledge about knowledge is both socially desirable (since it is knowledge or expertise that differentiates graduates from their fellow-citizens, and often gives them greater wealth and power) and is educationally and occupationally useful (in that it allows them to step outside the assumptions, practices and values of their own disciplines and see them from another angle). It is not so much a matter of depth and breadth, as of depth and perspective.

Some of this goes on already. Some scientific and professional courses (such as medicine and engineering) have options or require-ments dealing with the social and historical context of the discipline. The fact that such courses are much rarer in the arts and social sciences does not seem to me to be excused by the fact that such disciplines are often themselves social or historical. How many history or English graduates know how and when their disciplines became incorporated into the academic structures of higher edu-cation? And with what difficulties and struggles? The curriculum process – the individual lecturer and the departmental ethos – may steer students towards or away from such considerations. Philosophy used to be a lynchpin subject in Scottish universities and is still more central there than elsewhere. But developments of this kind are unlikely to go further, and the structural constraints of the system (the short bachelor's and master's degree) combined with the increasing vocational pressures described above may erode even the modest gains that were made in the 1960s and 1970s.

There are two consequences of the growing professionalization of the higher education curriculum. First, each course and each department is justified in terms of its own profession, academic or external, and there is therefore no general, institutional rationale. In fact, universities, polytechnics and colleges are largely administrative rather than academic entities; whereas the department embodies the discipline or field, the institution as a whole embodies nothing – it is a curious mixture of bureaucracy and ritual. This means that, for planning purposes, the essential unit is the department, so any central authority finds it easy to divide and rule. That process is becoming increasingly apparent in the current round of cuts.

Secondly, the professionalization of academic (as distinct from professional) curricula means that any shift of policy from the academic to the instrumental, such as we are now seeing, is merely a shift of orientation, from the internal to the external, rather than a profound change in the nature and purposes of higher education. By assimilating undergraduate courses to the norms and patterns of the academic professions themselves, in the form of the specialized honours degree, academics undermined their own defences against overly instrumental views of higher education, and cleared the way for the current economically oriented policies.

The system retains, however, in all its parts – universities, polytechnics and colleges – a capacity for rolling, pragmatic, undramatic innovation, which must qualify any general account such as this chapter has attempted to give, and also make one hesitant about broad predictions. Academics are almost always interested in *what* they teach, even if they display less concern with how they teach it, and to whom, and in what circumstances, than some might wish. Their subject or their field is in many ways their identity, even their life. That fact alone means that the curriculum in higher education is always likely to remain at the heart of the enterprise.

9

Teaching, Learning and Assessment

ERIC HEWTON

INTRODUCTION

In the mid 1970s, as a member of a research team (the Nuffield Group for Research and Innovation in Higher Education), I had the opportunity to visit several universities and polytechnics in the United Kingdom in order to discuss innovations in teaching and learning with the academics concerned. The impression I gained from this experience was of a predominantly subject-centred attitude to teaching and learning. As the name implies, this involves an approach to teaching that begins with the subject matter and seeks optimum ways of communicating it to students. The student is regarded as a relatively passive receiver of pre-specified knowledge. Progress is monitored throughout the period of instruction and final judgement is made on the basis of an examination, success in which usually leads to the award of a diploma or a degree. This traditional attitude is still an important influence on academic teaching.

In this chapter, I shall first examine this tradition in order to build up a picture of academic settings that have existed for a long time and also to suggest some of the reasons why teaching takes the form that it does. Then, in the second part of the chapter, I shall discuss some of the influences that are bringing about significant, if sporadic, change.

THE POWER OF THE SUBJECT

Until very recently, no training, other than that necessary to master a discipline, was required of those teaching in higher education. After an extensive review of teaching in universities and polytechnics, the Group for Research and Innovation in Higher Education reported:

> The belief is still widely held (and perhaps with some justification) that the good teacher is born, not made. There is also a good deal of scepticism about whether one can learn anything useful from others about how to teach. (GRIHE, 1975, p. 36)

Although there are now opportunities for training, there are still many lecturers who do not avail themselves of them. Beard and Hartley (1984) in a recent analysis of teaching and learning in higher education suggest that 'In Britain, except for brief courses for new teachers, programmes vary in success and tend to be ignored on the whole'. This pessimistic view is held by many of those involved with staff development in higher education. Matheson, who co-ordinated a national scheme for the training of university teachers in the 1970s, explains that for much of the decade there were both encouragement and resources for staff development but not a great deal to show for the effort in the end (Matheson, 1983).

It would seem that there is something inherent in the nature of a discipline that provides those who master it with not only a basis of specialized knowledge but also the means whereby this knowledge may be communicated to others. Bligh (1982) suggests:

> For many academic staff the starting point in planning their teaching is their academic subject. Decisions about the content of courses – what is to be taught – are uppermost in their minds. For some 'what is to be taught' consists of information to be learned. Others pay more attention to the skills, in particular the pattern of thought, the student must acquire. (Bligh, 1982, p. 14).

From this standpoint the subject and the teacher (who is master of that subject) dominate teaching, learning and assessment in several ways. As Bligh suggests, there is generally a set content that must be covered and, once this is accepted, there is a certain underlying logic that links the subject to the way in which it is taught.

The lecture (it is no coincidence that teachers in higher education are generally called lecturers) is the most widely used teaching method and there are two main reasons for this. First, the lecture is economical and efficient as far as teaching (though not necessarily learning) is concerned. It can be delivered to large groups of students (very large numbers if television monitors are used) and it can be repeated and recorded. Secondly, it is an important and seemingly effective means of giving information.

But other means may also be appropriate for mastering certain disciplines. Alongside the lecture, supporting and supplementing it, will be the textbook. This is usually regarded as an efficient means of providing information for pre-set areas of knowledge. Again, if intensive or extensive reading is required as a way of acquiring knowledge (as in history), then much of a student's time will be spent in a library or elsewhere alone with reference material.

In the case of a practically oriented subject, such as engineering, the acquisition of a large body of shared knowledge is necessary, but this is coupled with the need to be able to design, build and test items of various kinds. Almost inevitably, lectures will be regarded as the most effective way of presenting the background knowledge, and laboratories as the most appropriate places in which to practise the necessary skills. Wherever experimental or practical work is necessary, as in most scientific subjects, laboratory activities will take up a major proportion of formal teaching time.

In some subjects, such as archaeology, geology or social anthropology, much of the material for study is outside the institution and field work becomes a necessary part of teaching and learning. Students, therefore, will spend a part of their time carrying out surveys or investigations in areas of designated importance for their subject.

Finally, the idea of discussion, debate or disputation is regarded as important in some subjects. This is sometimes seen as an essential part of the discipline itself, as in law or politics or philosophy, where students in groups (which might range from three or four to thirty or more) are required to practise the art of expounding, attacking or defending a pre-specified position. But discussion, in what is usually called a tutorial or seminar group, has acquired a broader function and is often regarded as an important follow-up to lectures and reading, permitting lecturers to expand or emphasize important points and to test out, through questioning, the levels of students' understanding. Seminars also allow students to raise and discuss the issues or problems that are causing them difficulty. This form of teaching, whatever the size of the group, still tends to be subject-centred and teacher led. (Other ways in which such groups might operate are considered later.)

What the student actually receives in the way of teaching, then, depends upon a common view of the subject as perceived by lecturers in each subject area. Content (comprising facts, concepts, models and theories) is at the heart of the discipline and it is this that has to be conveyed as effectively and efficiently as possible.

Bligh (1982) makes a second point concerning the pattern of thought that a student is expected to acquire, and this further reinforces the subject-centredness of teaching. The student as novitiate is not simply absorbing a set of facts, concepts, theories or skills: he or she is also learning how to think, to behave like a subject specialist and to adopt the traditional norms associated with being, say, an economist, geographer or chemist. The subjects themselves act as socializing agencies administered by those who have achieved their mastery.

Knowledge and associated values are carefully controlled through the teaching process: they are filtered and packaged as they pass down through the various levels. This often provides a sense of security and certainty, which for many students and lecturers is both important and necessary. It is possible to pass to the next stage in the hierarchy of learning only by demonstrating the appropriate acquisition of knowledge and values in the earlier stages.

This careful control extends to the assessment procedures, each stage being based upon established criteria related to the achievement of specific competencies and attitudes. The unseen three-hour examination is at the heart of the formal system and students are normally examined at least two or three times, in each aspect of the subject. Generally, the examinations taken during their final year count for most of the marks awarded but there are usually other minor examinations throughout the course, some of which will count towards the final assessment and grading.

> This is the approach used in the overwhelming majority of courses in higher education. The method is for staff to make unilateral judgement of the learner's work and to decide on the award of qualifications. (Cunningham 1983).

The system is supported by demands for the demonstration of proficiency in accordance with clearly laid down, external standards. Equity requires public examinations in properly supervised situations. The written test, unseen to prevent 'cheating', has proved to be the most easily controlled and seemingly fair way of proving learning and of maintaining standards. More varied and open methods of assessment have been introduced into many courses in recent years: these are referred to later in this chapter.

In several ways, therefore, the demands of the subject have come to dominate the methods used in teaching it. The stereotype is largely predictable. Lectures are efficient means of disseminating facts to large groups. Laboratories are necessary for practising specific experimental skills. Libraries are essential depositories of written knowledge. Examinations are the most equitable way of demonstrating learning, and so on.

PRESSURES ON TRADITIONAL
PRACTICE

A closer examination of teaching and learning in higher education reveals three key pressures for change. These together produce significant and interesting variations on the traditional teaching and learning package already described.

The first is the notion that learning should be problem-centred rather than subject-centred. This approach stresses the importance of learning by doing and of working as closely as possible with real problems. The subject discipline is not the sole determinant of such activity. Demands from industry, commerce and the professions which together produce a concern for vocationalism are clearly associated with the problem-centred approach.

The second pressure comes from what is generally called educational technology. This attempts to provide a more systematic approach to the planning of courses. It involves identifying purposes – usually by specifying objectives; developing the appropriate learning experiences; evaluating the outcomes. Thus the emphasis is shifted away from content to be taught towards concern for aims or objectives for learning. In addition, the rapid development of new technologies, particularly microcomputers and advanced video equipment, has formed part of the educational technology approach. Its possible benefits have been clearly spelt out by the advocates of this approach during the last two decades, but the changes brought about as a result have been limited.

What is perhaps the most important challenge to the subject-centred tradition comes from a very different source. It places the student at the centre of the endeavour and predicates all decisions concerning teaching and learning with the question: what are the student's needs, individually and collectively? Student-centredness can lead to greater diversity in teaching methods; to a concern for how individuals learn; to independent, individualized or co-operative forms of learning. As Abercrombie (1981) suggests: 'The idea that learning is an active process is extended to the idea that students should learn to manage their own education.'

The pressures for change are, therefore, dealt with under three headings: problem orientation; educational technology; student-centredness.

Problem orientation
As already noted, the need or the desire to solve 'real' problems is often connected with vocational or professional preparation, which requires learning by doing rather than purely theoretical learning.

Practical work has always formed a part of many courses in higher education. Chemists, physicists and biologists experiment in laboratories, engineers build and test in workshops, architects design in studios, geographers spend time 'in the field', and so on. But to a large extent the traditional needs of the subject dominate the form that the practical work takes.

Laboratory work, for instance, is often highly formalized and devoted to solving set problems for which the solution is already known. Engineering design is often undertaken to demonstrate that the student is able to apply established theoretical procedures. The geographer will set out to verify knowledge learnt in the lecture theatre or through books. Thus, practical knowledge is employed to reinforce the understanding of the technical or theoretical knowledge associated with the subject.

One of the challenges to subject domination comes from the view that this traditional practice does not promote the skills necessary to tackle those problems likely to be met in performing a vocational role. There are skills in problem-solving that can only be learnt by actually doing a job and reflecting upon the outcomes. To a large degree this 'hands on' or vocational experience has been omitted from most undergraduate and much post-graduate work. The reasons seem to be that such skills are difficult to identify and codify and even more difficult to teach. Eraut (1985) comments:

> The language of syllabus construction prevails, accompanied perhaps by some homilies of the profession. Knowledge of the kind that does not normally get included in syllabi will not be considered, as attention is focused on the listing of topics or specialisms. To questions about the significance of a quality like 'getting on with people', the usual response is to treat it as an unchanging personal attribute or to assume that it will be acquired on-the-job with no need for special provision. In special circumstances it might be academicised and included in 'interpersonal skills' or 'psychology'. Thus knowledge is likely to be packaged according to traditional assumptions about where and how it will be acquired. (Eraut, 1985, p. 3).

Eraut goes on to give some examples of this kind of knowledge and know-how. For instance, he refers to knowledge about resources and how to get them; organizations, their norms and values and how to deal with them; how to get knowledge and store and retrieve it; how one learns; all kinds of 'coping knowledge' required to deal with the pressures and contradictions experienced at work.

Some courses now attempt to build in 'real' problems and to

183

expose students to the pressures of the workplace. The idea of the sandwich course with a major amount of time devoted to work experience is far from new – the technological universities and most polytechnics have used this idea extensively (although it is now under critical scrutiny by cost-conscious central and local authorities). Many other courses in advanced and non-advanced higher education espouse the virtues of work experience, which can range from work in the community (for those taking social work subjects) to work placement in a shop, office or factory (for those doing business or technically oriented courses).

The important aspect of this approach is the experience that it provides. But the question can reasonably be asked: what does the student learn? Because this can be so uncertain, time is usually devoted beforehand to preparing for the experience and, afterwards, to analysing it. The use of the individual experience of students in this way can considerably enhance learning, but it needs to be carefully integrated through reflection. If this does not happen there is a danger that the college-based and the work-based experiences will simply be regarded as two separate and unrelated parts of the programme.

A more specific form of learning by doing is described by Goodlad (1975) as 'education and social action', In discussing community service linked to the curriculum, he argues:

> Yet, however much one may value the specialist nature of the university's work, it is still necessary for the individual who works in the university, as student or teacher, to have some conception of the social relevance of his activity, to have a motive for being there at all: and this may best be achieved through some direct involvement with community problems. Only in this way can the subject of the university's intellectual activity be socially informed. (Goodlad, 1975, p. 24).

Relevant programmes range across subjects as diverse as education, engineering, theology, planning, sociology, law and liberal studies. In all cases students are involved in real community problems and provide help or advice to others. Examples cited include: the technical problems of providing hot food for house-bound old people; legal advice for fellow (non-law) students; helping children from deprived backgrounds with reading difficulties. In all cases the need for reflection upon and discussion of the experience gained is stressed.

But not all schemes concerned with learning by doing go as far as this. The idea of project work, although it might involve students in community affairs, is usually concerned with less ambitious activities. A project is generally an extended piece of work, which may last from a day to a year or more, involving students, singly or in groups, in the investigation or study of a situation, problem or theme. An outcome, such as a report, design, model or construction of some kind is usually expected and very often involves the solution to a problem.

Projects may take varied forms, but on the whole they seek to involve students in finding out something for themselves by engaging in a problem-solving activity for which there is no set answer. Such projects are to be found in many courses, even those that are still traditionally subject-based.

In some subjects, the idea of learning by doing is extended to include not only real-life problems but also simulated situations. It is argued that practice in problem-solving can be gained if conditions similar to those encountered in the workplace are created. Games and case studies have long been in use in business studies, but similar approaches are also found in medicine, social work, education, social sciences, law and many other disciplines. Again, it is regarded as important that experience gained in this way is understood and consolidated through reflection and analysis.

The problem-solving method offers a further challenge to subject domination in so far as the problems of real life usually require a multi-disciplinary approach. In some cases this is ignored as an unavoidable by-product of project work while in others it is acknowledged as useful experience and is built upon.

Finally, with regard to assessment, it may be that learning by doing is seen by teachers as a necessary contribution towards learning the subject and that no special assessment of the experience is required. It is assumed, in that case, that what has been learnt will automatically show in the quality of the answers in the normal examination. Increasingly, though, in those courses where problem-solving activities are regarded as important in themselves, an attempt is made to introduce some form of special evaluation. This will vary according to the nature of the experience, but will usually require some kind of report, presentation or product that demonstrates that learning has taken place.

The assessment of work of this kind, more than in most other forms of subject-dominated learning, involves an attempt to identify creative thought, ingenuity, application and tenacity. These are not always easily discernible in an objective way, and it is usually difficult to quantify them in a form that permits their transposition into a traditional marking scheme. As a result, a simple pass–fail system is often used. There are, however, some examples of more sophisticated methods. Some require student and supervisor to enter into a detailed 'contract' specifying intentions and methods to be used, students being judged against the fulfilment of the contract. Occasionally, the problem-solving activity is broken down into various phases and skills; the supervisor or tutor maintains a continuous marking scheme, so that the student is assessed upon plans, preliminary approach, setting up an experiment or fieldwork, general application, ways of dealing with unforeseen problems, originality and, finally, report writing or presentation. A few schemes allow students to play a part in their own assessment or to judge others. In such cases, the marks awarded usually form a small part of the overall assessment.

Problem orientation, therefore, can take many forms. Some, such as traditional laboratory work, fit neatly into the subject/teacher dominated stereotypes; others shift the learning into the experiential domain and, as a result, lessen the control of the teacher. What is learnt derives from the involvement of the student in a problem of some kind. This might arise from a work placement, a community action programme, a project, or some form of simulated experience within the college. The very nature of some of these experiences produces learning of a multidisciplinary form.

Educational technology
Educational technology tends to be associated, in the minds of many people, with visual aids, television, computers and programmed learning: indeed, at first, these were the stock-in-trade of the educational technologist and considerable sums were spent in the 1960s on various forms of hardware, particularly on television studios. But since then a gradual change has taken place:

> During the last twenty years, more and more sophisticated tools (like programmed learning and microcomputers) and teaching materials (like new curriculum packages) have entered the classroom. They have not always added much to the amount of learning taking place and have sometimes antagon-ised teacher and student alike. Hence, many educationalists have begun to look beyond the individual components and strategies of the teaching/learning system. They have become concerned with understanding the system as a whole. Identi-fying aims and objectives, planning the learning environment, exploring and structuring the subject matter, selecting appro-priate teaching strategies, helping students develop new ways of learning, evaluating the effects and effectiveness of the

teaching/learning system, and using the insights gained from evaluation to understand the system and, where possible, improve it – this is now the province of the educational technologist. (Rowntree, 1982, p. 3).

It is easy to see from this description that the traditional mould – subject to teacher to content to lecture to learner – would be broken if the systems approach were used. The notion of a systematic analysis of learning goals and the best ways of achieving them has often been supported, explicitly or implicitly, by validating bodies such as the CNAA and BTEC. Course planners have been exhorted to use a more systematic approach and to design learning experiences to suit the needs of the learners. This has often led to the introduction of non-traditional forms of teaching and learning, some of which were mentioned in the previous section: projects, games, simulations, 'hands on' experience, etc.

However, educational technology in the sense of learning systems design has not made a major impact on the teaching staff in higher education, despite external pressures and internal appointments of specialists with a brief to improve teaching and learning. The approach not only breaks with tradition but requires considerably more time to plan and execute. By and large, lecturers have not been convinced of its benefits.

The use of computers, video equipment and other forms of technology calls for separate mention. These have the potential to offer a major challenge to the status quo. Again, as with many innovations in teaching and learning, the possibilities have been seen and encouraged for some time (see Brynmor Jones, 1965), but a combination of refinements in technology and pressures on staff time have resulted in a resurgence of interest during the 1980s. Most institutions, sometimes with government help, have been able to find the capital necessary to finance developments, particularly in the introduction of computers.

Computer laboratories are now to be found on most campuses, and it is becoming increasingly difficult to complete a degree programme in higher education without some contact with the computer. Beard and Hartley (1984) suggest four possible uses: learning about the computer, its applications and how to use it; learning through the computer, involving drills and practice, diagnostic testing and feedback; learning with the computer, involving simulations, problem-solving and creative activities; finally, support systems in which the computer manages information, guides the student and generates instructions.

Computers are not the only aid used in the teaching and learning process. Video tapes, for instance, are increasingly used, and Watson (1977) has noted that when these are carefully planned and incorporated into a science course they can save staff and demonstrator time, produce presentations of a high quality and offer a flexible service to students, who can view and review them at any time. Other more traditional audiovisual methods of teaching and learning are also used, including tape slides, audio cassettes, film-strips, etc. These are sometimes combined into learning packages.

Thus technology, increasingly of a more sophisticated kind, is finding its way into teaching – for the most part providing a tool to assist the teacher. In one sense, though, teacher domination of the learning process is lessened because of the greater flexibility in pace and place of work that is permitted through the use of media. Video recordings of lectures and demonstrations, for instance, can be viewed by students in their own time and computer-assisted learning is an approach that allows a certain amount of self-pacing.

But it is perhaps the place of study that offers the greatest potential for change, particularly if students are enabled to learn at home or at work. In the 1960s this possibility was advanced, not as a cost-saving device but as a means of providing greater flexibility for students and for breaking institutional dominance over teaching and learning. The notion of 'open learning' was epitomized in the United States by the University Without Walls, and in the United Kingdom the Open University paved the way for its own brand of distance learning. It receives special mention in the 1985 Green Paper on Higher Education:

> Distance learning involving the use of audio-visual media as well as the written word and personal guidance has become an established part of higher education in this country primarily through the Open University (4.11) although other institutions, too, are taking welcome initiatives to develop teaching techniques and materials, including video tapes, that will enable employers to arrange for courses to be followed at the place of work. Distance learning may be not only the best but the only means of disseminating quickly and on a substantial scale expertise in new and rapidly expanding disciplines . . . There is scope for the wider application of distance learning in the updating of industry, commerce, the public services and the professions (including teaching). (DES, 1985a, paragraph 6.10).

The scope is not, however, limited to vocationally oriented pro-grammes. The potential for more distance education and training using combinations of learning materials, videos, computers and telecommunications (such as tele-conferencing) is clearly there: the possibilities of 'learning by appointment' and 'flexistudy' are already being tried in a number of colleges. But, for the present, the trend in this direction is slow and haphazard. Distance education materials are notoriously difficult and expensive to produce (Riley, 1984) and they become cost-effective only when produced for a large number of students.

In summary, there have been pressures for change towards a more systematized approach to course design and the use of the increasingly sophisticated technology now available. This has brought about some changes in the teaching and learning methods used, and has resulted in experiments in distance learning and the use of learning packages.

Student-centredness
The idea of student-centredness offers a direct challenge to subject/teacher domination. It is derived from a different philosophical standpoint, which is supported by a certain amount of empirical research. A key factor to emerge from the research is that different students learn in different ways and use different learning strategies. (Marton and Saljo, 1976; Pask, 1976). Whether these strategies are related to personality characteristics, to ingrained habits, or to expectations about what the student thinks is required, is the subject of much debate (Laurillard, 1979). Whatever the reason, it is clear that different students approach the same learning task in different ways. This throws doubt on the effectiveness of mass methods of teaching, such as lectures, which appear to expect all individuals to learn in the same way.

The basic assumptions that underlie a student-centred approach emanate from ideas about human growth, the psychology of learning, adult learning, the importance of experience and co-operative working. In all these the emphasis is upon the process of learning, the learner and the learning group, rather than upon the teacher and the subject. The influence of humanistic psychology is often apparent – particularly the work of Carl Rogers and Abraham Maslow and their concern with human potential and self-actualization.

As with subject-centredness, there are stereotypes that depict the approach and the attitudes that underpin it. Jenkins (1975), Davies (1976) and Beard and Hartley (1984) draw the distinction between the classical and romantic traditions. The classical tradition is based upon a pedagogy that is subject-centred and geared towards the certainty of knowledge; it is autocratic, conservative, teacher-dominated, competitive, and formally examined. The romantic tradition stresses individualized learning, inner-directedness, uncertainty, discovery, and co-operation. Assessment is related more to the learner's progress than to formally applied criteria and standards derived from the subject.

A similar set of ideas stems from the notion of 'androgogy' (the education of adults), as distinct from 'pedagogy' (the education of children). The claim is that adult thinking can be extended beyond formal operational processes related to a set body of knowledge, to a new stage at which learners become aware of their potential to originate their own thinking and feeling. Adults are more likely to learn if their motivation stems from a perceived learning need. Once established, this motivation will draw upon a student's ability to be self-directed. The most appropriate learning opportunities will be those in which learners are encouraged to tap their own experience and to reflect upon it. Knowles (1978) refers to androgogy as a process model, as opposed to the content model implied by subject-centredness.

Another approach to the learning process stresses the need for co-operation. Students can learn a great deal from each other. Collier (1985) notes that:

> the major fresh developments in academic discussion techniques have shown an increased concern with the emergence of the learner from dependence on his teachers and his taking responsibility for his own progress. This has been associated with a belief that close collaboration between students could promote such independence of thinking. (Collier, 1985, p. 7).

These ideas suggest a shift from the traditional notion of the student as a passive learner. Their adoption by a few teachers has led to some interesting developments, which are described later. In theory, they open up various possibilities for new relationships between teacher and taught. They call for less emphasis on content and upon the authority of the teacher that is derived from it. Courses or programmes of work could be jointly planned by teacher and student (through learning contracts and independent study programmes). Teaching would tend to focus upon activities involving discussion and critical appraisal (through peer group learning, seminars, tutorials and discursive essays); self-generated inquiry (through projects, field work and creative design); the conscious incorporation of experience into the learning process (through experiential learning, reflection and autobiography).

Research into the way students learn has not only stimulated but has also had a modifying effect upon a growing field of interest for academics and researchers alike – 'study skills' and 'learning to learn'. If students learn differently, then efforts to improve their ability to learn cannot proceed on the basis of uniform or stan-dardized techniques. Techniques to promote faster reading, better note-taking, improved writing skills, etc., will have no more than a marginal effect upon a student's ability to learn. More important, learning to learn involves students in reflecting upon their own motivation and approaches to study in order to understand and perhaps modify the way they approach educational activities.

Where does this all lead in terms of actual changes in institutions of higher education and the courses that they offer? Although most students in higher education are undergraduates, there is also a sizeable percentage of postgraduates (about 13 per cent) and, in their case, there is a greater chance that their programme will be directed along androgogic rather than pedagogic lines.

For instance, a PhD student, well adjusted to his or her role, would not feel uncomfortable discussing with a supervisor the focus and aims of the proposed research, the nature of the key research questions and the methodology needed to pursue them, and plans for a programme of action and its execution, sometimes alone and sometimes as part of a team. Nor would such a student baulk at the idea of presenting a research paper to a group, explaining the findings and defending the conclusions, challenging the views of 'experts' but also accepting criticism and rethinking ideas as a result.

Such a programme of study is to a large extent student-centred and is based implicitly on many of the ideas suggested above. But does such autonomy in learning extend to the undergraduate level? A single example will provide the flavour of a course that is built upon the principles of student-centredness.

The School for Independent Study at the North East London Polytechnic was created in 1974 and has since provided study facilities for more than a thousand students. Stephenson (1981) reports on the scheme as follows. The school has no predetermined syllabus, but instead aims to provide opportunities for students to:

1   formulate the problems of their own education and nego-tiate their own appropriate programme of study;
2   expose their proposals to rigorous external scrutiny prior to obtaining approval for their programme of study;
3   gain access to appropriate tutorial expertise and resources;
4   demonstrate their achievements;
5   gain public recognition for their work.

Stephenson stresses the importance of the planning process, which takes the whole of the first term, and argues that this not only ensures high commitment but is in itself a valuable educational experience. It results in a learning contract agreed between the student and the School, which sets out the student's intentions, the knowledge, skills and experience required, the proposed programme of study and the form of assessment that will be needed to demonstrate completion.

There is in this process a radical departure from the traditional, subject-dominated programme outlined earlier. A number of institutions have since provided similar opportunities; many courses go part of the way, encouraging students to make at least some of their own decisions about what to study and how to study it.

At another level, the domination of the subject and the teacher are reduced, permitting students a greater say in the direction of their learning. Collier (1985) describes the experience of syndicate work in several institutions. A large group is divided into smaller groups of four to eight students (syndicates) for all or part of a course. Assignments are carried out on a co-operative basis by the syndicates, working as teams, for much of the time in the absence of the tutor. Collier points to some of the benefits noted by those who have tried this approach. There is intensive debate within syndicates. There is a heightened motivation, increased satisfaction from the work, an active search for information, wide reading in the field of study, and the development of higher-order learning and research skills. The approach fits well with the student-centred ideals referred to earlier and incorporates many of the principles espoused by eductional researchers regarding motivation and co-operation.

Interesting innovations have extended beyond the teaching and learning process to ways and means of assessing students. The intentions have generally been to link assessment as closely as possible to the learning process, to stimulate learning by providing regular and relevant feedback to students throughout their studies, and to provide some opportunity for them to decide for themselves which forms are likely best to suit their particular needs.

Some schemes have, for instance, allowed students to read examination papers some hours before the formal examination time; others have permitted papers to be taken away and worked upon over several days. But the greatest change has come about as traditional examinations have either been abandoned or reduced to a less significant role in the overall scheme. This has encouraged what is often (wrongly) called continuous assessment. Such schemes provide for regular, but not continuous testing of student performance, sometimes over a three- or four-year period, and allow marks to be accumulated. They would thus incorporate marks gained for writing essays or dissertations, for project work, field work or laboratory work, and in some cases for practice in vocational situations.

A few schemes have moved still further away from traditional unseen examinations and allowed students some say in their own assessment. This may take the form of prior negotiation, in which the student agrees with supervisors how he or she will be assessed on certain learning tasks. Sometimes, also, students are encouraged to mark their own work and to negotiate a grade with their tutors.

Finally, the idea of a profile rather than, or in addition to, a final degree classification has been suggested (Klug, 1977). Such a profile would contain much more detail about a student's work and indicate progress and achievements in a range of areas. This approach has been tried in a limited number of courses.

To summarize, the idea of student-centredness in learning is an important influence for change away from the subject/teacher dominated stereotype described earlier. It is supported by a philosophy of education that places students and their needs before the demands of the subject. It recognizes that adults have different needs and motivations from those of younger learners. Empirical research into the psychology of learning adds further weight to student-centredness, stressing how different learners respond to differing approaches to or styles of learning. Several interesting and important changes have taken place in this direction and have proved themselves to be popular with both staff and students.

CONCLUSIONS

Some observers remain critical about the nature and quality of teaching in higher education:

> it is assumed that giving students information through 'telling' is an effective method of helping them learn ... Acceptance of such a view entails the belief that education is primarily a process of accumulating information which is then stored for use later. Several decades of research on learning have made little impact in changing this view despite the evidence produced ... that it is incorrect. (Stanton, 1978, p. 6)

In other words, the subject/teacher centred approach still prevails. The Group for Research and Innovation in Higher Education, to

193

which reference was made earlier, found a number of interesting developments but observed that 'change is noticeable but far from substantial'. The group offered the following explanation:

> We have already commented that academics do not, by and large, naturally engage in discussion of their teaching, or of any new curricular ideas they have in mind. The lone innovator was a common phenomenon we encountered during our visits. His isolation is reinforced both by the way in which many departments are organised and by the traditions of privacy which pervade attitudes to teaching. Lone innovators are often found in large departments, where, with more money, personnel and space available, there is sometimes more scope to experiment in teaching without all eyes being on the experimenter. This isolation has the advantage that failures are not necessarily blown up out of proportion, but the concomitant disadvantage that others do not learn from the experience. (GRIHE, 1975, p. 46).

There is another important reason why the status quo has been preserved. For a decade following the Robbins Report (Committee on Higher Education, 1963), the number of students in higher education grew rapidly and resources were increased to provide for this. New universities and polytechnics were built and new departments created: the way looked set for further growth. However, by the mid 1970s the trend had been slowed down and a period of economizing began, in which the amount of money made available to institutions was progressively cut back. The way this was done, the uncertainty surrounding the exercise and the overall effect upon universities, polytechnics and colleges has been discussed in earlier chapters. Here we are concerned specifically with the effects that retrenchment has had upon teaching, learning and assessment.

For most departments there was a general concern for standards and a growing feeling of pressure, but generally the cuts were absorbed by the system and very little changed: teachers worked that bit harder. However, new and possibly more demanding teaching methods became even less attractive than before. In the University of Sussex, for instance, one subject group – which, against the normal practice in universities, had mainly taught students in groups of five – appointed a working party to consider how savings might be made. A number of options were proposed, which included some lecturing and some seminar groups of 10 or 20 students. A decision was made to adopt each of these options for a trial period, and this led eventually to a shift from predominantly tutorial teaching to a mixture of large, medium and small group teaching.

But savings are not necessarily always concerned with increasing the size of groups. Elton (1983) describes attempts made in one university to increase the cost-effectiveness of laboratory teaching. Lecturers and educational researchers analysed the aims of first-year courses and the work patterns of students, and introduced a number of changes. 'Walk-in laboratories' were created in which students, using self-instructional materials, could carry out appropriate laboratory exercises in their own time and without the assistance of supervisory staff. In addition, parts of the course which integrated theory and practice were taught in a 'learning centre' where practical work was carried out without the need for expensive laboratory facilities. The content of the courses was also critically examined and it was found that in certain areas the syllabus, including laboratory work, could be reduced. It was shown that all these changes could result in improvements in cost-effectiveness – but the ideas were not taken up widely.

A general deterioration in staff:student ratios has also led to a number of experiments in which students have been encouraged to teach themselves. Many of the ideas that have been tried were developed in better times and for other reasons, but the pressure on resources had led to a renewed interest in their use. The syndicate groups mentioned earlier (Collier, 1985), for instance, although designed to foster co-operative learning, nevertheless offer structured learning experiences for students without the regular presence of a teacher. Other innovations in self-directed learning have arisen from the development of learning materials that enable students to work on their own or in groups through pre-set learning sequences. This approach was pioneered by the Open University, but the ideas became sufficiently widespread for the Council for National Academic Awards to set up a working party to advise colleges and polytechnics on the conditions necessary for the most effective use of resource-based learning. (CNAA, 1981).

In general, though, subject domination of the teaching process has survived the various pressures. Larger groups are regarded as more cost-effective than smaller ones. Schemes that allow greater choice and flexibility for students or attempt to combine separate disciplines in a creative way are ruled out as more costly than no-choice, single-subject programmes.

Willis (1983) suggests that the potential for change is undermined by the fact that the central units in universities and polytechnics that are meant to provide impetus and advice on educational technology have themselves been eroded by the financial pressures. He notes:

> The base upon which an innovative restructuring of the teaching methods and institutional structures of higher education might be built is being eroded before any attempt has been made to analyse ways in which new technology can be used to support radical change. (Willis, 1983, p. 113).

Willis also considers that the use of the new media still meets considerable resistance from teachers. To realize the potential of educational technology, new attitudes on the part of institutions and their staff will be necessary, and this seems unlikely in the present climate.

For the present, then, the subject-centred approach persists as the major influence on teaching and learning in higher education. But changes are taking place. Sometimes they are brought about when problems rather than subjects are given greater prominence in the process. Sometimes student-centred approaches, based upon the view that students can and should be given greater responsibility for their own learning, are introduced. Some changes have been stimulated by the creative use of educational technology. Further impetus for change might occur if, as seems possible, staff development programmes are introduced that help to promote new approaches to teaching and learning. What exists now, therefore, is a mixture – but a mixture that offers scope for discerning students to choose courses that provide, for them as individuals, interesting and appropriate learning experiences.

10

Conclusion

TONY BECHER

A BRIEF OVERVIEW

Every reader will have formed his or her own impressions of the accounts given in this book of different aspects of British higher education. Nevertheless, it may be useful in conclusion to draw together some of the salient points in each chapter, and to speculate on some of the considerations that may lie behind the working procedures of the system as a whole.

One of the issues that comes out most clearly is first pinpointed by Stuart Maclure in Chapter 2 – namely central government's heightened involvement in higher education policy during the past two decades. A large part of the explanation, as Maclure argues, derives from the spectacular rise in the costs of the system as a whole that followed the acceptance of the Robbins Committee's proposals for expansion – a problem that was exacerbated by the growing dependence (dating from prewar times) of higher education institutions on public funds. One aspect of the attempt to keep down government expenditure relates to student maintenance and tuition fees – a topic that is widely debated enough to need no further elaboration here. Chapter 2 also helps to underline the fact that government interest in higher education is not purely financial and, in particular, that the concern (in the ungainly jargon of manpower planning) to increase the output of qualified scientific manpower is of very long standing, even if it has so far met with little success. In this and other ways, Maclure suggests, the politicization (and consequent bureaucratization) of the higher education system has increased, is increasing, and must be presumed to increase still further.

The questions of management of the system, of changes in the role of the University Grants Committee in relation to the university sector, of the functions of the National Advisory Body in relation to the public sector, and of a possible unification of the two sectors, are touched on in Chapter 2 but are examined in greater detail in Chapters 3 and 4. In Chapter 3, John Farrant begins by exploring the constitutional rights of universities, as expressed in their Charters and Statutes, and the formal controls imposed by their Courts, Councils and Visitors. The main source of control, however – as exercised by the University Grants Committee and in lesser part by the research councils – is financial. Farrant points out that the universities have also voluntarily given up a measure of their independence to bodies that serve their collective interests, such as the Committee of Vice-Chancellors and Principals. Although some important areas of autonomy remain, a number – such as academics' rights to tenure of appointment – are under threat; the management structure of universities and their machinery for safeguarding standards have in recent years been externally determined; the balance between teaching and research is subject to outside constraint; even the subjects taught and the shape of future developments are matters for detailed negotiation with the UGC, which acts as an agency of the state. In the name of greater accountability, traditional freedoms have been eroded.

Nigel Nixon raises an interestingly different set of issues, reflecting some of the underlying contrasts between the autonomous and public sectors. Chapter 4 concentrates on the evolution of the polytechnics and colleges in the period following Anthony Crosland's Woolwich Speech in 1965 (which announced the government's plans to establish a dual pattern of universities on the one hand, and institutions 'under social control' on the other). Nixon's focus, like Farrant's, is on forms of control and accountability and their relationship to institutional freedom. He shows how successive attempts to achieve a satisfactory balance between them during the last two decades have continued to stumble over the contradictions inherent in the system. There are two strands to the argument, the first quantitative (relating to methods of allocating finance and controlling expenditure) and the second qualitative (relating to the maintenance of both academic standards and the validity of degree qualifications). Although not independent, they were largely treated as such until the establishment of the National Advisory Body. Nixon questions whether the connections should be further tightened by merging NAB with the main agency responsible for public sector quality control, the Council for National Academic Awards. In such a situation, NAB would presumably find itself in a situation similar to that of the UGC (as described in Chapter 3), in having to try to relate funding levels to a centralized assessment of academic worth: a notoriously tricky task, involving value-laden rankings within individual fields or disciplines and inherently questionable comparisons between one field or discipline and another. Nixon also notes the scope for mergers between individual institutions on opposite sides of the 'binary line', and the need for improved co-ordination, at the national level, between NAB and the UGC. Behind all this lies the idea of moving towards a unitary structure for higher education as a whole, reverting from the ideology of Crosland to the ideology of Robbins. Although that idea would commend itself to a number of people in the academic profession, it is likely to be seen by politicians and civil servants as a costly scheme with little in the public interest to commend it.

The changes at the level of national government and the central authorities are, as Chapters 5 and 6 show, reflected in the external demands made on individual institutions and their responses to such demands. Geoffrey Lockwood's account of university management in the 1980s rests on the twin notions of independence and competitiveness. Both enhance the proper individuality of the universities' roles and their internal structures – though there are common characteristics to be found as well, not least complexity and diffusion of responsibility. Management itself is, in Lockwood's metaphor, 'the skin on the drum: there to ... absorb the external pressure, protect the instrument and enable it to perform'. Part of its responsibility must be to ensure that the internal structures are adapted to cope with the growing burdens of expectation placed on them (creating new sources of funds, adjusting to changes in student requirements, incorporating new technologies, and so on). In this context, Lockwood discusses the recommendations of the Jarratt Committee on Efficiency Studies in Universities, which have sought to introduce a stronger sense of managerialism by giving Vice-Chancellors more executive power; urging (lay-dominated) University Councils to 'assert their responsibilities'; establishing small planning and resource committees; initiating budget delegation; developing performance indicators; introducing staff development, appraisal and accountability; and so on. The adoption of such recommendations – which would have seemed unthinkable a decade ago – is itself a measure of how far the earlier prevailing assumptions and practices within universities have been chipped away by a succession of financial and political hammer blows. But Lockwood remains optimistic, provided that universities are able to maintain (and where possible enhance) the quality of their leadership, their strategic planning, their institutional flexibility and their professional administration.

British Higher Education

In Chapter 6, Stephen Jones and George Kiloh, like Nigel Nixon, adopt a historical perspective for their review of the management of polytechnics and colleges, tracing the development of institutional frameworks from the early 1960s, when they were almost totally under local authority control, through the period of decolonization following the Robbins and Weaver Reports, to a level of autonomy that still falls well short of that enjoyed by the universities. The roles of the Governors, Director and Academic Board are seen as contrasting with their university counterparts mainly in terms of the continuing accountability to (and degree of interference exercised by) the local authorities. The pattern of administration and the functioning committees also clearly reflect the traditions of local authority control. Centralism is exacerbated by impossibly short budgetary horizons. The gulf between decisions about resources and decisions about academic quality is experienced as keenly at the institutional as at the national level. The main similarity of public sector institutions with the universities is seen in their need, in a period of contraction, to 'live with two conflicting cultures': that of an academic community, and that of a corporation able to implement hard decisions about how to cope with cuts. Jones and Kiloh end by outlining the case for preserving the distinctive characteristics of public sector higher education (especially their wide range of provision for students without conventional entry qualifications), and the need to encourage greater institutional autonomy and greater departmental commitment to this end.

Chapter 7 explores a less well-documented aspect of higher education, namely the part played in it by individual academics and the institutional and extra-institutional groupings to which they belong. It discusses some of the differences within and between different subject fields and the consequent possibilities of career choice and career mobility. A key motivating factor, it is argued, is scholarly reputation; the usual means of acquiring this is recognition by one's academic peers of high performance in research. From this viewpoint, the academic can be seen as a one-man business, dealing in intellectual property. However, by no means all academics stay active in research – the main alternatives are scholarship, teaching and administration. The chapter also notes an interplay between individuals and institutions, in that the research reputation of the one enhances that of the other, and vice versa. The relationships between individual academics and their departments or other basic units (like that between units and institutions) nevertheless remain loose, because of their specialized knowledge and their affiliations with independent external reference groups. Attempts to introduce greater managerial control are subject to the inherent unpredictability of student recruitment patterns and graduate employment opportunities, not to mention the outcomes of research. Existing incentive systems and accountability procedures would seem to allow for quite rapid responses to new needs. On this analysis, academic freedom has to be seen as functional rather than merely indulgent: to curtail it in the interests of good national housekeeping could serve to make British higher education as sterile and lifeless as a well-managed morgue.

It was stated in the introductory chapter that the clients of higher education – the students – figure only indirectly in this conspectus of the system. However, the provision that is made for them, in terms of curricular patterns, teaching and learning activities and forms of assessment, constitutes the theme of Chapters 8 and 9. Geoffrey Squires charts some national, sectoral and institutional variations in the undergraduate curriculum (for instance, the different forms of breadth of traditional Scottish degrees, of many public sector programmes, and of the Keele degree course with its unique foundation year), and draws out the distinctions between professional, academic and general courses. The main part of his discussion is given to an exploration of a number of key curricular problems, including those relating to interdisciplinary degrees, the notion of 'the trained mind', the difficult relationship in professional degrees between theory and practice, and the limitations imposed by modular courses. Squires' comments on policy hark back to Stuart Maclure's remarks in Chapter 2 about higher education and the economy, particularly in relation to the need to ensure that 'all graduates have a range of useful competencies'. His own preference would be for a broad and reflective curricular programme. He is, however, dubious about the viability of liberal education in its traditional form, and sees the increasing specialization and professionalization of degree courses as an undermining of the 'defences against overly instrumental views of higher education'.

In his discussion of teaching, learning and assessment in Chapter 9, Eric Hewton begins by reviewing the established sequence of subject-centred teaching: 'subject to teacher to content to lecture to learner.' Within this tradition, the subject itself acts as a socializing agency and imposes a control on the transmission and assessment of knowledge, attitudes and values. Although subject-centredness remains, in Hewton's view, the predominant approach, he identifies three significant departures from it. The first, problem-centred learning, calls for the incorporation into the undergraduate programme of 'real-life' problems, social action schemes, project work and the like. The second, educational technology, ranges from the design of learning systems (generally seen as over-ambitious) and distance learning techniques (pioneered by the Open University) to the use of computers and audiovisual equipment as aids to teaching and learning. The third, and perhaps most far-reaching, is student-centredness, which acknowledges individual differences, sees learning as a process of discovery, emphasises the autonomy of the learner, eschews competition and promotes co-operation. In effect, this means bringing down to the undergraduate level ideas that already obtain in large measure in postgraduate education. Related innovations include self-assessment or negotiated grading and the use of student profiles. New approaches along these lines are being adopted only slowly, Hewton argues, partly because of financial cut-backs and increased pressures on teaching staff, but also partly as a result of conservative attitudes towards teaching. None the less, the pattern of change here is 'significant, if sporadic'.

MEANS AND ENDS

The picture that emerges from these accounts of different aspects and levels of higher education is a complex one – not unexpectedly so, because the system itself is complex. But its various elements can (at the risk of over-simplification) be seen as interconnected in terms of the aims they espouse. In attempting to make the connections, I shall identify some of the key values and purposes that operate at given levels in the system, and also remark on certain of the means used to pursue them.

If we begin at the level of the individual, it can be argued that one of the ends pursued by students is to achieve a degree award of acceptable – if not excellent – quality: an outcome of the undergraduate course that serves both as a potential meal-ticket and as an acknowledgement of intellectual achievement while at college. The attainment of this end rests on marks for examinations and other assessed pieces of work (coursework essays, project reports and the like). Marks therefore become a major item of currency, playing a significant part in the strategies that students adopt – for example, activities that carry no marks are, like unpaid labour, relatively unattractive. Academic staff have different priorities. For them, as was noted in Chapter 7, reputation is the prime goal. Its attainment comes most commonly through prowess in research, and that in turn crucially depends on finding an adequate balance against the competing demands of teaching, administration and committee work. One might say, then, that the path to academic success starts from the successful management of time.

Basic units, also, regard academic reputation as being among their prime concerns – although here, the reputation is a collective one, closely bound up with the standing of their constituent members. It is not easy to achieve directly, since so much depends upon the more or less random comings and goings of individual academics. However, budgetary and political viability within the institution are prerequisites of effective research, and such viability is closely bound up with student recruitment. A department or other basic unit that is able to enrol students with good entry qualifications in adequate (but not excessive) numbers is thereby well placed to gain institutional support for the research requirements of its staff, and so further to enhance its prestige.

At the institutional level, the concern with reputation, which is a predominant value of individual academics and basic units, becomes generalized in the form of sustaining a good public image. The reference group goes wider here than the 'invisible colleges' of fellow-specialists to include potential applicants (and their parents), careers advisers in schools, actual and potential employers of graduates, and not least politicians and the press. This reputational goal again cannot be achieved directly, since it too depends on what the staffing profile happens to be like at any given time. However, most institutions put a premium on achieving a balance of subject specialisms, which between them can offset the vagaries of student recruitment, staff employment and the market for research funding. One might describe this strategy as developing a good investment portfolio.

The central agencies share the general emphasis, which runs through the other levels of the system, on maintaining standards of academic performance – though they are also taken up with issues of public credibility for the sector with which they are concerned. Their means of sustaining quality and continued governmental sponsorship lie in the effective deployment of the human and financial resources that are available – a job that (as Chapters 3 and 4 make plain) is more easily described than done.

Finally, government itself has to regard the system as a whole from an outside perspective, seeking to bring about the best negotiable match between institutional purposes and the social demands imposed by the polity at large. Its main instrument in achieving this goal is the blunt one of finance: blunt not only because higher education has to compete with other elements in the education service, and with many other calls on the public purse, so that its share may be inadequate for its needs, but also because whatever budget is allocated is then successively devolved to a level at which the original public purpose can become altogether lost to sight. The frustration resulting from this lack of direct managerial control has led, as Chapter 2 has suggested, to an increasing degree of detailed involvement of government in the affairs of universities, polytechnics and colleges.

What tends to be overlooked, in the concerns of ministers and mandarins to ensure that academic institutions and academics themselves are properly responsive to national needs, is that the system has a number of built-in mechanisms that help to promote this. No academic department, for example, that fails to attract students or that has a poor graduate employment record can expect to have a good prospect of survival. Few institutions will overlook the competitive opportunities afforded by the opening of a new market, whether this be in teaching or research. And, as we have seen, the individual academic is under steady peer group pressure to produce work of sufficiently good quality to enhance his or her standing – and hence that of the subject, the department, the institution, and ultimately of the system as a whole. Professional accountability, it can fairly be said, is endemic: so is a concern with the maintenance and improvement of standards.

CONTINUITY AND CHANGE

Two considerations need to be borne in mind by those who wish to advocate far-reaching changes in higher education. The first has already been underlined: namely, that there is a strong premium on the development of a professional reputation, which runs through virtually every level in the system and serves as an effective if informal means of quality control. It is important for outsiders to have some appreciation of this mechanism, lest it may need to be protected against over-zealous reform: for the values behind it lie at the heart of the academic enterprise.

The constant competitive pressure, taken together with the fact that academics are, almost by definition, intelligent people (even if their intelligence is limited in a particular direction), means that on the whole the system works well. The practices and procedures that have evolved over time, especially at the level of departments and other basic units, are ones that reasonably match the demands of the job.

The second consideration relates to those features of an

academic's life that involve frequent changes – and in particular students and subjects. The impact of an annual exodus of roughly one-third of each institution's population, together with a corresponding influx of new inhabitants, is a significant part of the context of higher education. It presents fresh challenges and brings in novel ideas in a steady flow, militating against stagnation and complacency. Academic disciplines are, in their turn, in a constant state of development. The larger the national and international research community becomes, the more rapidly the world of academic knowledge grows. New theories and new interpretations are advanced; new sub-specialisms emerge; new fields of enquiry hive off from the old. Those concerned to enhance their research reputations cannot afford to ignore the fruits of this activity; no more can those who take a pride in their scholarship, or those whose teaching requires them to keep abreast of current trends. It is perhaps understandable that, in relation to other aspects of their lives, academics hanker after some stability. They do not in general seem enthusiastic for institutional reform, or for changes at the level of the system as a whole – perhaps because they see them as irrelevant (as well, quite often, as potentially threatening).

If these arguments are valid, it would seem to follow that there is little need and even less scope for external involvement in the affairs of academic institutions and their constituent elements. This conclusion sounds suspiciously like the response of any and every professional group that finds itself under public scrutiny: 'our affairs are in good order, thank you – and even if they were not, we would be perfectly capable of putting them to rights ourselves'. It would be going much too far to suggest that higher education ought to be immune from outside criticism or from any form of governmental action. However, in the light of the explanation that this book has attempted to give of how the system works, some issues would seem to be more in need of attention than others, and some forms of intervention more productive than the rest.

Looking at some of the lessons of previous experience, it has been argued (Becher and Kogan, 1980) that successful changes in the structure of higher education – as well as in its primary processes of teaching and research – seem generally to depend on going with the grain. That is to say, those seeking to promote new values and to embody them in new practices had best avoid a direct challenge to the existing norms of the academic profession: indeed, they should in some aspects seek to reinforce them. It has in any case to be remembered that reforms in managerial structures can permit but will seldom generate changes in practice. Orders from higher

205

authority are generally capable of being ignored. Academics share with other professionals the resilience afforded by their expertise, which no lay outsider is in a position to gainsay. Would-be reformers may do well, therefore, by setting out to understand the perspectives of those whose ways they seek to mend, so that they can enlist their support rather than try to crush their resistance.

SOME ISSUES FOR CONSIDERATION

The various contributors to this book have, between them, highlighted a number of issues calling for change. Two such issues may deserve a further mention here. The first is the inadequate recognition afforded within the system to excellence in teaching, as opposed to research; the second is the apparent distancing of institutions of higher education from the outside world in general, and their own local and regional communities in particular.

It is not generally contested within academia that teaching capability remains too little recognized and rewarded. One reason commonly advanced is that the quality of a teacher is hard to assess, not only because teaching is a largely private activity but also because it lacks the tangible products of research and consultancy; another is that nearly all teaching is localized in its effects and implications, and hence cannot achieve the national and international visibility of significant research findings. Be that as it may, the very strong premium placed on research activity makes it difficult for the more ambitious and capable academics to give full weight to the demands of their students, and leaves without any comparable career rewards those who have opted to devote their main efforts to undergraduate teaching. As Chapter 9 indicated, the lack of any systematic training of academics for their teaching duties – as compared with a long initiation into research – perpetuates the view of a secondary and somewhat amateur activity. It also serves to play down the significance of innovations in curricula and teaching and learning methods, and thus limits the pace and extent of pedagogic change. But new developments herald a possible shift in values. As and when academic salary scales are more directly related to the assessment of professional capability, competence in teaching – however it may be judged – is likely to be given greater weight, and academics themselves are likely to demand the means and opportunity, through suitable training, to enhance that competence. A reform along these lines is unlikely to jeopardize the prime position accorded to research, but it could help redress the balance to some extent, and give good teaching a fairer degree of recognition than it currently enjoys.

Turning now to the second issue, the charge of remoteness is a long-standing one, and is not lacking in justification (indeed, the very existence of this book, as an attempt to make more plain what happens in British higher education, serves to underline the point). The plea that the universities, polytechnics and colleges have many better things to do than cultivate public understanding and appro-bation becomes increasingly difficult to sustain. The taxpayers – and the politicians who represent them – do not seem nowadays to consider that they automatically owe the academic world a living. As a sizeable consumer of public funds, the higher education system cannot reasonably contest a demand for accountability; one way to meet it is to become more accessible, more open to scrutiny, and less aloof in attitude. Changes along these lines have already begun to take place, as the writing on the wall has become harder to ignore: but there remains a fair way to go before academic institutions are as responsive as many primary and secondary schools are to the wider public interest.

ENVOI

It is no matter for debate that British higher education (among, inci-dentally, its counterparts in several other countries) enjoys less poli-tical confidence and less public esteem than it did twenty years ago. The reasons are various, but must include the student troubles of the late 1960s (which, although a worldwide phenomenon, appeared to make a particular impact in Britain); the continuing – and frequently reported – pattern of unrest in a few universities and polytechnics; and the seeming arrogance of senior university management in refusing to respond to governmental proposals for reform in 1969 (labelled at the time as Shirley Williams' Thirteen Points). The media, as is their prerogative, have given fairly generous publicity to what has gone wrong, but have not regarded the positive features of the system as newsworthy enough to mention. Even the now fairly sizeable body of fiction written by insiders about college life, with Kingsley Amis' *Lucky Jim* as its unforgettable prototype, generally portrays the academic world as peopled with amiable rogues and colourful eccentrics (or even, as in Malcolm Bradbury's *The History Man*, rogues who are not particularly amiable).

The effects of the largely unfavourable press that higher education has experienced have been complemented (as noted above) by the failure of universities, polytechnics and colleges themselves to encourage a general awareness of their aims and what they are doing to meet them. A greater openness to view would seem particularly important during a period of frequent and substantial upheaval, encompassing not only significant advances in knowledge on several fronts but also major structural reforms initiated from the outside and very substantial shifts in market conditions (in terms of both student recruitment and graduate employment). The nature of higher education, as the previous chapters have attempted to show, is markedly different from what it was at the starting-point of massive expansion two decades ago. By no means all the changes have been for the worse, though it is generally the negative effects that have caught the attention of those outside the academic world.

Following this line of argument, the undervaluing of higher education can be seen as the joint product of a persistently negative image and an apparent lack of responsiveness by academic institutions to outside concerns. One way of preventing the two factors from feeding off each other must be to explain, to a wider public, what the enterprise is actually about. As Burton Clark has contended, 'a sector is taken seriously when we seek its own ways of dividing work, promoting belief, and distributing authority, its own ways of changing and its own conflict of values' (Clark, 1983b, p. 276). To understand the ways of academic life is, one might hope, to become more appreciative of its concerns and more sensitive to its needs. Certainly, many of the external demands that have been made on universities, polytechnics and colleges in recent years would appear to have stemmed from an inadequate awareness of what they can and cannot reasonably be expected to do.

The attempt to show what the academic world looks like to those within it, and hence to create a more enlightened perception among those outside of what it stands for, has formed an important part of the rationale for this book. If readers – both those who are already involved in one way or another with higher education and those who are not – come away better informed about the system than they were before they read it, then, as was remarked in the introductory chapter, one of its main objectives will have been achieved.

Contributors

Tony Becher is Professor of Education at the University of Sussex. He served for some years on the editorial staff of Cambridge University Press while teaching philosophy at Cambridge, and was subsequently Assistant Director of the Nuffield Foundation with special responsibility for its educational programme. Between 1970 and 1975 he was Director of the Nuffield Higher Education Group. He has served on a number of national bodies concerned with higher education, including the Educational Research Board of the SSRC, the Committee on the Training of University Teachers of the CVCP, and the Council for the Accreditation of Teacher Education. He edited *Studies in Higher Education* between 1975 and 1979. His principal publications include: (with Jack Embling and Maurice Kogan) *Systems of Higher Education – United Kingdom*, 1978; (with Stuart Maclure) *The Politics of Curriculum Change*, 1978, and *Accountability in Education*, 1979; (with Maurice Kogan), *Process and Structure in Higher Education*, 1980.

John Farrant is Planning Officer at the University of Sussex. After reading history at Oxford and working for a brief spell in local government, he has held various posts in the University of Sussex administration since 1968. In 1984 he was seconded to the University Grants Committee's secretariat to assist in preparing the Committee's advice on 'A strategy for higher education into the 1990s'. He has acted as consultant to the University of Malawi and to the Eastern and Southern African Universities Research Project. He has a particular interest in statistics on higher education and their utility for planning purposes, as reflected in his paper for the Leverhulme Study on student access and demand, and his membership of the UCCA Statistics Committee.

Eric Hewton is Reader in Education at the University of Sussex. After extensive experience in commerce he spent some time as a member of the Nuffield Higher Education Group. He has been a member of various national bodies concerned with higher education, including the CNAA, SRHE and UCET. He has a particular interest in student learning and has for some years worked with groups of students concerned to improve their study skills. His principal publications include *Re-Thinking Educational Change*, 1982, *Education in Recession*, 1986; and various journal articles on student learning, assessment and staff development.

Stephen Jones was, until December 1985, Assistant Provost at the City of London Polytechnic. In the late 1960s and early 1970s he held posts in the Ministry of Defence and the Foreign and Commonwealth Office, and from 1973 worked in the Department of Education and Science (where, in 1977 and 1978, he was Private Secretary to Shirley Williams, the then Secretary of State). Apart from a spell at the University Grants Committee, his other posts at DES were concerned with policy and finance in public sector higher education. Since January 1986 he has been attached to HM Inspectorate as Staff Inspector, Higher Education, although it is not in this capacity that he contributes to this book. His career has brought him into contact with most of the major national bodies in public sector higher education, including the National Advisory Body, the Council for National Academic Awards, the Committee of Directors of Polytechnics, and the National Association of Teachers in Further and Higher Education. He has contributed to conferences on issues of general policy as well as of institutional management.

George Kiloh is a professional administrator in the higher education sector. He is currently Academic Secretary of the City of London Polytechnic. He has also worked at the University of Sussex, the Open University and Canberra College of Advanced Education. He serves on a number of bodies concerned with public sector higher education and student admissions.

Geoffrey Lockwood graduated at the London School of Economics in 1959. Since then he has spent twenty-seven years as a professional university administrator, initially at the University of Manchester and then at the University of Sussex, which he joined before its formal foundation. He has published extensively on university planning and management, is an international consultant in that field, and teaches that subject (mainly to university administrators in the UK and abroad, but also on Masters courses). He is active on a variety of relevant national bodies and was a member of the Jarratt Committee. His publications include (with J. L. Davies) *Universities: The Management Challenge*, 1985; (with J. Fielden)

Planning and Management in Universities, 1973; a number of OECD reports, and several articles.

Stuart Maclure has been editor of *The Times Educational Supplement* since 1969, having before that been editor of *Education* from 1954–69. He was awarded a CBE in 1982. In addition to occasional journalism and work for radio and television, his publications include: *Educational Documents: 1816 to the Present Day*, various editions 1965–85; *A Hundred Years of London Education*, 1970; (with Tony Becher) *The Politics of Curriculum Change*, 1978 and *Accountability in Education*, 1979; *Educational Development and School Building*, 1984.

Nigel Nixon is Assistant Registrar for Development Services at the Council for National Academic Awards. A modern linguist by background, he taught at the University of Paris in the late 1960s and subsequently (from 1971 until 1984) was Senior Lecturer in French and Linguistics at the City of London Polytechnic. While at the City of London Polytechnic he developed an interest in higher education policy-making and undertook postgraduate work at the University of London Institute of Education and subsequently at the University of Sussex.

Geoffrey Squires is a Lecturer in the Department of Adult and Continuing Education at the University of Hull. After taking degrees at Cambridge and Edinburgh, he worked in higher education in France and the United States before joining the Nuffield Higher Education Group from 1972–76, during which time he also taught at the University of Sussex. He participated in the Leverhulme Studies of higher education in the early 1980s, and has been a consultant to the OECD for ten years, contributing to reports on 16–19, higher and adult education. He was for some time reviews editor for *Studies in Higher Education* and is a consulting editor for *Studies in the Education of Adults*. His principal publications are *Innovation Through Recession*, 1983, and *The Curriculum Beyond School*, 1987.

List of abbreviations

ABRC	Advisory Board for Research Councils
AC	Audit Commission
AFE	Advanced further education
AFEC	Advanced Further Education Council
APT	Association of Polytechnic Teachers
AUT	Association of University Teachers
BE	Board of Education
BTEC	Business and Technician Education Council
CAE	Colleges of Advanced Education (in Australia)
CAG	Comptroller and Auditor General
CAT	College of Advanced Technology
CATS	Credit Accumulation and Transfer Scheme of CNAA
CBURC	Computer Board for Universities and Research Councils
CDP	Committee of Directors of Polytechnics
CERN	European Council for Nuclear Research
CHE	Committee on Higher Education
CIT	Cranfield Institute of Technology
CLEA	Council of Local Education Authorities
CNAA	Council for National Academic Awards
CONTACT	Consortium for Advanced Education and Training
CPRS	Central Policy Review Staff
CRAC	Careers Research and Advisory Centre
CSM	Committee on Scientific Manpower
CVCP	Committee of Vice-Chancellors and Principals of the Universities of the United Kingdom
DENI	Department of Education for Northern Ireland
DES	Department of Education and Science
DoE	Department of Employment
DSIR	Department of Scientific and Industrial Research
DTI	Department of Trade and Industry
EEC	European Economic Community
FE	Further education
FHE	Further and higher education
GCE	General Certificate of Education
GMP	Study Group on the Management of the AFE Pool
GRIHE	Nuffield Group for Research and Innovation in Higher Education
HE	Higher education

212

HMI	HM Inspectorate
ILEA	Inner London Education Authority
LA	Local authority
LEA	Local education authority
MoE	Ministry of Education
MSC	Manpower Services Commission
NAB	National Advisory Body
NAFE	Non-advanced further education
NATFHE	National Association of Teachers in Further and Higher Education
NCTA	National Council for Technological Awards
NEDC	National Economic Development Council
NFER	National Foundation for Education Research
NIESR	National Institute of Economic and Social Research
NUS	National Union of Students
OECD	Organization for Economic Co-operation and Development
ONC	Ordinary National Certificate
OU	The Open University
PSHE	Public sector of higher education
RAC	Regional Advisory Council
RCA	Royal College of Art
SCUE	Standing Conference on University Entrance
SED	Scottish Education Department
SRHE	Society for Research into Higher Education
SSR	Student–staff ratio
SSRC	Social Science Research Council
STEAC	Scottish Tertiary Education Advisory Council
TDG	Technical and Data Group of the National Advisory Body
THES	The Times Higher Education Supplement
UAP	Universities Authorities Panel
UCCA	Universities Central Council on Admissions
UCET	Universities Council for the Education of Teachers
UCNS	Universities Committee for Non-teaching Staffs
UGC	University Grants Committee
USR	Universities Statistical Record
VAT	Value added tax
WAB	Wales Advisory Board
WO	Welsh Office

References

Abercrombie, M. L. J. (1981), 'Changing basic assumptions about teaching and learning', in D. Boud (ed.), *Developing Student Autonomy in Learning* (London: Kogan Page).

ABRC and UGC (1982), *Report of a Joint Working Party on the Support of University Scientific Research*, Cmnd 8567 (London: HMSO).

Aitken, R. (1966), *The Administration of a University* (London: University of London Press).

Ashby, E. (1970), *Masters and Scholars* (London: Oxford University Press).

Ashby, E. (1974), *Adapting Universities to a Technological Society* (San Francisco: Jossey-Bass), p. 14.

Ashby, E. and Anderson, M. (1974), *Portrait of Haldane at Work on Education* (London: Macmillan).

Association of Polytechnic Teachers (1981), *Higher Education: Towards a More Rational System* (Portsmouth: APT).

Bailey, F. G. (1977), *Morality and Expediency: The Folklore of Academic Politics* (Oxford: Blackwell).

Balderston, F. E. (1974), *Managing Today's University* (San Francisco: Jossey-Bass).

Baldridge, J. V. (1971), *Power and Conflict in the University* (New York: Wiley).

Baldridge, J. V. *et al.* (1978), *Policy Making and Effective Leadership* (San Francisco: Jossey-Bass).

Barnett, C. (1986), *The Audit of War* (London: Macmillan).

Barnett, R., Becher, T. and Cork, M. (1987), 'Models of professional preparation', *Studies in Higher Education*, vol. 12, no. 1, pp. 51–63.

Baron, G. (1975), 'The changing political context of higher educational administration in England', in A. Ross Thomas, R. H. Farquhar and W. Taylor (eds), *Educational Administration in Australia and Abroad: Analyses and Challenges* (St Lucia: University of Queensland Press).

Beard, R. and Hartley, J. (1984), *Teaching and Learning in Higher Education* (London: Harper and Row).

Becher, T. (1981), 'Towards a definition of disciplinary cultures', *Studies in Higher Education*, vol. 6, no. 1, pp. 109–22.

Becher, T. (1984), 'The cultural view', in B. Clark (ed.), *Perspectives on Higher Education* (Berkeley, Calif.: University of California Press).

Becher, T. (1987), 'The disciplinary shaping of the profession', in B. R. Clark (ed.), *The Academic Profession* (Berkeley, Calif.: University of California Press).

Becher, T. and Kogan, M. (1980), *Process and Structure in Higher Education* (London: Heinemann).

Bell, R. (1971), 'The growth of the modern university', in R. Hooper (ed.), *The Curriculum* (Edinburgh: Oliver and Boyd).

Berdahl, R. O. (1959), *British Universities and the State* (Berkeley, Calif.: University of California Press).

Billing, D. (1974), *Notes for Guidance on the Design of Modular Courses* (London: Council for National Academic Awards).

Bligh, D. (ed.) (1982), *Professionalism and Flexibility in Learning* (Guildford: Society for Research into Higher Education).

Bocock, J. (1980), 'Union view', *The Times Higher Education Supplement*, 8 August 1980.

Bosworth, S. R. (1985), *National Negotiating Arrangements for University Staff* (np: CVCP Administrative Training Committee).

Bramer, M. (1984), 'New information technologies in teaching and learning', *Teaching News*, Newsletter of the Educational Development Advisory Committee, University of Birmingham, vol. 23, pp. 3–4.

Braybrooke, D. and Lindblom, C. E. (1963), *A Strategy of Decision* (New York: Free Press).

Brooks, G. E. and Rourke, F. E. (1966), *The Managerial Revolution in Higher Education* (Baltimore, Md: Johns Hopkins University Press).

Brosan, G. *et al.* (1971), *Patterns and Policies in Higher Education* (Harmondsworth: Penguin).

Brynmor Jones (1965), *Audio-Visual Aids in Higher Scientific Education*, UGC/DES report (London: HMSO).

Carswell, J. (1985), *Government and the Universities in Britain: Programme and Performance 1960–1980* (Cambridge: Cambridge University Press).

Central Policy Review Staff (1980), *Education, Training and Industrial Performance* (London: HMSO).

Chickering, A. W. (ed.) (1981), *The Modern American College* (San Francisco: Jossey-Bass).

Church, C. (ed.) (1983), *Practice and Perspectives in Validation* (Guildford: SRHE).

City of London Polytechnic (1970), *Bye-laws* (London: City of London Polytechnic).

Clark, B. R. (1983a), 'Governing the higher education system', in M. Shattock (ed.) *The Structure and Governance of Higher Education*, Leverhulme 9 (Guildford: Society for Research into Higher Education).

Clark, B. R. (1983b), *The Higher Education System* (Berkeley, Calif.: University of California Press).

Cohen, M. D. and March, J. G. (1974), *Leadership and Ambiguity: The American College President* (New York: McGraw-Hill).

Collier, G. K. (1985), 'Teaching methods in higher education: the changing scene, with special reference to small-group work', *Higher Education Research and Development*, vol. 4, no. 1, pp. 3–27.

Committee of Directors of Polytechnics (1980), *The Planning and Control of Higher Education*, Paper 80–18 (London: CDP).

Committee of Vice-Chancellors and Principals (1985), *Report of the Steering Committee for Efficiency Studies in Universities*, Jarratt Report (London: CVCP).

Committee of Vice-Chancellors and Principals (1986), *Academic Standards in Universities* (London: CVCP).

Committee on Higher Education (1963), *Higher Education*, Robbins Report, Cmnd 2154 (London: HMSO).

Commonwealth of Australia (1964), *Report of the Committee on the Future of Tertiary Education in Australia*, Martin Report (Melbourne: Government Printer).

Commonwealth of Australia (1966), *Report of a Committee of Enquiry into the Need for a College of Advanced Education in the Australian Capital Territory*, Burton Report (Canberra: The Prime Minister's Department).

Corson, J. J. (1973), 'Perspectives on the university compared to other organizations', in J. A. Perkins (ed.), *The University as an Organization*, Carnegie Commission on Higher Education (New York: McGraw-Hill), p. 155.

Council for National Academic Awards (1975), *Partnership in Validation: A Discussion Paper* (London: CNAA).

Council for National Academic Awards (1979), *Developments in Partnership in Validation* (London: CNAA).

Council for National Academic Awards (1981), 'The use of learning resources in higher education', CNAA Learning Resources Working Party, *British Journal of Educational Technology*, vol. 12, no. 2, pp. 84–97.

Council for National Academic Awards (1986), *Handbook 1986* (London: CNAA).

Council of Local Educational Authorities (1981) *The Future of Higher Education in the Maintained Sector: A Consultative Paper* (London: Association of County Councils/Association of Municipal Authorities).

CRAC (annually, revised biennially), *Degree Course Guides* (Cambridge: Careers Research and Advisory Centre).

Crane, D. (1972), *Invisible Colleges* (Chicago: Chicago University Press).

Cronin, B. (1985), *The Citation Process* (London: Taylor Graham).

Crosland, C. A. R. (1965), Speech at Woolwich Polytechnic, 27 April 1965, quoted in J. Pratt and T. Burgess (1974), *Polytechnics: A Report* (London: Pitman), pp. 203–7.

Crosland, C. A. R. (1967), Speech at Lancaster University, 20 January 1967, quoted in J. Pratt and T. Burgess (1974), *Polytechnics: A Report* (London: Pitman), pp. 208–13.

Cunningham, I. (1983), 'Assessment and experiential learning', in R. Boot and M. Reynolds (eds), *Learning and Experience in Formal Education* (Manchester: Department of Adult and Higher Education, University of Manchester).

Davie, G. (1961), *The Democratic Intellect* (Edinburgh: Edinburgh University Press).

Davies, I. K. (1976), *Objectives in Curriculum Design* (London: McGraw-Hill).

Department of Education and Science (1966a), *A Plan for Polytechnics and Other Colleges: Higher Education in the Further Education System*, Cmnd 3006 (London: HMSO).

Department of Education and Science (1966b), *Report of the Study Group on the Government of Colleges of Education*, Weaver Report (London: HMSO).

Department of Education and Science (1967), *Polytechnics*, Administrative Memorandum 8/67 (London: DES).

Department of Education and Science (1970), *Government and Conduct of Establishments of Further Education*, Circular 7/70 (London: DES).

Department of Education and Science (1972), *Education: A Framework for Expansion*, Cmnd 5174 (London: HMSO).

Department of Education and Science (1973), *Development of Higher Education in the Non-University Sector*, Circular 7/73 (London: DES).

Department of Education and Science (1978), *Report of the Working Group on the Management of Higher Education in the Maintained Sector*, Oakes Report, Cmnd 7130 (London: HMSO).

Department of Education and Science (1981), *Higher Education in England outside the Universities; Policy, Funding and Management*. A consultative document (London: DES).

Department of Education and Science (1985a), *The Development of Higher Education into the 1990s*, Cmnd 9524 (London: HMSO).

Department of Education and Science (1985b), *Academic Validation in Public Sector Higher Education*, Lindop Report, Cmnd 9501 (London: HMSO).

Department of Education and Science (1985c), *Higher Education: Funding Comparisons across Sectors* (London: DES).

Department of Education and Science (1985d), *Student Numbers in Higher Education – Gt Britain: 1970–1983*, Statistical Bulletin 9/85 (London: DES).

Department of Education and Science (1987), *Higher Education: Meeting the Challenge*, Cm 114 (London: HMSO).

Elton, L. (1983), 'Cost-effectiveness in laboratory teaching', in G. Squires (ed.), *Innovation in Recession* (Guildford: Society for Research into Higher Education).

Eraut, M. (1985), 'Knowledge creation and knowledge use in professional contexts', *Studies in Higher Education*, vol. 10, no. 2, pp. 117–33.

Fielden, J. and Lockwood, G. (1973), *Planning and Management in Universities* (London: Sussex University Press).

Fowler, G. (1978), 'Non-university higher education', *New Statesman*, 31 March 1978, pp. 424–5.

Gibbs, G., Morgan, A. and Taylor, E. (1984), 'The world of the learner', in F. Marton, D. Hounsell and N. Entwistle (eds), *The Experience of Learning* (Edinburgh: Scottish Academic Press).

Goldman, R. (1973), 'No way to run a college', in R. Bell *et al.* (eds), *Education in Great Britain and Ireland: A Source Book* (London: Routledge and Kegan Paul in association with Open University Press).

Goodlad, S. (1975), *Education and Social Action* (London: Allen and Unwin).

Goodlad, S. (ed.) (1984), *Education for the Professions* (Guildford: Society for Research into Higher Education and NFER–Nelson).

Gosden, P. H. J. H. (1976), *Education in the Second World War* (London: Methuen).

Gouldner, A. W. (1957), 'Locals and cosmopolitans', *Administrative Science Quarterly*, vol. 1, pp. 281–306, vol. 2, pp. 444–80.

Government of New South Wales (1968), *Report of a Committee to Investigate the Proposal to Establish a College of Advanced Education at Wagga Wagga*, Heath Report (Sydney: NSW Government Printer).

Griffiths, F. (1985), 'Funding for inequality', *NATFHE Journal*, no. 7, November 1985, pp. 14–16.

GRIHE (1973–76), *Newsletters 1 to 7* (London: Group for Research and Innovation in Higher Education, The Nuffield Foundation).

GRIHE (1975), *The Drift of Change: An Interim Report of the Group for Research and Innovation in Higher Education* (London: The Nuffield Foundation).

Halsey, A. H. and Trow, M. (1971), *The British Academics* (London: Faber).

Heath, R. (1978), 'Personality and the development of students in higher education', in C. A. Parker (ed.), *Encouraging Development in College Students* (Minneapolis: University of Minnesota Press).

Hencke, D. (1978), *Colleges in Crisis* (Harmondsworth: Penguin).

Hirst, P. H. (1974), *Knowledge and the Curriculum* (London: Routledge and Kegan Paul).

HM Treasury (1981), *The Government's Expenditure Plans 1981–82 to 1983–84*, Cmnd 8175 (London: HMSO).

HM Treasury (1986), *Supply Estimates: Class XII – Department of Education and Science*, HC 284–XII (London: HMSO).

Hollenstein, H. (1982), *Economic Performance and the Vocational Qualifications of the Swiss Labour Force compared with Britain and Germany* (London: National Institute of Economic and Social Research).

House of Commons (1972–73), *Further and Higher Education*, Report from the Expenditure Committee (Education and Arts Sub-Committee), HC 48 (London: HMSO).

House of Commons (1976), *Local Government Finance*, Layfield Report, Cmnd 6453 (London: HMSO).

House of Commons (1980), *The Funding and Organisation of Courses in Higher Education, Volume II: Minutes of Evidence*, Fifth Report of the Education, Science and Arts Committee, Session 1979–80, HC 787–II, September 1980, p. 44.

Howell, D. A. (1980), 'The Department of Education and Science: its critics and defenders', *Educational Administration*, vol. 9, no. 1, pp. 108–33.

Inner London Education Authority (1985), *Report of the Polytechnic of North London Committee of Inquiry 1985*, Browne Report (London: ILEA).

Jackson, J. (ed.) (1970), *Professionals and Professionalization* (Cambridge: Cambridge University Press).

Jedamus, P., Peterson, M. W. and associates (1980) *Improving Academic Management* (San Francisco: Jossey-Bass).

Jenkins, D. (1975), 'The classical and romantic in the curriculum landscape', in M. Golby, J. Greenwood and R. West (eds), *Curriculum Design* (London: Croom Helm).

Kay, R. (1985), *UCCA: Its Origins and Development 1950–85* (Cheltenham: Universities Central Council on Admissions).

Keller, G. (1983), *Academic Strategy: The Management Revolution in American Higher Education* (Baltimore, Md: Johns Hopkins University Press).

Kerr, C. *et al.* (1979), *Twelve Systems of Higher Education: Six Decisive Issues* (New York: International Council for Educational Development), p. 158.

Klug, B. (1977), *The Grading Game* (London: National Union of Students).

Knowles, M. (1978), *The Adult Learner: A Neglected Species* (Houston, Tex.: Gulf).

Kogan, M. (1971), *The Politics of Education* (Harmondsworth: Penguin).

Kogan, M. with Kogan, D. (1983). *The Attack on Higher Education* (London: Kogan Page).

Laurillard, D. (1979), 'The processes of student learning', *Higher Education*, vol. 8, pp. 395–410.

Lehman, H. C. (1953), *Age and Achievement* (London: Oxford University Press).

Leverhulme Studies of Higher Education (1983), *Programme of Study in Higher Education* (Guildford: Society for Research into Higher Education and NFER–Nelson).

Levine, A. (1978), *Handbook on Undergraduate Curriculum* (San Francisco: Jossey Bass).

Lewis, R. (1982), 'Funding versus validating', in A. Morris and J. Sizer (eds), *Resources and Higher Education*, Leverhulme 8 (Guildford: Society for Research into Higher Education).

Lindley, R. (ed.) (1981), *Higher Education and the Labour Market*, Leverhulme 1 (Guildford: Society for Research into Higher Education).

Livingstone, H. (1974), *The University: An Organisational Analysis* (Glasgow: Blackie).

Lobkowicz, N. (1967), *Theory and Practice* (Notre Dame, Ind.: University of Notre Dame Press).

Locke, M., Pratt, J. and Burgess, T. (1985), *The Colleges of Higher Education 1972 to 1982: The Central Management of Organic Change* (Croydon: Critical Press).

Lockwood, G. and Davies, J. L. (1985), *Universities and the Management Challenge* (Slough: NFER–Nelson).

Lukes, J. R. (1967), 'The binary policy: a critical study', *Universities Quarterly*, vol. 22, no. 1, pp. 6–45.

McCaig, R. (1973), 'Role perception by members of university governing bodies', in W. G. Walker, A. R. Crane and A. Ross Thomas (eds), *Exploration in Educational Administration* (St Lucia: University of Queensland Press).

Mansell, T. *et al.* (1976), *The Container Revolution: A Study of Unit and Modular Schemes* (London: The Nuffield Foundation).

Marton, F. and Saijo, R. (1976), 'On qualitative differences in learning. I – Outcome and process', *British Journal of Educational Psychology*, vol. 46, pp. 115–27.

Mathieson, C. C. (1981), *Staff Development Matters: Academic Staff Training and Development in the Universities of the United Kingdom, 1961–1981* (London: Co-ordinating Committee for the Training of the University Teachers, CVCP).

Matterson, A. (1981), *Polytechnics and Colleges* (London: Longman).

Merton, R. K. (1973), *The Sociology of Science* (Chicago: University of Chicago Press).

Miller, T. G. (1980), 'Miller's tale', *The Times Higher Education Supplement*, 1 February 1980.

Ministry of Education (1945), *Higher Technical Education*, Percy Report (London: HMSO).

Ministry of Education (1956), *Technical Education*, Cmnd 9703 (London: HMSO).

Ministry of Education (1960), *Grants to Students*, Anderson Report, Cmnd 1051 (London: HMSO).

Moodie, G. C. and Eustace, R. (1974), *Power and Authority in British Universities* (London: Allen and Unwin).

Mortimer, K. P. and McConnell, T. R. (1978), *Sharing Authority Effectively* (San Francisco: Jossey-Bass).

NAB (1983), *NAB Bulletin*, Spring 1983 (London: National Advisory Body).

NAB (1984a), *A Strategy for Higher Education into the Later 1980s and Beyond* (London: National Advisory Body).

NAB (1984b), *Report of the Continuing Education Group* (London: National Advisory Body).

NATFHE (1981a), Secretarial Discussion Paper on the DES Paper 'The Management of Public Sector Higher Education in England', Paper 2196–81, 20 February 1981 (London: NATFHE).

NATFHE (1981b), An Association Commentary on the DES Paper 'The Management of Public Sector Higher Education in England', Circular 13/81, 2 March 1981 (London: NATFHE).

National Audit Office (1985), *Redundancy Compensation Payments to University Staff*, Report by the Comptroller and Auditor General, HC 598 (London: HMSO).

National Union of Students (1981), *Public Sector Higher Education: Why the DES is Wrong* (London: NUS).

NEDC (1984), *Competence and Competition* (London: National Economic Development Council/Manpower Services Commission).

OECD (1972), *Interdisciplinarity* (Paris: Organization for Economic Co-operation and Development).

OECD (1979), *State of the Art in University Management in Europe* (Paris: Organization for Economic Co-operation and Development).

Open University (1982), *Report of the Vice-Chancellor 1981* (Milton Keynes: The Open University Press).

Pask, G. (1976), 'Styles and strategies of learning', *British Journal of Educational Psychology*, vol. 46, pp. 129–48.

Perkin, H. (1969), *Key Profession: The History of the Association of University Teachers* (London: Routledge and Kegan Paul).

Perry, W. (1976), *Open University* (Milton Keynes: The Open University Press).

Powell, J. P. (1966), *Universities and University Education: A Select Bibliography* (Slough: NFER).

Pratt, J. and Burgess, T. (1974), *Polytechnics: A Report* (London: Pitman).

Price, D. J. de S. (1963), *Little Science, Big Science* (New York: Columbia University Press).

Richards, C. (1984), *Curriculum Studies: An Annotated Introductory Bibliography*, 2nd edn (London: Falmer Press).

Riley, J. (1984), 'The problems of drafting distance learning materials', *British Journal of Educational Technology*, vol. 15, no. 3, pp. 192–238.

Robbins, Lord (1980), *Higher Education Revisited* (London: Macmillan).

Robinson, E. (1968), *The New Polytechnics* (London: Cornmarket Press).

Rothblatt, S. (1976), *Tradition and Change in English Liberal Education* (London: Faber).

Rowntree, D. (1982), *Educational Technology in Curriculum Development* (London: Harper Row).

Sanderson, M. (1972), *The Universities and British Industry, 1850–1970* (London: Routledge and Kegan Paul).

Sanderson, M. (ed.) (1975), *The Universities in the Nineteenth Century* (London: Routledge and Kegan Paul).

Scott, P. (1984), *The Crisis of the University* (London: Croom Helm).

Scottish Tertiary Education Advisory Council (1985), *Future Strategy for Higher Education in Scotland*, Cmnd 9676 (Edinburgh: HMSO).

Shattock, M. (ed.) (1983), *The Structure and Governance of Higher Education*, Leverhulme 9 (Guildford: Society for Research into Higher Education).

Shinn, C. H. (1986), *Paying the Piper: The Development of the University Grants Committee 1919–1946* (Barcombe: Falmer Press).

Smith, P. M. (1981), 'The exclusive jurisdiction of the university visitor', *Law Quarterly Review*, vol. 97, pp. 610–47.

Smith, P. M. (1986), 'Visitation of the universities: a ghost from the past', *New Law Journal*, vol. 136, pp. 484–6, 519–20.

Squires, G. (1979), 'Innovations in British higher education and their implications for adult education', in OECD, *Learning Opportunities for Adults*, vol. 2 (Paris: Organization for Economic Co-operation and Development).

Squires, G. (1980), 'Individuality in higher education', *Studies in Higher Education*, vol. 5, no. 2, pp. 217–26.

Squires, G. (1986), *Modularisation* (Manchester: Consortium for Advanced Continuing Education and Training in the Universities of Manchester and Salford, University of Manchester Institute of Science and Technology and Manchester Polytechnic (CONTACT)).

Squires, G. (1987), *The Curriculum beyond School* (London: Hodder and Stoughton).

Squires, G. *et al.* (1975), *Interdisciplinarity* (London: The Nuffield Foundation).

Squires, G. *et al.* (1976), *Breadth and Depth* (London: The Nuffield Foundation).

Staffordshire County Council (1985), *Report of the Working Party on Collaboration between the University of Keele and North Staffordshire Polytechnic* (Stafford: University of Keele/North Staffordshire Polytechnic).

Stanton, H. E. (1978), *Helping Students Learn: The Improvement of Higher Education* (Washington: University Press of America).

Stephenson, J. (1981), 'Student planned learning', in D. Boud (ed.), *Developing Student Autonomy in Learning* (London: Kogan Page).

Taylor, P. H. and Richards, C. (1985), *An Introduction to Curriculum Studies*, 2nd edn (Slough: NFER–Nelson).

Tight, M. (1985), 'Academic freedom re-examined', *Higher Education Review*, vol. 18, pp. 7–23.

Trow, M. (1975), 'The public and private lives of higher education', in *American Higher Education: Towards an Uncertain Future, Daedalus*, vol. 2, Winter 1975, pp. 113–27.

Trow, M. (1976), 'The American academic department as a context for learning', *Studies in Higher Education*, vol. 1, no. 1, pp. 11–22.

Trow, M. (1983), 'Defining the issues in university–government relations: an international perspective', *Studies in Higher Education*, vol. 8, pp. 115–28.

University Grants Committee (1968), *University Development 1962–1967*, Cmnd 3820 (London: HMSO).

University Grants Committee (1979), *Report on Russian and Russian Studies in British Universities* (London: UGC).

University Grants Committee (1982) *Annual Survey 1980–81*, Cmnd 8663 (London: HMSO).

University Grants Committee (1984a), *A Strategy for Higher Education into the 1990s: The University Grants Committee's Advice* (London: HMSO).

University Grants Committee (1984b), *Report of the Continuing Education Working Party* (London: UGC).

University Grants Committee (1985a), *University Statistics 1983–84, Volume 3: Finance* (Cheltenham: Universities Statistical Record).

University Grants Committee (1985b), 'Rationalisation', Circular Letter 18/85 (London: UGC).

University Grants Committee (1985c), 'Planning for the late 1980s: the resource allocation process', Circular Letter 22/85 (London: UGC).

University Grants Committee (1986), 'Planning for the late 1980s: recurrent grant for 1986–87', Circular Letter 4/86 (London: UGC).

Wade, E. C. S. and Bradley, A. W. (1985), *Constitutional and Administrative Law*, 10th edn (London: Longman).

Wade, H. W. R. (1982), *Administrative Law*, 5th edn (Oxford: Clarendon Press).

Waitt, I. (ed.) (1980), *College Administration: A Handbook* (London: National Association of Teachers in Further and Higher Education).

Watson, J. R. (1977), 'Videotapes in undergraduate teaching laboratories', *Education in Chemistry*, vol. 14, no. 3, pp. 84–6.

Wiener, M. (1981), *English Culture and the Decline of the Industrial Spirit, 1850–1980* (Cambridge: Cambridge University Press).

Williams, G. and Blackstone, T. (1983), *Response to Adversity*, Leverhulme 10 (Guildford: Society for Research into Higher Education).

Willis, N. (1983), 'The potential of educational technology', in G. Squires (ed.), *Innovation through Recession* (Guildford: Society for Research into Higher Education).

Zuckerman, H. (1977), *Scientific Elite: Nobel Laureates in the United States* (New York: Free Press).

Zuckerman, H. and Merton, R. K. (1971), 'Patterns of evaluation in science', *Minerva*, vol. ix, no. 1, pp. 66–100.

Index